D1051212

CATASTROPHE

The Story of Bernard L. Madoff, The Man Who Swindled the World

DEBORAH AND **GERALD STROBER**

PHOENIX BOOKS

ISBN-10: 1-59777-640-8
ISBN-13: 978-1-59777-640-0

Library of Congress Cataloging-In-Publication Data Available

Book & Cover Design by Sonia Fiore
Bernard Madoff Photo by Brendan McDermid/Reuters/Corbis

Printed in the United States of America

Phoenix Books, Inc.
9465 Wilshire Boulevard, Suite 840
Beverly Hills, CA 90212

10 9 8 7 6 5 4 3 2 1

WE DEDICATE THIS BOOK TO
THE VICTIMS OF THE MAN WHO
SWINDLED THE WORLD.

CONTENTS

Part Four
The Shakeout

Appendices

FOREWORD

O n the chilly morning of Thursday, December 11, 2008, we were both at home, battling a nasty, twenty-four-hour flu. Not really in the mood to read but craving distraction, we tuned in to one of the cable news channels and sat there taking in one soft news piece after another, as well as innumerable commercials.

Suddenly there was a "breaking news" flash. A wealthy former chairman of NASDAQ was under arrest in what the media was touting as "the biggest Ponzi scheme ever," even as the accused man was being driven downtown to the federal courthouse for arraignment.

The following days brought startling revelations: major charitable organizations, institutions, and boldface names scammed by the once highly respected founder and head of Bernard L. Madoff Investment Securities and now nearly destitute.

How could so many organizations and individuals have been taken in? And what sort of person could have so coldly stolen from those who had entrusted him with their funds and, in many instances, with their life savings?

On Friday, December 19, eight days after we had been jolted out of our flu-induced fog, we could stand it no longer. We were going to obtain answers to our questions. We would write a book about Bernard Madoff, and we would do it now, while the ink on Bernard Madoff's complaint document was still drying!

Deciding to do so was the *easy* part; now we would have to find a publisher willing to take a flyer on such an ambitious undertaking. That afternoon, we e-mailed Michael Viner at Phoenix Books. Within hours, we had his reply.

We were now off and running on the most challenging assignment of our twenty years as a husband-and-wife writing team: to chronicle the immediate days and weeks following the apprehension of the Wall Street entrepreneur who had so cruelly devastated so many lives.

Deborah Hart Strober
Gerald S. Strober
January 12, 2009

ACKNOWLEDGMENTS

*C*atastrophe: The Story of Bernard L. Madoff, the Man Who Swindled the World* could not have come to fruition without the participation of our interviewees, all of whom responded to our request, made on very short notice over the Christmas and New Year holidays of 2008–09, to speak with them.

We would also like to thank the following individuals who either provided us with useful background information or facilitated certain interviews: Rafi Rothstein, Myron Strober, Scott Strober, and Betty Yarmon.

At Phoenix Books, we want to express appreciation to our publisher, Michael Viner, for his initial enthusiasm for our project, as well for his understanding and support at every stage of the process. And we also wish to thank Michael's very able colleagues at Phoenix Books, Henrietta Tiefenthaler, Darby Connor, copy editor Jennifer Hoche, and attorney Mitra Ahouraian, who carefully examined our text.

It goes without saying that our close friends and family deserve a great measure of our gratitude. Among the latter are our siblings and their partners, Judith and Dr. Mortimer Civan, Joseph Hochstein, Ruth Hockstein, and Mindy and Myron Strober.

Lastly, we want to express our deep affection and appreciation to our children, their partners, and our adorable grandchildren: Gabi and Jeremy Benjamin, parents of Eyal and Ran;

Lori and Bryan Sterling, parents of Kai and Marley; Jon Strober; and Michelle Meyers and Robin Strober.

Part One
December 11, 2008

For the very latest news on the Madoff saga, to access our archive of stories, or to add your own comments, please visit our Web site:

www.madoffbreakingnews.com

CHAPTER ONE

THE CONFESSION AND ARREST
OF BERNARD MADOFF

"Is there an innocent explanation for what happened?"
—FBI agent Theodore Cacioppi on Thursday,
December 11, 2008, on arriving at
Bernard Madoff's apartment to arrest him

"There is no innocent explanation."—Bernard Madoff

So begins the tragic and incredible downfall of seventy-year-old Bernard Madoff, the much sought-after Wall Street adviser, trader, and former NASDAQ chairman, known for his social graces and "soft-sell" approach to potential investors.

Madoff knew when he awoke on that chilly December morning that it was only a matter of time before there would be a knock on the door of Apartment 12A, the elegant duplex penthouse he shares with his wife, Ruth, at 133 East 64th Street—he served as chairman of the cooperative's board—in the heart of Manhattan's Silk Stocking district. He also knew that he would be arrested by FBI agents and taken away in handcuffs.

We were told that earlier in the month, Madoff had informed his two sons—Mark, 44, a graduate of the University of

Michigan and the director of proprietary trading of Bernard Madoff Investment Securities, LLC (BMIS), and Andrew, 42, a graduate of the University of Pennsylvania and the firm's director of trading—that in the wake of the continuing financial meltdown seizing the country, "clients had requested approximately $7 billion in redemptions" and that he was frantically trying to find enough liquid assets to meet his obligations.

Then on Tuesday, December 9, Madoff, who, according to his sons, had been very stressed out for several weeks, said that he wanted to pay company bonuses immediately. The following day, Mark and Andrew met with their father in his inner sanctum on the 17th floor of 885 Third Avenue, known as the Lipstick Building—a 453-foot-high, 34-story, red granite and steel tower designed by the John Burgee firm with the doyen of American architects, Philip Johnson, and so named due to its distinctive oval shape and color. They wanted to know about the status of the bonuses.

Refusing to divulge any information on that subject in the office, Madoff said that he had "something" to tell them, but doubted that he could "hold it together" if they pressed him for information in the office.

And so Madoff brought Mark and Andrew, as well as Madoff's younger brother, Peter, BMIS's senior managing director, home to Apartment 12A. There the man who had launched BMIS in 1960, with an initial investment of $5,000, confessed to them that his $50 billion enterprise was, in reality, "just one big lie, basically a giant Ponzi scheme."

The term *Ponzi scheme* is named after Charles Ponzi, an Italian immigrant who from 1919 to 1920 collected millions of dollars by convincing thousands of people to buy postage stamps using international coupons. He promised a fifty-percent gain in ninety days, based on the fact that an international reply coupon purchased at European currency rates could be redeemed at a higher price in the United States—and, as the money poured in, he diverted late investors' money to support payments to earlier investors. Though his activities earned him the namesake term, Ponzi didn't originate this scheme.

In fact, according to Mitchell Zukoff, a biographer of Ponzi, the type of fraud he would come to perpetrate on his victims was first committed by one William Miller, a New Yorker who in 1899 swindled investors after having promised them an astounding 520-percent return annually. Miller would make payouts to the first of his investors, so as not to arouse their suspicions, and then solicit new investments, using the additional funds to continue his nefarious activity. Operating in the days before governmental regulatory agencies, Miller managed to collect nearly one million dollars before his fraud was exposed during the course of an investigation by a newspaper. He was sentenced to ten years in prison.

Twenty years later, Ponzi's scheme would collapse when he failed to attract a mass of new money due to the shortage of circulating coupons, and the criminal whose name would be forever attached to such a scam was found guilty, jailed, and in 1934 deported to his native Italy.

That Tuesday, Madoff was actually confessing to the biggest Ponzi scheme ever. As of December 26, 2008, the *Wall Street Journal* printed a staggering list of victims: wealthy individuals; charitable foundations and their founders; Jewish secondary schools and universities; domestic and international insurers and pension funds; investment management firms; hedge funds; U.S. and international banks; and, most distressing, many "little people"—trusting individuals seduced by Bernard Madoff.

Could Mark, who, coincidently, had been served with divorce papers by his wife that very day, Andrew, and their Uncle Peter have suspected as much? After all, they were highly skilled professionals, educated in the ways of Wall Street. Now, as they heard—supposedly for the first time—from Madoff's own lips the extent of the fraud he had perpetrated on his unsuspecting clients, the stunned Mark and Andrew wasted no time in distancing themselves from their father's enormous moral sin, the breaking of the biblical commandment "Thou shalt not steal."

Madoff then answered his sons' question about the bonus payments. In his arrogance, he informed them that he would wait a week before surrendering to authorities, as he wanted to distribute the remaining $200 to $300 million of his once enormous, ill-gotten gains to certain employees, friends, and relatives. As if he could orchestrate the timing of his arrest!

We are led to believe that Mark and Andrew were not swayed by their father's intimation that he wished to take care of *them* financially, hence his delaying tactic, and that they were shocked by Madoff's confession. That may very well be the case. If so, Mark and Andrew deserve much credit for having had the courage to make the early evening telephone call to their attorney that would lead to their father's disgrace. On hearing from Mark and Andrew, the attorney immediately alerted the FBI and the Securities and Exchange Commission (SEC) to Bernard Madoff's terrible deception.

In the wake of Madoff's arrest the next morning, Agent Cacioppi stated that BMIS had "deceived investors by operating a securities business in which [Madoff] traded and lost investor money, and then paid certain investors purported returns on investment with the principle received from other, different investors, which resulted in investors' losses of approximately $50 billion."

In fact, Madoff had succeeded in bilking such boldface names as Senator Frank Lautenberg, filmmaker Steven Spielberg, husband and wife actors Kyra Sedgwick and Kevin Bacon, Holocaust survivor, author, and playwright Elie Wiesel, Mets owner and partner in Sterling Equities Fred Wilpon and his associate Saul Katz, the cofounder of Sterling, and media mogul Mort Zuckerman. He also swindled Yeshiva University and other highly respected educational institutions; banking giants like HSBC and the private, Geneva, Switzerland-based Union Bancaire Privée, which has ties to Fairfield Greenwich Group, a New York-based investment firm that was the largest supplier of money for Madoff (having brought him $7.2 billion and collecting in excess of $500 million in fees); hedge fund directors, including Ezra Merkin, a respected second-generation philanthropist; and the French-born R. Thierry Magon de la Villehuchet, a cofounder of Access International Advisors and the manager of a $1.4 billion fund, who, on the morning of December 23, took his life in his Manhattan office because he "could not cope" with his failure to make good on his clients' losses.

Andrew M. Calamari, associate director of enforcement in the SEC's New York office, said that Madoff has perpetrated "a stunning fraud that appears to be of epic proportions," and as the days go by, names are being added to the long list of those whose trust has been violated by the man they knew as "good old Bernie."

Taken downtown to be arraigned and charged with a single count of securities fraud, Madoff arranged to post a $10 million bond, secured by his duplex, as well as by his homes in Palm Beach, Florida, and Montauk, New York, and was immediately released on his own recognizance. Interviewed by the authors on December 27, Ira Lee Sorkin, Madoff's lead attorney and a partner at the white-shoe firm Dickstein Shapiro, declined to discuss his defense strategy or even his client's state of mind as Madoff remained confined to his duplex, awaiting his next court appearance.

"I can't talk about the case; that about sums it up," Sorkin said. "I could talk to you about the New York Giants, but not about Mr. Madoff, or the case."

When asked to at least release some information about Madoff's background—his parents' names, their occupations, where the family had lived when he was coming of age—Sorkin was adamant, insisting, "I cannot go into *anything* involving Mr. Madoff. You can ask about his mood, but I can't go into *that* either."

Sorkin *was* willing to speak about the statute under which Madoff was granted bail, however. "The purpose behind the Bail Reform Act is to ensure two things," he said, "one, that an individual does not flee the jurisdiction; and two, that the individual is not a danger to the community. That's the basis behind bail, pure and simple. It is not *punitive* and was never intended to be *punitive*."

Mark and Andrew Madoff refused to participate in the bail scheme, however. Thus it falls upon Ruth Madoff and her brother-in-law, Peter, to secure the disgraced financier's freedom while he awaits an array of further legal proceedings.

The following day, Madoff had his second court appearance. En route home afterward, with the media in hot pursuit and passersby gawking at the latest tabloid celebrity, "good old Bernie" demonstrated his bonhomie by doing a "walkabout" on Lexington Avenue, smiling and waving as if he had not a care in the world.

Photographs taken of Madoff during his walkabout capture his almost detached, slightly quizzical expression, as if he is thinking, *Who are all these people? Why are they staring at me? And what am I doing here?*

"If you analyze his demeanor when he was returning to his apartment, he was almost light and jumping around," former federal prosecutor Douglas Burns observed. "It was really weird."

The court didn't buy Madoff's act and promptly reined him in, confining him to 24-hour-a-day house arrest under the watchful eyes of round-the-clock security personnel, paid for by his wife, as well as video surveillance in the form of cameras trained on the front door of Apartment 12A.

Declining to comment on the court's action, lead attorney Sorkin said only, "I can't go into why the government changed the terms of the house arrest."

Were the court's newly imposed restrictions intended to protect as well as confine Madoff?

That would appear to be the case, based on unusual language in a letter sent by prosecutors to U.S. Magistrate Judge Gabriel W. Gorenstein, in which it stated that round-the-clock guards were necessary in order "to prevent harm or flight."

"That's nonsense," said attorney Barry Slotnick, a shareholder in the Manhattan firm Buchanan Ingersoll & Rooney, who is representing many of Bernard Madoff's victims. "A lot of people are very angry. But would they *kill* him? I don't think so."

But in fact, Madoff is reported to have received threats because, as a recent *New York Post* headline proclaimed, he is "The Most Hated Man in New York."

"I have heard rumors that he is very afraid for his life, as well he should be," said Jon Najarian, a professional investor and founder of the Web site optionMONSTER. "I would think that many of the people whom he stole from have connections to very bad people. I would be surprised if Mr. Madoff survives to see the inside of prison."

Threats against the accused Ponzi schemer notwithstanding, some of Madoff's victims are upset that he is enjoying the comforts of home rather than being confined to a jail cell.

"The fact that he was given bail has enraged my clients," said attorney Mark Mulholland, who represents many of Madoff's victims throughout the United States.

"People are shocked that he's out on bail," said Tara Pearl, a prominent Palm Beach realtor and businesswoman who knows Madoff and many of those who are deeply affected by his treachery.

"Imagine how his victims feel!" Pearl exclaimed, her voice rising with emotion. "To have your world go and knowing you cannot deal with that; knowing that you can't put your grandkids through college because your kids lived off of you; knowing you can't provide for your own health care or for the pills you're taking now. Seeing him walk out of court with a big grin on his face? It's emotionally devastating."

"I can't imagine why anybody gave him a free pass," said Bette Greenfield, of Deerfield Beach, Florida, who, along with her two brothers, is a victim of Madoff's Ponzi scheme. "The only thing I can think of is that the judge was afraid someone would kill him. They really need him secure to find out what he did. There has to be somebody who wrote that program and somebody who ran the numbers. There's a back room; it can't be just one person."

On the day of Madoff's arrest, U.S District Judge Louis L. Stanton had signed an order freezing all of Madoff's assets and ordering him to provide a written list by December 31 of all of his assets and liabilities to the SEC.

Madoff complied with Judge Stanton's order on the appointed date, but did so only minutes before the deadline. Those of his victims who wanted to know the contents of the list and had anxiously awaited Madoff's filing were sorely disappointed, however, as the SEC promptly embargoed the material.

Placing a telephone call to the SEC's Emergency Line on the evening of the 31st to inquire as to why the list had *not* been made available to the public, the authors were told only that the court, not the regulatory agency, had ordered the embargo.

As to why that information was not released on that day, victims' attorney Barry Slotnick responded with a question: "What would happen if you discovered [hypothetically] that Bernie Madoff owns the Waldorf Astoria? If everybody were to go after such assets, life would be very disrupted."

The court's action raised the specter of Madoff's having concealed huge assets in offshore accounts, thereby remaining solvent, or—more distressing to his many victims—that the court, in collusion with the SEC, was showing favoritism to the self-confessed Ponzi schemer, or that the SEC had pressed the court to withhold the accounting in order to conceal that agency's failure to heed the red flags posed over the years concerning Madoff's operational methods. Does Bernard Madoff have friends at both the SEC and the court? Is that why lead attorney Ira Sorkin was able to broker such an unprecedented deal for his client?

And so began the complex task of untangling the sordid details of Bernard Madoff's decades-long Ponzi scheme.

The only other individual besides his wife and brother who voiced support of Bernard Madoff was Dan Horwitz, another partner at Dickstein Shapiro and a member of Madoff's legal team, who maintained that his client "is a long-standing leader in the financial services industry with an unblemished record."

Madoff's confession and the testaments of many of his victims notwithstanding, Horwitz insisted that his client "is a person of integrity; he intends to fight to get through this unfortunate event"—an event that has already more than decimated a network of distinguished Jewish philanthropic organizations, destroyed the confidence of many wealthy Wall Street investors, robbed individuals of relatively modest means of their financial security, and has even driven one conscientious hedge fund manager to suicide.

CHAPTER TWO

THE VICTIMS OF THE SCANDAL THAT COULD WIPE OUT A GENERATION OF JEWISH WEALTH

"It's devastating, even for those of us who aren't directly affected."

—Ivy Barsky, director of Manhattan's Museum of Jewish Heritage

"I can't think of anything since the Great Depression that had an impact of this size."

—Melissa Berman, president of the New York-based Rockefeller Philanthropy Advisors

"The Shapiro Family Foundation was shocked and horrified to learn about allegations against Mr. Madoff, who has long been considered a trusted and effective leader in the investment field."

—Shapiro Family Foundation statement

"It's like finding out that your father is a felon—this is bad news for the family."

—Gary Tobin, president of the Institute for Jewish and Community Research and an expert on Jewish philanthropy

"You'll see organizations going out of business. Staff will get fired, programs will get slashed.... We just don't know yet."

—Mark Charendoff, president of the
Jewish Funders Network and
adviser to Jewish philanthropists

"This is a much more draconian hit on American philanthropy than the generalized credit crunch has been. This one man has demonstrated a capacity to radically impact American Jewish philanthropy and, even more important, elements of American civil society."

—Mark Rosenblum, director of the
Jewish Studies Center, Queens College

"The loss to Jewish philanthropy is catastrophic— there's no other word. The Jewish community will look different when this is all over."

—Jonathan Sarna, Brandeis University

"I did not know Bernard Madoff. I may have been one of the few in the Jewish community not to know who he was. I did not understand initially just how extended so many in the Jewish community, both individually and institutionally, were because of him. So for me there was a bit of a learning curve here to understand the extent of the damage he did to the Jewish community and within the Jewish community."

—David Harris, executive director
of the American Jewish Committee

"It's devastating. Lives have been ruined and communities have been changed forever."

—Robert L. Lappin, founder of the
Robert L. Lappin Charitable Foundation

These were but a few of the anguished cries of disbelief and prophecies of doom uttered by individual philanthropists and officials of a wide range of Jewish philanthropic organizations, whose very existence now hangs in the balance in the wake of a loss of between $600 million and $1 billion.

"It's an embarrassment, but the real opposite side of the question is the fact that he stole from the *Jews,*" said Harry S. Taubenfeld, a New York attorney specializing in real estate transactions and a former member of the Board of Governors of the Jewish Agency for Israel. Noting that "most of the organizations were Jewish ones," Taubenfeld excoriated Madoff for having "taken advantage of his Jewish connections to steal. It is unfortunate that communities honor the people for the money they donate rather than the quality of the people they are dealing with. But this is something that has been going on for ages."

"On the other hand," Taubenfeld observed, "the leaders of the Jewish Agency for Israel were chosen on the basis of achievement, as opposed to just donating money. These people fought very hard to protect the assets of the organization because they felt they were guardians of the Jewish people. This fellow was a criminal who went to the softest spots available; his friends, his golfing partners. He was not really representative of the Jewish community."

"One point that's being missed is that he didn't target charities," maintained writer Lawrence Leamer, whose latest book, *Madness Under the Royal Palms: Love and Death Behind the Gates of Palm Beach*, was published in January 2009. "It's that Jewish Americans are overwhelmingly generous and charitable. In fact, if you are Jewish and you are wealthy, you *have* to give to charity or you are ostracized. Let's say this happened at an overwhelmingly WASP country club—that it was a WASP swindler. Millions and millions of dollars in charity *wouldn't* be bilked."

"As someone who studies Jewish philanthropy and would know most of the major players—either personally or by research—in every major Jewish community in North America, [Madoff] is not a person who popped up on the screen [for me]," said Gary Tobin, president of the Institute for Jewish and Community Research.

In fact, Tobin noted, "For mostly everybody outside of a very small circle, he was off the radar. He was not a person who was going to meetings of the Conference of Presidents of Major American Jewish Organizations. He might have served on boards of institutions like Yeshiva University, but most people would not have heard of him before the scandal broke."

Professor Jonathan Sarna of Brandeis University, an expert on American Jewish history, has a somewhat different view. "The reduction of billions—not millions, but billions—in the Jewish economy means that there is just not going to be enough money to sustain all the institutions and initiatives that have been created," he said. "We will be a poorer community for that. What's been wiped out is an infrastructure that was particularly important in sustaining these institutions. The people who were invested with Madoff were the generation that not only supported institutions like Yeshiva University or the Holocaust museums, but that created them."

"This is not at all an unusual case, procedurally," said Douglas T. Burns, a former federal prosecutor and an expert in white-collar criminal defense. "Anybody who has spent time in the federal courts, in white-collar criminal law, which is my bailiwick, has seen every type of fraud under the sun. All it is, if I can be glib, is basically taking stuff that ain't yours."

The Madoff case, though, according to Burns, "is a bit different. This is not someone who sat down and said, 'I am going to steal fifty billion dollars.' That's not what happened. What happened in the case is that this is a guy who started robbing Peter to pay Paul."

As the news of Madoff's arrest hit the airwaves, wealthy individuals and institutional heads from New York to Boston to Florida to Los Angeles to Europe to the Middle East to the Far East learned that their assets, if not totally wiped out, had been severely diminished.

In New York City, home to the largest Jewish community in the United States, Holocaust survivor Elie Wiesel, a distinguished author and playwright and founder of the Elie Wiesel Foundation for Humanity reported the loss of $15.2 million, representing "substantially all of the Foundation's assets," according to a statement released by the foundation.

Established by Wiesel and his wife, Marion, soon after he was awarded the 1986 Nobel Peace Prize, the foundation, according to its mission statement, seeks to "combat indifference, intolerance, and injustice through international dialogue and youth-focused programs to promote acceptance, understanding, and equality."

The foundation's leadership, expressing the sort of determination that enabled Elie Wiesel to survive the horrors of the Nazi Holocaust and to achieve great success as a writer and humanitarian, vowed to continue the organization's activities, possibly including the operation of its study centers in Israel for Ethiopian Jewish children.

One hundred and ten million dollars of the $1.2 billion endowment of Yeshiva University, the 122-year-old private institution that offers religious and academic curricula, was lost. Most of that amount was invested from hedge funds initially controlled by J. Ezra Merkin, a Yeshiva trustee and chairman of the university's investment committee.

In a curious coincidence, both Ezra Merkin and Bernard Madoff played important lay leadership roles for Yeshiva University.

Madoff, a university trustee who received an honorary degree in 2001 and was elected the institution's treasurer the next year, served as chairman of the university's Sy Syms School of Business, an appointment that came about as a result of a major financial donation. And Merkin, also a Yeshiva trustee, served as chairman of the university's investment committee.

It is difficult to understand how and why the university's senior administrators and trustees did not regard Merkin's role on the investment committee as a blatant conflict of interest.

While the financial damage to Yeshiva will likely lead to a curtailment of some programs, university officials said that its scholarships, financial aid, and staff pensions would not be affected.

Still, the university retained the law firm Sullivan & Cromwell, as well as the investment adviser Cambridge Associates, to review the institution's policies and procedures. Yeshiva's president, Richard Joel, said in a statement: "We will be working closely with our advisers over the coming weeks and months and I'm confident that we will emerge stronger than ever."

Elsewhere in New York City, Ramaz, a Jewish-sponsored secondary school located about ten blocks north of the Madoff residence, is out $6 million, while Congregation Kehilath Jeshurun, the Orthodox synagogue with which Ramaz is affiliated, has lost $3.5 million. Among the philanthropic groups with national headquarters located in the city, Hadassah, the women's Zionist organization founded nearly a century ago at Manhattan's Temple Emanuel, and which funds Jewish day camps in the Unites States and supports medical research and hospitals in Israel, lost $90 million of its worth.

In response to Hadassah's loss, the organization's president, Nancy Falchuck, issued a message from Hadassah House, the group's headquarters on West 58th Street in Manhattan, in which she wrote: "Like all of America's citizens and institutions, Hadassah has felt the impact of the global financial crisis. And as I am sure you have heard by now, Hadassah was also one of many philanthropic organizations that fell victim to Bernard Madoff."

Nowhere in her fifteen-paragraph statement, however, did Falchuck explain why Hadassah placed almost one fifth of its total assets with one investment firm. Instead, and despite the serious issue of a gap in stewardship, she asks for *additional* financial support, stating that: "Protecting our mission and our values takes more than planning. That's why we need every member of Hadassah, and generous non-members as well, to be involved. This is a critical moment in which your financial support is so urgent. I'm asking every one of you to give as much as you can."

On the evening of Thursday, December 18, the more than 1,000 attendees at the United Jewish Appeal-Federation's annual Wall Street Dinner managed to raise approximately $18.8 million, down from the previous year's $21.6 million. Fortunately UJA-Federation, which supports more than 100 health, education, and community organizations, had not invested any of its funds with Madoff. Donors glancing through the event's program must have been chilled to read the name of Bernard Madoff on page two: He is listed as a member of the organization's executive council.

Across the Hudson River, in New Jersey, Senator Frank Lautenberg, a Democrat and a wealthy philanthropist, learned that $12.8 million of his foundation's $13.8 million in assets invested with the Madoff firm are no more. Thus the Lautenberg Foundation would not likely be able to match its largest single contribution to date, the $352,500 donated in 2006 to the United Jewish Appeal of Metro West, located in Whippany, New Jersey.

In New England in 1971, Carl Shapiro sold his women's clothing business, Kay Windsor, Inc., and established the Carl and Ruth Shapiro Family Foundation. With assets of $345 million, the foundation became a major donor to the Jewish-sponsored Brandeis University in Waltham, Massachusetts, as well as to Boston's Museum of Fine Arts. At the end of 2008, 45 percent of the foundation's endowment was gone.

Shapiro, now in his nineties, was so close to Bernard Madoff that he regarded him as a son. The philanthropist is so devastated by the Ponzi schemer's betrayal that when called by the authors and asked to comment on Madoff's enormous breach of trust, he refused to do so.

"How do you think Carl Shapiro feels?" asked Tara Pearl, a Palm Beach realtor and businesswoman. "He is one of the biggest philanthropists in the country, if not the world. He took this man under his wing; they played with each other's children and grandchildren. And now he finds that this person has betrayed him beyond his wildest imagination. That's *emotional rape.*"

In Brookline, Massachusetts, the Maimonides School, an Orthodox Jewish day school, may have lost as much as $5 million. In Swampscott, on the coast, Robert L. Lappin, founder of the Robert L. Lappin Charitable Foundation, acknowledged on December 23 that his organization had lost $8 million, "with more by myself."

Lawrence Leamer, a writer who learned of the debacle when he received a call from a member of the Palm Beach Country Club late on the afternoon of December 11, went that evening "to a dinner party at an Asian fusion restaurant, hosted by a dear friend of mine, Herb Gray. When I arrived I told the gathering. Herb stood up, took out his cell phone and called Bob Lappin, a very generous man who has given tens of millions of dollars to charity."

At that point, Leamer said, "Bob, whose foundation and all of his company's retirement plans were managed by Madoff, was preparing to probe through the wreckage."

Assessing the damage to the foundation, Lappin said, "In my community, the effects of the Madoff scandal are disastrous. Programs for Jewish teens, Jewish educators, and families have been aborted. Activities that bind the community together around the celebration of Jewish living and learning have ceased, and their future is uncertain." While emphasizing that "The foundation is not dissolving at this time," Lappin said "all but two programs have ceased because the money to fund them is gone. The staff of seven talented professionals who ran the programs has been terminated. I am not sure which programs, if any, will resume. I am in the process of assessing what can be salvaged."

"Aside from my family, the work of the Foundation has been one of the greatest joys in my life," Lappin said. "I dedicated decades to the Jewish youth of our community and beyond, which is why I am heartsick and devastated about the situation."

Among the programs sponsored by the Robert L. Lappin Foundation was Youth to Israel, a free, two-week summer trip for Jewish teenagers to the Jewish state, in which Helen Simons's fifteen-year-old daughter was scheduled to participate.

"It would have touched her heart to be in the homeland and see for herself what her father and I are trying to instill in her," the girl's disappointed mother said in an interview with the *Boston Globe*.

In Florida, the Jewish community of Palm Beach, especially hard hit by the debacle, "is in such shock," Tara Pearl reported on December 24, nearly two weeks after Madoff's arrest. "The streets are half empty and people are trying to figure out what happens tomorrow," she said, adding that "many of the people are in their seventies and eighties. You have billionaires who have lost a lot of money; people who have many millions—$30 to $50 million—who have lost a chunk of their money and have to readjust their lifestyle; and then you have people who are wiped out."

"It is a plague beyond imagination, the sheer numbers that have come is nothing compared to how many people were affected," said Leamer. "Some people are too embarrassed to say anything. Some people are so devastated they can't even talk."

"At first, people thought it was a joke; they didn't believe it was really happening," Tara Pearl said, recalling the moment the news hit the airwaves. As it became apparent that the bulletins were real, however, and the extent of the financial and emotional devastation began to sink in, people scrambled to "find out what proportion of their money was involved; then they started to find out that it was real, and they learned on television that all their money with Madoff was gone."

Sydelle Meyer, another resident of Palm Beach, suffered doubly: Her husband died in October 2008, just two months before Madoff's arrest, and then she learned on December 11 that her fortune was entirely wiped out.

"I had several foundations; they are not now functioning," she told the authors on December 28, 2008. "Anybody who had invested everything they owned with him was just wiped out. If you were completely involved with him, it was a sad day.

"What happened? I don't know. I just can't imagine. It's a mystery to me," Meyer said. "He came into the [Palm Beach Country] Club—one of its requirements is that you give X amount of dollars a year to charity and everybody did what they were supposed to do. That's one of the things that makes the club so outstanding— and gradually we all knew him. He was very quiet, very reserved, very laid-back. The Madoffs were just like all the rest of us, but they did not get involved with too many people on the social scale that I'm aware of.

"When I first heard the news, I was stunned, I couldn't believe it," Meyer added. "But when I called up my CEO, I was informed that everything we had heard was the truth. Everybody was in a state of shock."

Meyer did not know Bernie Madoff well. "My husband, who knew him much better than I did, seemed to have every confidence in him at that time—we are talking about ten years ago," she said.

Meyer found Madoff to be "very pleasant, very nice, very honorable; all the things that you would expect in a gentleman of his stature at that time, not ostentatious in any way." She continued, "I have no idea what his lifestyle was; I never questioned it. He was very low-key—he was all over the world, I guess. Everybody was interested in getting to know him. I never thought much about it until all this happened."

"Everybody in Palm Beach is quite upset," Meyer said. "A lot of people did not understand what Madoff was doing, so they did not involve themselves. At the time, my husband apparently seemed to understand."

"Palm Beach is devastated beyond imagination," said Lawrence Leamer, noting that "Even *before* [the news about] Madoff struck, most people I know had lost about half of what they had, so the stores were already empty, people were already depressed. Madoff has taken it to another level. It has spilled over and affected everybody."

Leamer described an acquaintance "who was worth six hundred million dollars and even before Madoff, his worth was down to five hundred million dollars. Instead of taking people to expensive Palm Beach restaurants, he took his guests to a pizza place in West Palm Beach. It's just bizarre, because there is no way he could spend all the money he had, but he felt he had to economize."

Other Madoff victims with homes in Florida include seventy-two-year-old Marilyn Lane and her eighty-one-year-old husband, William, who own a Chevrolet and Saturn dealership in Manassas, Virginia, as well as a place in Palm Beach. During the summer of 2008, they invested in excess of $1 million with Madoff.

Now, the Lanes are trying to figure out how they could have entrusted Madoff with their hard-earned savings. "He certainly had a track record," Ms. Lane told Bloomberg correspondents Mark Clothier and Oshrat Carmiel over a meal at Green's Pharmacy and Luncheonette, a well-known Palm Beach spot for breakfast or lunch. "Everyone you spoke to highly recommended him. It wasn't like you were going with a fly-by-night scheme." Or so the Lanes thought.

Bette Greenfield, who once worked for the brokerage firm Merrill Lynch, and her two brothers, an accountant and an attorney, are also trying to figure out how they will survive—not only financially, but emotionally.

"I never met Madoff," Greenfield said. "It was my father, who lived in Lake Worth. Friends of friends recommended that he invest with Madoff because Madoff's reputation was stellar. My father, who was a CPA, was very knowledgeable. He was involved in securities and knew exactly what was going on. But something about Madoff made him feel that this was really the right place to put his money.

"At that point, the early 1990s, he had enough to go into one of Madoff's trusts. He believed in Madoff, who was apparently the king of Palm Beach at that time. My father felt very, very comfortable about putting his money there.

"For about ten years, he apparently took income to support himself and my stepmother. So there was something coming in. My father was not a big investor by any means, not in the millions the way everybody is talking about. He was comfortable enough to have a nice income for the two of them.

"My stepmother died, and then in 2003, he died. He left the trust in my brothers' and my names. It was a revocable trust for ten years, so in 2013, my brothers and I would be in our seventies and would benefit from the trust.

"We never took any money from the trust. By this time there was about half a million dollars in it and we thought that this would be just perfect for us: We would be able to have that money because none of us had ever worked in those kinds of companies where there would have been a pension or an IRA or a 401(k). This was the way we had to save our money. I was a single parent and I spent all my money on colleges and other expenses. When I retired in March, my thinking was that I would be able to sell my house, come down to Florida, buy another place, and, when the time came, I would have money for my future.

"Just this past September, my brothers and I talked about how maybe it's time to take some of the earnings. We decided we were going to ask for the earnings every quarter. That was really going to help me and one of my brothers, who is retired. We thought that between this money and our social security, we wouldn't be rich by any means, but we would be *comfortable*. At least we wouldn't have to worry about our bills."

In September 2008, Greenfield and her brothers asked Madoff for their first check. "Of course, that's the *last* check that we ever got," she said. "We now think that lots of people were asking for their checks at the same time. We hadn't had the election yet, the talk was about the awful economy, and it scared us all; we had never been scared of this kind of thing. When you are younger, you don't think about it. All of a sudden, when you are faced with the fact that you have no income other than social security, which is like being on relief, which is what our grandmothers used to talk about, it began to really frighten us, so we decided to take some money out. That's what happened. I get an e-mail from my brother and that was *it*."

Greenfield said that she and her brothers "never thought that the money was not secure; we never thought that it was a razzle-dazzle, a Ponzi scheme. It never dawned on us. My father received these accounts every single month and confirmations of all the sales. I used to read the reports.

"Of course, now I see that *everybody* got the same reports; they must have come out of a big computer," Greenfield surmised. "I can't imagine that Bernie Madoff sat there and wrote computer programs. It doesn't make sense. So somebody knew exactly what he was doing. I wonder if somebody's out there with that computer story.

"It looks like everybody was buying the same stocks, only if my father had a million, and somebody else had fifty million, it showed my father with fifty Home Depot shares and the other guy with five thousand Home Depot shares," Greenfield said. "The statements looked very legitimate. They showed that when the market went down, the money went into Treasuries. And how could you mistrust Treasuries? There were dividends from these ten top companies: GE, Merrill Lynch, Home Depot, Coca-Cola."

Also among the "little people" devastated by Madoff's scam are Joan Sinkin, a seventy-five-year-old physical therapist, now retired, and her husband, Arnold, of Boynton Beach, not far from the elaborate homes of Palm Beach, who were recently interviewed by the Jewish weekly newspaper the *Forward.*

Thirty-two years ago, acting on their accountant's advice, the Sinkins began to invest with Madoff. Once they had paid for their children's education, the Sinkins increased their investment, several thousand dollars at a time, until they had amassed a considerable amount of money. Now, that money, their life savings, is almost gone. Joan Sinkin still can't believe what happened. She said that Madoff explained his investment philosophy. "We really couldn't lose."

Tara Pearl's heart goes out to one individual, an eighty-six-year-old doctor, "a man who worked his whole life, invested properly, and decided a few years ago that he was going to put everything in *this* investment. There is noting you can say to a person in this situation." Pearl added, "someone who has no earning ability anymore, who will not be able to start a business again; someone who has worked very hard and sacrificed to provide a future for his children, a person who hasn't even a certain degree of comfort and may not survive.

"Unlike death, where there is a grieving period and then finality, here there was only confusion," Pearl said, "'Oh, my God! What do we do? We can't pay our cable; we have to let our housekeeper go.'"

For Pearl, the most poignant aspect of the Madoff scandal is the plight of the housekeepers, cooks, chauffeurs, and gardeners who depended on employment in the homes of the wealthy residents of Palm Beach to pay their rent, put food on their tables, and save for their children's education. "Now they are out of work and unable to feed their families," Pearl said.

As for the plight of the once wealthy and now nearly destitute, many of them are turning to Pearl for assistance in selling off their remaining assets. "It's an emotional holocaust for a certain segment of people," Pearl observed, adding that a close friend, a psychiatrist who treats mostly very wealthy people, said that "the only other time she saw a situation like this from an emotional perspective was during Hurricane Katrina."

"I just can't imagine how he slept at night," Bette Greenfield said. "How long had this been going on? What did he think he was doing? I am dumbfounded. My initial reaction when I received my brother's e-mail about the fraud was, 'Oh shit!' I couldn't believe it."

"Palm Beach will recover financially. America is always creating wealthy people," Lawrence Leamer predicts. But, he believes, "Palm Beach has been humbled and broken. Whether the fantasy of Palm Beach can be rebuilt is an open question."

As news of Madoff's thievery spread throughout Florida, rumors abounded concerning the extent of the financial devastation suffered by organizations and foundations.

Supporters of the Gift of Life Bone Marrow Foundation, based in Boca Raton, near Palm Beach, believed that the foundation has lost $1.8 million. Established in 1991 as a donor recruitment organization to help save the life of Jay Feinberg, a leukemia victim from New Jersey (who received a bone marrow transplant in 1995), the foundation serves as the sole donor registry in North America dedicated to Jewish recruitment, with more than 128,000 donors, and serves people in thirty-three countries. Fortunately, the initial, shocking media reports of the foundation's loss were false. On December 13, 2008, two days after Bernard Madoff's arrest, the foundation informed the public that its registry operations remained "sound and secure," that its finances were not managed by Bernard Madoff's firm. The foundation did caution, however, that "losses by some of our contributors understandably impacted their charitable giving plans and commitments." As a result, the foundation vows to seek alternative means in order to fulfill its recruitment goals.

Elsewhere in Florida, donors to the Jewish Federation of South Palm Beach County suffered significant losses. Several dozen contributors to the Jewish Federation of Broward County had invested with Madoff, two of them each contributing tens of thousands of dollars annually.

Eric Stillman, the federation's CEO, noted, "We were going through a terrible economic recession already. This scandal is just worsening the situation." Particularly upsetting to Stillman is the impact of Madoff's thievery on some of the Federation's elderly donors. "They won't have time left to recoup losses," he said.

Across the nation, in California, the Los Angeles Jewish Federation, whose 2008 budget was approximately $50 million, may have suffered a loss of $6.4 million, constituting eleven percent of its endowment.

Also hit was the Jewish Community Foundation of Los Angeles, typical of Jewish community foundations in many American cities. Established in the summer of 1954 through the efforts of a small group of leaders, the foundation sought to serve the needs of the city's rapidly growing Jewish population. According to the founding chairman, Judge Isaac Pacht, the foundation's ultimate objective was "to build up a substantial fund for capital and special needs as they arise in the community." Today the foundation is a multifaceted institution, assisting philanthropists with all aspects of charitable giving in the Jewish community and beyond, though their ability to continue operations is now questionable. Might they meet the fate of the Chais Family Foundation? Established in 1985 and dedicated to the advancement of educational excellence in Israel, as well to the deepening of Jewish identity throughout the world, the organization was forced to cease operations on Sunday, December 14, three days after Bernard Madoff's arrest.

Jerry Reisman, a partner in the law firm Reisman, Peirez & Reisman, based in Garden City on New York's Long Island, met Bernie Madoff several years ago at the Glen Oaks Country Club in

Westbury, Long Island. In an interview distributed by Bloomberg News, he said he found Madoff to be "very personable, very charming, probably one of the best social networkers in America, who moved in the best circles—he was a pro at it."

Now, Reisman said, he is representing ten of Madoff's victims, whose losses amount to $150 million.

"Long Island seems to be something of an epicenter for this whole tragedy," observed Mark Mulholland, an attorney who is representing victims of Bernard Madoff's treachery throughout the United States. "The fact that Madoff traveled the country club circuit here on Long Island, and also had homes here, where many of his victims have homes and businesses, made it a likely spot. Literally hundreds of people who were victimized had direct outreach into my law firm.

"I had never even heard his name," said Mulholland. "My first reaction was: How could so many sophisticated individuals be so drawn to this man, and so willing to trust him with their life fortunes?

"My partners and I have spoken with well over a hundred victims—heading toward two hundred. Many of them represent not just *themselves*; they will call on behalf of an entire family. John will call and say that he's calling on behalf of himself and his wife and his father and his two children, all of whom are invested with Madoff," Mulholland added.

"The theme that came out in dozens and dozens of those calls was that this man was masterful in creating a mystique, an aura about himself as this brilliant investment strategist.

"There were two things that added to his aura," Mulholland observed. "One was that he took advantage of so-called black box investment strategy, which the SEC condones—I don't know if they will condone now—and is a strategy whereby the SEC will allow an investment manager like Madoff to maintain his particular strategy as proprietary, and on the basis of competitive ownership and the need to maintain proprietary custody of his secretive strategy, the SEC will allow him to avoid disclosing it."

Will any of Bernard Madoff's victims receive financial restitution?

Under a program initiated by the Securities Investor Protection Corporation (SIPC), a government agency that maintains a special reserve fund authorized by Congress to help investors at failed brokerage firms, there could be some relief: The program allows victims to claim compensation up to a maximum of $500,000, with no more than $100,000 of that amount distributed in cash. Those investors seeking compensation must prove that they sent money to Madoff in the twelve months prior to his arrest on December 11, 2008. Those seeking compensation beyond that which can be provided by the SIPC must pursue separate lawsuits, however, or join one of the many class-action claims arising from the scandal.

Federal District Court Judge Louis L. Stanton, who is in charge of the civil case against Madoff, was asked to broaden access to SIPC compensation for those individuals who had invested in "feeder funds," which in turn were invested with Madoff.

In a letter to the judge, one of those investors, Daniel R. Goldenson of Bremen, Maine, wrote: "This was an intertwined system of deceit and theft within our financial markets that has left retirees like ourselves having to sell our homes and raise any money we can."

On December 15, 2008, SIPC announced that it was liquidating Bernard Madoff's company under the Securities Investor Protection Act. That same day, the SIPC filed an application with the U.S. District Court for the Southern District of New York for a declaration that the customers of the Madoff firm were in need of protections under the SIPA. The court granted the application and appointed Irving H. Picard as trustee, and the law firm Baker & Hostetler as counsel to Picard.

In a statement, Stephen Harbeck, SIPC's president and CEO, acknowledged, "It is clear that the customers of the Madoff firm need the protection available under federal law." Harbeck cautioned, however, that the scope of the misappropriation and the state of the defunct firm's records would make this more difficult than in most prior brokerage firm insolvencies.

"It is unlikely that SIPC and the trustee will be able to transfer the customer accounts of the firm to a solvent brokerage firm," the SIPC's statement concluded. "The state of the firm's records may preclude a transfer of customer accounts. Also, because the size of the misappropriation has not yet been established, it is impossible to determine each customer's pro rata share of 'customer property.'"

A complicating factor for the Madoff firm's brokerage clients is that on December 2, 2008, forms were mailed by the SIPC to 925,000 customers and creditors of Lehman Brothers. Thus the Madoff's firm's many victims would have to wait in line after them in order to receive any compensation.

As to whether Sydelle Meyer will likely join that queue, she said, "We don't expect to get any restitution at all. I don't believe it is the government's responsibility to bail out the Madoff investors. It's bad enough we have to give to the automobile companies and everybody else. We should have done our own due diligence a lot sooner."

Observing that the impact of the implosion of Bernard Madoff Investment Securities is "global—I know people in New York, Los Angeles, and in London who were affected, but not anybody who's not Jewish who lost money with him," Tara Pearl said, adding that "sixty-five percent of my client base is international, and we are currently selling paintings owned by Palm Beach collectors to someone in Russia."

Gary Tobin, somewhat of a contrarian on the issue, maintained that "The way the story is being told in the Jewish community is that this is a person who was very involved in Jewish organizational life and is seen through the lens of the Jewish community, when, in fact, he is a former chairman of NASDAQ and was involved in financial and communal institutions of all kinds.

"The *real* story here is what he has done to American and world financial institutions, rather than what he has done to American Jewish philanthropy. This is not a Jewish story, as much as the hysteria you see in the Jewish press tries to make it out to be," Tobin insisted. "The idea, as has been expressed, that this is a catastrophe for an entire Jewish generation is just nonsense; it's *silly*. For example, if you take a look at the Forbes 400 list and look at the net worth of the Jews on that list—the hundred wealthiest Jews in America—they have a net worth of about $400 billion," Tobin observed.

"So if you are talking about generations of Jewish wealth being wiped out when there might be two or three or four billion dollars gone—perhaps more, but not likely—and think of the hundreds of billions of dollars that the Jewish community has, while it is tragic that some nonprofits are going to be hurt badly, it is not a tragedy for the *Jewish people.*

"That does not mean that some Jewish organizations have not been hurt badly, like Hadassah and Yeshiva University," Tobin added. "But for the most part, if you look at the thousands and thousands of Jewish organizations out there, 99.9 percent of them have not been touched in any serious way by this."

But, Tobin predicted, "Over time, there will be a tremendous loss to *American* philanthropy. If you look at where some of the Jewish-founded foundations that have gone out of business gave their money—the Picower Foundation, for example [based in Palm Beach, with an office in New York], gives ninety-six percent of its dollars to non-Jewish institutions—it is the range of non-Jewish institutions, universities, hospitals, and cultural organizations that are going to be hurt by this," Tobin explained, "because the majority of dollars that Jews give go to secular institutions, not to Jewish ones."

Soon after the disclosure of Madoff's thievery, the Picower Foundation, which in 2007 reported assets of $552 million, and was described by the *New York Times* as being "one of the nation's leading philanthropies," was forced to close its doors. Established in 1989 by Barbara and Jeffrey M. Picower, the foundation engaged in grant-making in education, medical research, and in the promotion of an equitable and inclusive society. The foundation's efforts in that regard consisted of supporting projects related to human rights, reproductive rights, and Jewish continuity. In 2002, the foundation extended a grant of $50 million to the Massachusetts Institute of Technology to build and staff a center for brain research. That grant, fortunately, had been fully funded.

In a statement, Barbara Picower said that this "act of fraud has had a devastating impact on tens of thousands of lives, as well as on many philanthropic foundations and nonprofit organizations."

As the days and weeks wear on, the list of Madoff's individual, profit-making, and not-for-profit victims grew larger. One investor, Robert Chew, wrote an article for *Time* magazine, entitled "How I Got Screwed by Bernie Madoff," in which he stated that he and his wife had been playing in "the Bernard Madoff Investment Securities, LLC Fantasy Financial League."

Chew recalled his wife's incredulous response to their investment adviser's telephone call informing them that their life savings had gone up in smoke: "You're joking! This is a joke, *right?*"

Investing "with a combination of pleasure and trepidation," the Chews had placed their life savings in the care of Madoff middleman Stanley Chais. In his *Time* article, Chew spelled out the extent of his family's involvement with Madoff: "We lost $1.2 million on paper, and my wife's family's combined losses are close to $30 million.... We are talking to old ladies, and men, lawyers, children with Madoff trusts, students in college, and an array of others who thought they had the world beat—and they did, at least for a *time.* Now, we and they and everyone in this fraud are all wiped out."

As for Stanley Chais, who suffered the loss of his foundation as well as significant personal wealth, he was sued by Eric Roth, a screenwriter, whose latest film credit was for *The Curious Case of Benjamin Button.*

In an action filed in Los Angeles Superior Court, Roth blamed Chais for the loss of a "substantial amount of money." It is likely that Chais will face additional legal actions in the months to come.

Also wiped out is New Jersey State Senator Loretta Weinberg. Her late husband had a saying, "If you make a dollar-and-a-half, you put seventy-five cents in a savings account and you live under the other seventy-five cents."

Senator Weinberg followed that maxim. Now, her $1.3 million nest egg is gone. As she stated in an interview with the Associated Press, "I had never heard of Bernie Madoff. My money was invested, along with [that of] many extended family members, with a financial adviser in Los Angeles."

That adviser was Stanley Chais.

Another major individual investor was ninety-five-year-old Carl Shapiro, who considered Madoff a son and sustained a $145 million loss to his foundation, as well as a huge personal loss.

Steering investors to BMIS was Robert Jaffe, Shapiro's son-in-law and a middleman for Madoff. Jaffe, a major Palm Beach philanthropist in his own right, was dubbed "the receiver," according to the *New York Post*.

While there is speculation as to whether Jaffe took any commissions for his activities on behalf of Madoff, he has become something of a controversial figure in Palm Beach—so much so that at a recent party held at the exclusive Mar-a-Lago Club, he and Jerome Fisher, the cofounder of the women's apparel chain Nine West and also one of Madoff's victims to the tune of $150 million, nearly came to blows.

The authors telephoned Jaffe's residence only to be told to contact his public relations representative. A few days later, the authors received a telephone call from Joshua Hochberg, a senior vice president of Sloane & Company, a firm specializing in, among other things, "crisis counseling," who read the following, terse statement: "[Mr. Jaffe] had no knowledge of the fraud, like so many others of the victims of those tragic events. Mr. Jaffe has known Mr. Madoff for forty years and was, like others, completely shocked at the disclosure of the fraud."

Should Chais and Jaffe be considered to be among Bernard Madoff's many victims?

As victims' attorney Mark Mulholland sees it, "Chais and Jaffe *are* innocent victims, but to the extent that they took it upon themselves to recommend an investment course for friends or colleagues, they took on something of a duty, and whether they're now responsible under local state laws or if they were acting as an investment adviser, then there may be some problems for them.

"Yes, they *are* victims," Mulholland exclaimed. "But they took it upon themselves to entice others into this mess. I've seen that theme play out in this mess repeatedly, where people who are victims are wearing multiple hats."

How has the American Jewish community reacted in the wake of the Madoff scandal?

"With embarrassment, frustration—the same thing happens any time a prominent Jew is involved in scandal," said Gary Tobin. "I remember when Ivan Boesky and Michael Milken were involved in financial scandals and the Jewish community was worried about a backlash. Yet ninety-nine percent of Americans didn't know that Boesky and Milken were Jewish.

"Now, with Bernie Madoff, there has been such a big story about how many Jewish organizations have been hurt that more people will know that. Certainly in the Jewish philanthropic world, everybody knows it."

This story has legs, and certain sectors of the media are having a field day tinged with just-under-the-radar anti-Semitism. For instance, in a story entitled, "Standing Accused: A Pillar of Finance and Charity," published in the Business Day section of the *New York Times* two days after Madoff's arrest, the fact that Madoff is Jewish was mentioned three times at the beginning of the piece.

Taking the *Times* to task in a letter to the editor published on December 21, American Jewish Committee (AJC) executive director David Harris pointed out that the *Times* did not make mention of the religion of Governor Rod Blagojevich when referring to his "shenanigans." He added: "...to refer to the 'Jewish T-bill,' 'the clubby Jewish world,' and the 'world of Jewish New York' within four paragraphs near the top of the article on Mr. Madoff was over the top."

On Tuesday, December 23, twelve days after Bernard Madoff's arrest prompted daily front-page headlines and thousands of comments posted on Internet sites, Harris told the authors, "I don't know if one can easily draw conclusions as yet if the media is portraying this in a way that strengthens anti-Semitism."

Harris was reacting to "an early story in the *New York Times* that was not meant to be about [Madoff's] *Jewishness*. In this article, the seeming obsession with his being Jewish came through in a way that I thought was inconsistent with what the article was purportedly attempting to do."

Attorney Barry Slotnick also took issue with the tone of the *Times* article, saying that he was "deeply upset by it."

The victims' representative is also troubled by the singling out of Jews as somehow being *different*. Describing a post-Madoff encounter with an acquaintance, Slotnick recalled, "He said to me 'you people' and I said, 'Do me a favor.' 'What's that?' he asked. 'Never again say the words *you people* to me.'"

Has the Madoff scandal in fact unleashed a new wave of anti-Semitism? "What the story will do is give all the anti-Semites the fuel on their financial conspiracies about Jews controlling the world," Gary Tobin predicts. "Then the question is: Does it create anti-Semitism?

"The answer is no," he said. "The vast majority of Americans are going to consider Bernie Madoff's religion irrelevant. The real issue is that this is the biggest financial scam in American history."

"The notion that this criminal reflects upon the Jewish community is a crazy message," Tobin continued. "It shows some level of insecurity, or discomfort, that Jews still have about their place in American society—that they have to make excuses for him. Many racial and ethnic religious communities respond this way;

it's not that unusual. But for Jews to go public with laying their embarrassment out for everybody to see is an overreaction."

"I can't say more broadly yet that this has unleashed a new wave of anti-Semitism or that the media is feeding it," David Harris said. "On the other hand I can't exclude it because it still remains to be seen." The AJC official added that "the mail that I have received as a result of the letter I wrote to the *Times* is voluminous. I've written a lot of letters to the *Times* over the years and I'm usually happy if *my mother* notices."

Most of the responses to Harris's letter were from Jews. "Many agree with me but a number *don't*," he said. "The reasoning is quite thoughtful. The real question they argue is: Wasn't the fact that Madoff is Jewish central to his ability to ingratiate himself and enter into various offices and clubs and institutions as a member of the Jewish community?"

From Harris's point of view, "If he were of another faith or ethnicity—if his name were O'Connor or Santini—if he had the same returns year after year, would the same people and institutions have flocked to him? I would like to think the answer is *yes*. But there is a dispute of people who argue: 'No, you are being unfair to the *Times*, Mr. Harris. His being Jewish was important to the story. So we condemn him but we don't condemn the *Times*.'"

On the other hand, Harris said, "I saw the story in today's *Times* [December 23, 2008] about Mr. Noel"—a principal in Fairfield Greenwich Group, a Madoff client with a $7.3 billion loss—"and I said to myself, 'Aha! Am I going to learn his religion in the story?' The answer is, I did *not*."

Morton Klein, an economist and the president of the Zionist Organization of America (ZOA) said, "I've never seen someone's religion invoked repeatedly toward somebody who has committed a serious crime as has Madoff's. They keep emphasizing that he's a *Jew*. We don't know what O.J. Simpson's religion is; we don't know what the governor of Illinois' religion is, and none of us care. That's because neither Simpson nor Blagojevich committed a crime in the name of his religion."

Harris said that the article he would like to see is one revealing "how Mr. Madoff, who believed himself to be an active and proud member of the Jewish community, could engage in business practices that could inflict such cataclysmic damage on the community of which he professed to be a proud member.

"How could he do that?" Harris asked. "What was going through his mind? Was he posturing all those years? Was it nothing more than a *front*? When he went to these meetings at Yeshiva University or anywhere else, was he *totally* insincere?"

"What has happened with Madoff is very disturbing," Klein said. "It has led to the ugly haters of Jews coming out from under their rocks and accusing the Jews of destroying the economy, of stealing money, and of sending it to Israel—of *Madoff* stealing money and sending it to Israel, which is rather astonishing in that he was destroying Jewish organizations to give it to a Jewish country.

"It makes no sense," Klein continued, "But making sense is not an important part of being an anti-Semite. I have actually heard people say that they become concerned about giving to Jewish causes if Jewish organizations are not being more conservative in their investments."

Asked how he responds to those who ask why organizations that invested with Madoff failed to perform due diligence, Klein said, "I say to them: If someone came to you and said, 'There is this fabulous financial adviser. It's very hard to place your money with him because he is overwhelmed with people who want to invest with him, he's the former head of NASDAQ, he's treasurer of Yeshiva University, he's head of the Sy Sims School of

Business, and Ira Rennert, Ezra Merkin, Elie Wiesel's foundation, and Hadassah all invest with him,' would I really worry that there's a problem? 'If you're lucky enough for him to take your money, this guy has been averaging ten to fifteen percent a year. And he's been doing it for thirty years.' If I heard that and invested with him, I'm not sure I could be fairly portrayed as doing something idiotic. I can see how you could be involved with him without investigating it thoroughly. I can see it because of this guy's *bona fide*, his incredible credentials."

The AJC's Harris said that Madoff's success in bilking such a large sector of the Jewish community "raises a number of profound questions for institutions, be they Jewish or non-Jewish, of issues of governance, of conflicts of interest, of lack of due diligence, of asset allocation."

Concerning the last question, Harris said, "Asset Allocation 101, for example, would tell you [to] never put more than ten percent of assets in any one instrument. That is the way we govern ourselves here. Yet in the case of a number of institutions, that clearly was *not* the case."

Regarding conflicts of interest, Harris observed that "people who watch over your money are not the people who should benefit from your asset allocation. In some cases that seems to have been neglected.

"To be fair, in addition to looking at the larger questions of the losses which are catastrophic, the larger questions of what the Jewish landscape will look like in the months ahead, I think there are internal questions that every institution has to ask. The fact that we at AJC dodged a bullet doesn't mean that we can sit pretty."

While the list of Jewish organizations taken in by Madoff's amazing performance is seemingly endless, the ZOA was one of the three bodies—the others being the AJC and the UJA-Federation of

New York, the nation's largest local philanthropy—that read the warning signs, saw the red flags, and did their due diligence.

In the days following the disclosure of the thievery, Klein said that he had been called "by many of my major donors, asking, 'Did you take the funds I gave you and invest them with Madoff?' Of course I *didn't*.

"I have had hedge fund people ask me to invest ZOA money in their hedge funds. I would look into it but couldn't quite figure out what they do. So I kept ZOA money away from hedge funds because their operations looked too complicated," Klein explained, adding that he had "never heard of pushing your money off to some other group without letting the donor know what you are doing. And then charging a fee for handing money over to Madoff? It's outrageous. To me, there is no other word for it but *theft*."

While ZOA saw the red flags, one of its donors did not. "He was with Madoff for thirty years, getting twelve percent a year," Klein said. "Did he worry for a second? Of course not! He said that 'every quarter, like clockwork, the check was there. And if at times I needed extra money, within four days I got the check.'"

As for the AJC's having avoided the temptation to entrust its funds with Madoff, David Harris said that after the story broke, "I was reminded by colleagues here that the Madoff name had come up in the AJC's investment committee some months ago, when someone had suggested we ought to explore investing some of our endowment money with Madoff. And the chairman of our investment committee actually said, 'No, I think it's a Ponzi scheme.' He actually used *those words* to the ten or fifteen people in the meeting."

Concerning UJA-Federation's decision not to invest with Madoff, the organization released a statement on December 16, 2008, five days after Madoff's arrest, in which it was explained that

"UJA-Federation does not make any new investments without the manager meeting with, and responding to questions from, members of the Investment Committee to give them an understanding of the manager's strategy and execution." One of the members of the Investment Committee was Ezra Merkin.

Mark Seal, a longtime Jewish organizational foot soldier, recalled in an interview with the *Forward*, the weekly Jewish newspaper, having observed Madoff, who was brought in by board members, giving pitches to the organization on two occasions, the first in the early 1990s and the second ten years later.

"Unlike other financial consultants who came in with flashy suits and elaborate presentations, Madoff was modest and kept things simple," Seal said, adding that Madoff displayed "a couple of pieces of paper with annualized returns. You got an explanation of covered options. It wasn't slick, and that, in some ways, endeared him to people. It was almost like he didn't need your money. Everyone else always seemed a little hungry and eager to get your business."

Madoff's winning presentation notwithstanding, UJA-Federation decided against entrusting BMIS with its considerable funds. "UJA-Federation would insist that securities be held by our independent custodian [JPMorgan]," the organization's statement explained. "That alone would have prevented investment in Madoff's securities, as we understand Madoff's structure depended on his firm also acting as the custodian."

Regarding the actions of hedge fund managers taken in by Madoff's scheme, attorney Taubenfeld said, "Having been involved in real estate investments, I can tell you that these people were almost criminal in that they did not perform due diligence."

As for Madoff's clients' inordinately high yields, Taubenfeld observed, "Anyone in the financial world or the real estate business knows that you can't guarantee an equal return every year. They were getting returns that they *couldn't* get, yet they never doubted that he could achieve these returns."

Then there is the ethics issue: "These people who gave Madoff hundreds of millions—and in some cases billions—were making a fortune through commissions from him for bringing money in," Taubenfeld said. "Most hedge funds pay their managers based on a percentage of their assets. So they were double-dipping and, in many cases, were violating their requirement that they protect their investors."

What of the prognosis for the Jewish organizations defrauded by Madoff? "This scandal has rocked the nonprofit world. Nonprofits that were directly impacted, if they were not forced to close, have to do business differently," said Robert Lappin, adding that "the scandal is putting more stress on Jewish agencies and on philanthropists to attempt to save what has not been destroyed by Mr. Madoff."

Observing that "Jewish philanthropy has been hurt in obvious and unforeseeable ways," Lappin said that "it's been increasingly difficult for the Jewish nonprofit world to raise funds, coupled with a declining Jewish population and smaller pool of potential funders. The impact has been described as cataclysmic, and I believe that this is an honest and fair assessment of the damage that has been caused by this case."

The ZOA's Klein is guardedly optimistic about the long run. He noted that Jews are "historically blamed for all the societal tragedies." At the present time, he said, "people are having great concern about giving money to charities because a number of them have not taken care of the money well." This concern, he predicts, "will dissipate."

The AJC's Harris had a less sanguine prediction. "As far as Jewish philanthropy is concerned, the dust has to settle, but right now the prognosis is not great. The conventional wisdom is that a year from now the organized Jewish community may look a bit different as a consequence of this Madoff meltdown, which comes on the heels of an economic slowdown. Either one by itself would have been major. If you put the two together, they are potentially catastrophic for many. Whether this leads to the closing of more organizations, consolidation, mergers, and the rethinking of goals and priorities of institutions that have been hard hit and need to shrink, clearly there will be consequences."

How did Bernard Madoff manage to pull off such massive fraud, and for so long?

David Harris believes that "The nation, and perhaps the world, became tantalized by notions of quick and sustained profits, where everyone wanted to get in on the deal."

"Those who cast judgment on Bernard Madoff's victims would do well to consider the experience of one of them," said Dr. Stephen Greenspan, a clinical professor of psychiatry at the University of Colorado.

In an article first appearing in the online newsletter *eSkeptic,* he wrote that he was attracted to the Madoff scheme by its promise of "small, but steady returns, high enough to be attractive but not so high as to arouse suspicion."

In making his investment—with the Rye Prime Bond Fund, part of the Tremont family of funds—Greenspan believed that he was dealing with some very reputable financial firms. Thus he had the impression that such investments "had been well researched and posed acceptable risks." While Greenspan never met Bernard Madoff, he did meet and come to like and trust the investment adviser who was authorized to sign people up to participate in the Rye, a Madoff-managed fund.

"The real mystery in the Madoff story is not how naive individual investors such as myself would think the investment safe," Greenspan stated, "but how the risks and warning signs could have been ignored by so many financially knowledgeable people, ranging from my investment adviser who sold me and my sister [and himself] on the investment to the highly compensated executives who ran the various feeder funds that kept the Madoff ship afloat.

"So should one feel pity or blame toward those who were insufficiently skeptical about Madoff and his scheme?" Greenspan asked. "It would be too easy to say that a skeptical person would, and should have, avoided investing in a Madoff fund. The big mistake here was throwing all caution to the wind, as in the stories of many people, some quite elderly, who invested every last dollar with Madoff or one of his feeder funds."

"I don't have the right as a manager of money to take on risk that I believe is inappropriate," said venture capitalist Fred Adler. "The Madoffs of this world are different. Apparently he had no sense of responsibility to his people or, at least, he lost it along the way.

"Most hedge funds report to investors that they work hard, meet with different investors, and do their best to check things out," Adler noted. "It seems to me that many of these people didn't do that. I can't understand why they wouldn't want to get significant information.

"This is a how-could-this-have-happened situation. It is so monstrous in its impact. In all fairness to the early investors who went in," the venture capitalist observed, "they started with a guy who was very successful in this computerized trading operation, so I can understand them."

What is it about Bernard Madoff, a man who could have done so much good for his community and society at large, that prompted him to dissipate his boundless energy and squander his skills for nearly fifty years, and then lose his nerve and confess to having committed what may go down in financial annals as the crime of the century?

Is Bernard Madoff mentally disturbed?

Is he a sociopath?

Or is he completely rational, but totally amoral?

CHAPTER THREE

THE JEWISH COMMUNITY IS NOT THE ONLY VICTIM

"I am not rich, or Jewish. I grew up below the poverty level, worked for twenty years for the same company. My job was outsourced in 1998. I lost approximately seventy percent of my life's savings in this mess. I am angry and pray that justice will be served on Madoff. However, to watch so many people play armchair QB is amazing. I don't have time for it. I have to start over and try to recoup as much as I can of my losses."

—Mike

"My 80 yr. old mother just lost her husband six months ago, and now every penny that she has had as a result of investing with Madoff. I'd love to help out, but I recently lost my position working on site in real estate sales. We are devastated! Where do we go now?"

—Sherrie

"Hey. There are many of us who loved and respected Bernie and he [has] stolen EVERYTHING from us. I cannot believe he was a monster, but I will never forgive him for stealing my family's money. Still, he was brilliant in many ways. He has a wonderful family who deserve our support. Something [probably his ego] made him dig this hole for us. Let us try to be human beings, not judges!"—Eliz

"I lost all my savings. I would like to be part of a class action lawsuit. Could somebody please give this info. I wonder even if my name shows up in any of this crook's books."—Kaat

"My family has been devastated by this. This year our 70-year-old family business shut down and now we are dealing with this. We reside in Metro Detroit, the nation's open wound. Madoff should do the right thing and rid the world of his presence. Read: The Asian executives that took their own lives because of bad judgment and errors that cost so many people so much!"—Howard

"Bernard Madoff is a terrorist, a financial terrorist whose actions will bring down the trust Americans have on a system which is supposed to shield us from such nightmare[s]. He does not deserve to [sic] privilege to be called a son of America. I am speaking on behalf of my family and the American people who's [sic] work ethics, hard work and dreams where shattered by such a traitor. In this time of world instability I've always thought a stranger could do us harm. But to think that one of us could have done this is unbearable, God help us."

—Jorge and Clara

"The Madoff affair is the last straw we needed in this crisis and it is more severe than 9/11 to the Financial System of the world. It destroyed not only billions of assests [sic], but the trust needed in any kind of investment business."—Joh., Pfister, Switzerland

"We are witnessing true 'terrorism.' No one has to attack this country. We will do that ourselves. The USA is truly becoming the real joke of the civilized world."

—John Welch

The Internet communications medium of the Web log, known popularly as the blog, is being used by thousands of individuals wishing to discuss the Madoff scandal.

Lest it be assumed that the bulk of Madoff's crimes were perpetrated against his own community, gentiles, too, suffered greatly: Witness the blogs of individuals, apparently of relatively modest means, displayed above.

These blogs, as well as those to be found in later chapters, represent a cross section of views of the vox populi and are reproduced on these pages exactly as they appeared on the Internet, abbreviations, sentence structure, and punctuation reflecting not only the bloggers' haste, but their strongly felt emotions as well. Some of them were written anonymously, others by people signing only their first names.

Wealthy individuals also suffered major losses. Near the top of that roster is Lilliane Betancourt of Paris, the eighty-six-year-old daughter of Eugene Schueller, the founder of L'Oréal cosmetics.

Betancourt, who, according to Bloomberg.com is "the world's wealthiest woman," invested part of her $22.9 billion fortune in a fund managed by Access International Advisors, founded in 1994, which had placed $1.4 billion with BMIS.

One of the firm's partners was Philippe Junot, the former husband of Princess Caroline of Monaco. A cofounder was Thierry Magon de La Villehuchet, who had been based in New York since 1983. Magon de la Villehuchet lost his personal fortune as well as his clients' and was found dead in his Manhattan office on December 24, 2008, a likely suicide. He had taken sleeping pills and cut his biceps and wrists, and a box cutter was discovered near his body, as was a garbage bin, which he had strategically positioned to collect his blood as his life ebbed away.

Access International Advisors told investors in September 2008 that it carried out "extensive" due diligence on the funds to which it allocated money, even boasting that it had hired private investigators to run "extensive background checks" on fund managers.

Other hedge funds caught up in Bernard Madoff's fraud include Austin Capital Management, Fairfield Greenwich Group, Kingate Management, Tremont Capital, and Union Bancaire Privée.

One of the funds particularly hard hit is Ascot Partners, headed by J. Ezra Merkin, which lost $1.8 billion. Ascot Partners is certain to face an avalanche of lawsuits, as are other hedge funds involved with Madoff.

In October 2006, Merkin sent a document to prospective investors with a minimum participation of $500,000. In the document he outlined both a strategy and a program, "consisting of capital appreciation and income by investing in a diversified portfolio of securities."

In the offering, Ascot Partners promised that Merkin, as general partner, "intends, to the extent circumstances permit, to adopt a selective approach in evaluating investment situations generally concentrating on relatively fewer transactions that *he* [italics added] can follow more closely."

It was also stated that Merkin retained the right to give over assets to other third-party managers who "engage in investment strategies similar to the Partnership's."

If ever there was a cautionary tale about reading the fine print, Merkin's offering statement is it.

For its services—now revealed as mostly turning over its investment assets to Madoff—Ascot received an annual fee of 1.5 percent. Adding insult to injury, Merkin had told prospective investors that a decision to use third-party managers necessitated higher fees. Apparently, neither in written form nor in conversations with clients did Merkin inform his investors that *Madoff* was, in essence, handling their money.

When the fraud was revealed, Merkin sent the investors a three-page "Dear Limited Partner" letter, in which he stated that as "one of the largest investors in our fund," he shared their pain—scant consolation to his clients.

The gentile financial establishment, too, has been rocked to its very core.

For instance, while the Connecticut-based Fairfield Greenwich Group, a hedge fund advisory company, turned handsome profits during its association with Bernard Madoff—collecting in excess of $500,000 million in fees since 2003—Fairfield lost $7.3 billion in the wake of the implosion of BMIS.

Rather than sharing the wealth, Fairfield disbursed its largesse to its top executives, among them the fund's founder, Walter M. Noel. He had used his share to support a jet-set lifestyle, with five luxurious, multimillion dollar homes: a pied-à-terre at 812 Park Avenue in Manhattan; his primary residence in Greenwich, Connecticut; and houses in Southampton, an exclusive Long Island enclave, as well as in Florida and the Caribbean; together worth more than $20 million.

"The way it worked," said attorney Mark Mulholland, "is that Fairfield set up Century Fund, which was the fund that invested in Madoff. Investors in Century Fund signed an agreement with Fairfield that allowed Fairfield a twenty percent performance fee for monies earned on the monies invested by Century.

"Let's take a hypothetical $1 billion, because it's an easy number to work with. If Century puts a billion with Madoff in 2000, and over the next one-year period Madoff reports that he's earned a hundred million [ten percent], Century Fund will now book a

$100 million accrual income on its financial statements and $100 million to its investors.

"Even though that income is phantom income that Madoff didn't really *earn*, Fairfield and Century are booking it as $100 million of income. They then turn to their investors and say: 'We are entitled to our twenty percent performance fee.' So they are able to take the twenty percent performance fee out of that $100 million in real, actual dollars," Mulholland explained. "And, of course, it was not a billion, it was *seven* billion."

Mulholland continued: "If you multiply this out over a period of years and years, you will see that Fairfield was able to extract hundreds of millions of dollars in performance fees, using accrual accounting to its advantage, and taking those fees based on bogus, fictitious income that no one had really earned.

"If you ask why they didn't see the red flags, well, there's your answer," said Mulholland. "There was this enormous, glowing carrot of the twenty percent performance fee blinding their eyes.

"Fifty billion is the fictitious amount reported on all the phony monthly statements issued to the several thousand Madoff victims," Mulholland noted. "So if I invest a million with him in 1980, and he reports to me that over the years that million has grown to five million, that five million dollar figure is phantom. If you add up all those five millions you get your fifty billion. So the true number, once it's discovered, will be half or less than the fifty billion."

In the wake of revelations about Fairfield's association with Madoff, questions arose concerning its performance—the hedge fund had assured its own investors that any transfer of their funds to BMIS would require two signatures—and even about whether Fairfield was involved in the carrying-out part of Madoff's Ponzi scheme.

Did Fairfield fulfill its fiduciary responsibilities to its own clients by making good on its pledge to monitor and track Madoff's investments? Was Fairfield a victim of Madoff's fraud, as it is now claiming? Or was there collusion with Madoff in the scamming of the financial establishment?

Early in 2008, several private equity and investment firms were approached by Fairfield: Would they be interested in purchasing shares in the hedge fund? A partner in one of the firms actually considered Fairfield's proposition—to purchase shares amounting to anywhere from one third to one half of Fairfield's value, which, the partner was told, was estimated to be between $1 and $1.5 billion.

The prospective buyer demurred about twenty minutes into an initial meeting with Fairfield managers, however, finding their team to be "just incredibly squishy and vague, even during the warm-up." When asked about the manager of the fund Fairfield fed into, he was told, "We don't really need to talk about him."

Ten days after the public revelation of Madoff's Ponzi scheme, Thomas Mulligan, a Fairfield spokesman, had only the following to say: "Fairfield Greenwich Group is in the process of gathering and reviewing all of the factual information relevant to its having been defrauded by Bernard Madoff."

Another Connecticut banking institution, Westport National Bank, has come under scrutiny as well. The *New York Times* broke the story on December 31, 2008, that attorneys as far away as Florida were investigating the role that Westport may have played in funneling money to BMIS.

The attorneys, Adam T. Rabin, a partner at McCabe Rabin in West Palm Beach, and co-counsel Craig Stein, a partner in Stein, Stein & Pinsky in Boca Raton, said that their clients, a middle-aged professional couple living in South Florida, had assumed for more than a decade that they had their accounts with the Westport National Bank, a division of Westport's Connecticut Community Bank, where they had invested after being approached by a "promoter," and from where they had received their statements for many years showing deductions for "custodial and record-keeping fees" amounting to four percent annually. That would not turn out to be the case, however. In an early "Christmas present," the clients learned in a letter from Westport National Bank, dated December 12, 2008, and delivered to their doorstep via Federal Express, that their money had, in fact, been entrusted to Bernard Madoff. Thus they joined the ranks of wealthy individuals and institutions that have also learned of the transfer of their funds without their knowledge and were filing lawsuits.

Beginning with the salutation "Dear Custodial Services Customer," the letter went on, in an attempt at face-saving, to state that the couple had given "full discretionary authority" over their account at the bank to BMIS. "You may have learned of the recent allegations involving Bernard Madoff's firm," the letter continued. The couple was then asked to notify the bank as to whether they desired it to request that BMIS "return assets of yours to the bank."

Now beleaguered bank officials appear to be struggling to play catch-up, claiming on December 31 that Westport's only role had been to maintain "a custodial account for a number of individuals and entities" invested with BMIS.

The bank's president, Richard T, Cummings Jr., issued a statement on that day that "As custodian, Westport National Bank served in a ministerial capacity only," and that the bank neither offered investment advice nor invested its own assets with BMIS.

Madoff's long arm of fraud reached around the globe, from the Man Group, the British financial services company and sponsor of the prestigious Man Booker literary prize, with approximately

$360 million invested in funds linked to BMIS, to major international banks, including Bank Medici of Austria, KBC Group NV of Belgium, Natixis SA and BNP Paribas of France, UniCredit SpA of Italy, Banco Espirito Santo of Portugal, Fortis of the Netherlands, Banco Santander of Spain, Nordea Bank AB of Sweden, Union Bancaire Privée and UBS AG of Switzerland, and Barclays PLC, HSBC, and the Royal Bank of Scotland in the United Kingdom, to numerous hedge funds, brokerage firms, and pension funds in Europe and Asia.

The Madoff meltdown also ensnared major accounting firms that oversaw many of the feeder funds that channeled billions of dollars in ill-gotten gains into the biggest Ponzi scheme ever. Investigators want to know how and why such prestigious firms as Price Waterhouse Coopers and KPMG ignored red flags that were raised during their audits of those funds.

Austria's Bank Medici had placed $2.1 billion in Madoff's hands with two of their funds, Herald USA and Herald Luxemburg. With a focus on asset management, investment banking, and international, private banking, the bank was founded in 1994 by Sonja Kohn, who is reportedly close friends with Madoff. The bank's Web site, which obviously was produced before the Madoff crisis erupted, contains the text: "It is this most unusual mixture of financial strength and tradition, of sophisticated know-how and technological expertise, and of entrepreneurial flexibility, creativity, and team spirit, that makes BANK MEDICI a powerful and valuable partner"—a bitter lesson for the bank's investors to not necessarily believe everything they read. The bank has since been taken over by the Austrian government.

Spain's Banco Santander, whose $3.3 billion investment with Madoff accounts for about one fourth of the total potential loss to European investors, was the recipient only this past July of a financial publication's "Best Bank in the World" award. Adding to the bank's misery over entrusting its funds with Madoff is the comment made at the awards ceremony by its chairman, Emilio Botin, that "If you don't fully understand an instrument, don't *buy* it."

Insurance companies, banks, and funds in Israel, Japan, the United Kingdom, and Switzerland have also been caught up in Bernard Madoff's machinations.

Lest one assume that no one escaped unscathed, there were individuals who saw the warning signs and heeded the red flags raised by BMIS over the years, among them bloggers who continue to post their comments as the scandal unfolds:

> "I was 'privileged' few months ago to be financially capable of investing with Bernie Madoff. Due diligence was sent to my home before meeting with 'rep. It was MY money and read every word. RED FLAGS were up all over the place. Accounts not backed by any regulatory body!!!!!!! No association, verbally or on paper with Bernie Madoff???? Yet, HE was mastermind behind consistent returns. Statements? Would I like to checkout [sic] trading details on a daily basis? Could I get duplicate reports? Thank God for red flags."
>
> —Roxie

> "In 2002 I did Due Dilligence [sic] on Madoff for a large Swiss institution. We had been advised before by several large hedge funds not to invest with him; mainly because there was no independent fund administrator, which could have meant we would always have been in doubt whether the reports would be correct. In the end we followed this very simple, logical argument and did not want to invest. Even so, my personal interview with Madoff was excellent, his

brokerage offices were incredibly well organized and spotless clean [the only truly paperless trading floor I have ever seen, and I have seen about a hundred] the staff all looked young and preppy, almost like actors. Maybe this was part of the scam as well? His explanation for his performance was that through his supposedly largest US wholesale brokerage activities he knew the market flows and could thereby time the S&P100, calibrating the risk by using bull-call spread trades. This seemed somewhat plausible. However, with our outside confirmation of his trades, we decided not to invest. In short: By applying some simple operational risk controls, it was easy to evade this trouble."—Nick

As the various investigations of BMIS, and of the banks, feeder funds, accountancy firms, and individuals enticed into Bernard Madoff's web continued, one thing is certain: There will be many civil lawsuits and criminal indictments.

Part Two
The Madoff Family

CHAPTER FOUR

THE MAN BEHIND THE SHAMELESS VIOLATION OF THE COMMANDMENT "THOU SHALT NOT STEAL"

"I met with Mr. Madoff once in 1998, and again in 2003, in Palm Beach, Florida. I had a nodding acquaintance with him and I considered him to be a paragon of virtue, and his strategy a paradigm for conservative investing."—Robert L. Lappin

"He and his wife were nice golfers. He and his wife seemed lovely."
—Denise Lefrak Calicchio, a social acquaintance of Ruth and Bernard Madoff

"For me, he was a gentleman. What he did outside, it was news to me."
—Senio Figliozzi, Bernard Madoff's Palm Beach barber for seventeen years

"He is a very troubled man, very sociopathic."
—Tara Pearl, Palm Beach realtor and businesswoman who is now helping Bernard Madoff's victims to sell their remaining possessions

"I met Bernie Madoff once, in a restaurant with one of my clients, and we shook hands—that was all. Then I went to my table and had dinner. Thank God I didn't give him a check!"

—Barry Slotnick, attorney for
some of Madoff's victims

B ernie Madoff was born on April 29, 1938, into a middle-class family in New York. Growing up in Laurelton, in Queens, one of the five boroughs comprising New York City, he attended Far Rockaway High School, graduating in 1956.

Surprisingly, while acquaintances of Bernard Madoff the financier vividly recalled many aspects of his personality, several high school classmates and a teacher with whom we spoke only vaguely remembered him as a teenager.

Arthur Traiger, who taught at Far Rockaway High School from 1949 to 1956, said, "It's peculiar, but I cannot place Madoff at all. He graduated in 1956, at the time I was teaching advanced classes in the English department. When I look over the lists of students who attended the school, I usually can put a face on dozens and dozens of students, even though we've had these intervening years."

"When his name came up—that he had been a Far Rockaway student—I thought that I would search my memory and see if I could find out if I had taught him. But I just don't see him at all. He may have been a very nondescript, average kind of student."

Stephen Pine, a classmate of Madoff's who grew up in Rockaway Beach and commuted to Far Rockaway High School by public bus, said, "I didn't know him. If I did, I don't remember him."

Bob Nessoff, who grew up in the neighborhood of Arverne and commuted by bus to school, said that "people in the Rockaways all knew each other. It was a big small town." Following Madoff's arrest, Nessoff said, "Somebody e-mailed me and said, 'How about Bernie!' I remember his name; it immediately struck me. I realized that we went to high school together. But we weren't social friends or anything like that."

"I know he was on the swim team," Nessoff added. "He worked at the Silver Point beach club in Atlantic Beach. The swimming coach got him the job. It's possible he was from Laurelton, since kids from Laurelton and Rosedale either went to Andrew Jackson or Far Rockaway High School."

"A lot of kids did what he did, working as a life guard or a cabana boy at a beach club." Traiger noted. "If Bernie Madoff was on the swimming team, I would not have had much contact with him. The phys ed department was not a strong group of people intellectually; they were jocks. But they had a lot of control over the student body because sports were very important."

What would life have been like for Bernie Madoff in the mid-1950s?

The authors were struck, in conversations with several of Madoff's high school classmates, by their near idyllic recollections of life in the Eisenhower era, a time when young people were thought to be complacent.

"I can tell you that growing up in the fifties was great; Far Rockaway High was a perfect school, and Bayswater, where I lived, was the perfect place to live," said Carol Solomon-Marston, another schoolmate of Bernie's.

"We had a good football team, a good swimming team, and a good rifle team. It was a big family; everybody knew everybody," Bob Nessoff observed. "If you want to understand the atmosphere there, think of *Happy Days*. We all dressed like Fonzi, except that Fonzi was a little later than we were. Very few people wore jeans to school; chinos would be the thing. Your belt buckle was off to the side, your collar was up, your sleeves were rolled up. That was de rigueur. If you weren't dressed like that, you were what would later be called a nerd."

Arthur Traiger recalled that the female students "were bobby-soxers who wore pleated skirts and Lana Turner—type sweaters."

"The students came from Far Rockaway, Rockaway Beach, Belle Harbor, Neponsit, and Arverne. It was a very good high school, one of the top high schools," Stephen Pine said. "It always had a high rating academically, and had a very good swimming team, and a good football team that won the PSAL championship one year. Our graduating class had six or seven hundred kids. All my friends went on to college. They had their careers and were successful people."

"In a way the school was stratified," Traiger said. "We had academic classes, commercial classes, and general classes. But there was no strife; I can't remember one single incident due to the school's diverse population."

"Laurelton students were not in the Far Rockaway High School district," Traiger noted. "Many of them wanted to go to Far Rockaway, however, because our school was a better one—a premier high school at that time—and in order to do so, a lot of those students opted to take Hebrew. I would stack it up with any private school in America. That's how good the top-ranked students were at that time." Among Far Rockaway High's exceptionally bright students were three Nobel Prize winners, psychologist, author, and television personality Joyce Brothers, and industrialist Carl Icahn.

Bob Nessoff recalled Far Rockaway High as having been "predominately Jewish, but it was a mixed school. There were a lot of people who were not Jewish, but on a Jewish holiday the school was virtually empty. There were a number of black students also, and everybody got along pretty well. We didn't know that there was such a thing as racism at that time."

According to Arthur Traiger, "In those days, the Rockaway peninsula was quite stratified. At the extreme western end was Belle Harbor, a rich Jewish community. Next to Belle Harbor was Rockaway Park, which had a similar, if not quite as rich, population. Then came an Irish section. Below the Irish group, in Hammels, there was a black group. Then in Arverne there was a Jewish group. Then you had Edgemere with a large summer population. Finally, there was Far Rockaway with a predominately Jewish population."

There *were* social divisions, however, said Nessoff. "The kids from Belle Harbor and Neponsit were the richer kids," Nessoff explained. "The ones from Rockaway Park were a step or two down. Bayswater was upper middle class. Arverne, where I came from, was strictly middle class, with many blue collar families. We used to refer to the people who lived in the many bungalow colonies as 'summer trash.'"

Fletcher Eberle, a cocaptain of Far Rockaway High's swim team, said in an interview with Doug Feiden of the *New York Daily News*, "The Bernie I knew was a good-natured, happy-go-lucky guy, always smiling and kidding, who swam the butterfly very well and never got overly serious. If you had said to me that Bernie was going to be chairman of NASDAQ and make all that money, I never would have believed it possible."

After graduating from Far Rockaway High, Bernie attended Hofstra University. Founded in 1935 with funds provided by William Hofstra and located in Hempstead, Long Island, twenty-five miles from New York City, the school was a branch of New York University until 1939. It would become known as Hofstra University in 1960, the year of Bernie Madoff's graduation.

"At that time Hofstra did not have the kind of reputation that some of the Ivy League schools had," Arthur Traiger observed. "The top Far Rockaway students went to the Ivy League schools. The 1956 class was exceptional; there were a lot of bright, bright students, and I taught most of them."

Among Hofstra's celebrity graduates are movie director Francis Ford Coppola, actress Madeline Kahn, and the best-selling novelist Nelson DeMille. Bernie Madoff would himself come to be regarded as a celebrity alumnus, becoming a trustee of his alma mater in 2004.

All that ended on December 12, 2008, as Madoff's enormous Ponzi scheme was revealed to the world. On that day he was suspended from his post. In a statement issued by the university at the time, it was emphasized that "the charges against Mr. Madoff have nothing to do with his prior role at the university; the university is in no way involved in the dealings of Mr. Madoff's firm, and has no investments of any type with the Madoff firm.

"After learning of the charges against Mr. Madoff through public reports," the statement continued, "on December 12, 2008, the university's board of trustees voted unanimously to place Mr. Madoff on leave. As of January 1, 2009, Mr. Madoff will no longer be a member of the board of trustees."

Much earlier in his career, Bernie Madoff attended Brooklyn Law School for a time—a "fact" noted on page four of BMIS's Web site (see Appendix A).

A murky area is whether Madoff ever served in the military. At a time when the Cold War military draft was in full force and service was compulsory unless the Selective Service determined otherwise, there seems to be no record of military service by Bernie Madoff, either following his graduation from high school in 1956 or from college in 1960, the year he established BMIS. It is conceivable, although unlikely, that he did a six-month tour of active duty in the Army Reserve.

Somewhere along the way, Bernie married a high school friend, Ruth Alpern. A graduate of Queens College, class of 1961, Ruth earned a master's degree in nutrition from New York University. In 1996, she co-edited a cookbook, *The Great Chefs of America Cook Kosher.*

In 1960, at the age of twenty-two, after graduating from Hofstra University with a degree in political science and briefly attending law school, or so his clients were told, Bernie decided to use the $5,000 he had earned as a lifeguard and installer of sprinkler systems to establish a securities investment firm in Manhattan, which he called Bernard L. Madoff Investment Securities, LLC, or BMIS.

Ambitious yet disarmingly affable, clever but low-key, Bernie took to his new calling with enthusiasm. While basically serving as a middleman between buyers and sellers of shares, Bernie also ran an investment advisory business, managing hedge funds, the money of wealthy individuals, as well as that of Jewish and non-Jewish organizations and financial institutions.

"He was very personable," Jon Najarian recalled, adding that he first heard of Madoff in the late 1980s. "The reason was that back in those days, we were paying a lot of money to trade stock and I was being charged between five and six cents per share," Najarian said. "Then in 1989, I began to see articles in *Barrons* talking about this guy in New York who was buying order flow [aggregated, small securities orders that brokers send to dealers often in return for cash payments], not from the customer directly, but from a firm—let's say, for example, from Charles Schwab. He would buy some order flow, buying on the bid or selling to customers on the offer in S&P 500 stocks. The reason he did it was that back then, the spread between the bid and the offer was quite large. If you are doing this hundreds or thousands of times a day, it is a printing press of money.

"He may have been one of the first people to get into that payment for order flow business," Najarian continued. "It was probably a profitable business for him—he may have been running his Ponzi scheme at that time—it remained a profitable business for him during the next decade, when virtually every firm on Wall Street got into that business.

"And although volumes went up dramatically, the spread—the edge, if you will—went down dramatically. Looking back on it now," Najarian said, "my theory is that he started seeking publicity after everyone started getting into the game. The reason that would make sense to me is that if you had a secret, or alchemy, and a way to make money from making fuel from seawater, for example, you wouldn't tell me about it. You would only do it after the practice became well known and you had no secret to sell anymore. At that point, he used the story as the hook to get people into his clutches."

Monica Gagnier, a reporter for the financial paper *Investor's Business Daily* and for the newsletter *Trading Systems Technology*, who covered Bernard and Peter Madoff during the 1980s, recalled both brothers' "street smarts and their charm."

In a posting on BusinessWeek.com, Gagnier wrote:

> *Bernie was the elder statesman and Peter the young visionary. They were generous with their time, whether it was explaining the intricacies of market structure to a fledgling reporter or striving to improve the competitiveness of the NASDAQ Stock Market. It was thanks to the efforts of people like Bernie Madoff that NASDAQ was able to attract listings from top-tier tech companies such as Apple, Sun Microsystems, Cisco Systems, and later search powerhouse Google.*

It wasn't long before certain wealthy would-be investors were joining clubs Madoff belonged to just so they could get close enough to the seeming wizard in order to beg him to let them invest their ample funds with BMIS. Bernie Madoff didn't take on just any wealthy investor, however. One of his favorite tactics was to refuse certain supplicants, thus engendering exclusivity about BMIS.

But Bernie Madoff was no mere financial wizard. In an era when stock trades were still laboriously conducted by telephone, we are told that he intuitively grasped the need for a rapid way of conducting and finalizing transactions in an ever more computer-driven world. In turn he fully automated BMIS so that a transaction would take only four seconds from start to finish. And in doing so, Bernie Madoff set off the computerization of the entire financial industry.

Not everybody agrees that Bernie Madoff was the technology pioneer he is reputed to be. Jon Najarian said, "I don't know that he was an innovator in true electronic trading. I did not see anything about him, or his background, that would have led me to believe that he was on a par with other electronic trading firms that I know very well, ones that are populated with geniuses. I didn't see that from him, but I didn't see him as a crook either. In hindsight about many of the things I saw back then, I could say, 'Oh my God! This was a *red flag.*'"

So impressive were the Madoff firm's computer trading programs to others, however, that the brothers were mentioned in a 1996 scholarly paper entitled "Quotes Order Flow and Price Discovery." The paper's co-author, Marshall Blume, the Howard Butcher III Professor of Financial Management at the University of Pennsylvania's Wharton School, told the authors that "at that time, anybody that was interested in the trading world would have been derelict if they hadn't gone to the Madoff office. They had a substantial portion of the NYSE listed trading and NASDAQ trading. They were a major player."

Blume was interested in the computerized system for order flow that the Madoffs had put in place. "They found a niche that they exploited that helped customers a lot. Remember that at that time there were fixed, high commissions, and the Madoffs found a way in which retail customers could trade with some benefits. They were able to interface computer-wise with the retail brokerage firms and reduce costs all over the place."

Blume said that the Madoff brothers were "very personable" and that they got along very well and worked as a pair. There was a division of labor, the professor said: "Peter was highly skilled technically and was able to implement some of the systems; Bernie was very astute in understanding the regulatory environment."

"I was late to the game," said venture capitalist Fred Adler. "I invested with Madoff more than ten years ago, when I came to Palm Beach. I had never heard of him before. I had joined the Palm Beach Country Club and he was talked about there; his name came up with people saying what a genius he was and that he had made all this money from, what I gathered, was a trading operation.

"I wouldn't say he had 'boosters' in Palm Beach, but he had people who really loved and respected him," Adler observed, adding that, "I wasn't part of that circle. I bumped into him in an Italian restaurant on Second Avenue in Manhattan. All I can say is that he was a very nice man. I never discussed investments with him. His wife is a perfectly lovely, sweet woman and I never discussed investments with her, and I never met his sons.

"I put some money in, along with two fellows who work with me," Adler recalled. "We said, 'Let's look and see what he's doing.' After a year or so, we didn't have any more idea [of what he was doing] than at the beginning, so, when you don't know enough, you go home. It was luck that I got into it and *good luck* that I got out of it."

According to Jon Najarian, Madoff was somewhat of an innovator: "He was one of the first to figure out that bid spread. I suspect that he did make money for at least a decade on that legitimate scheme, even though many of us thought that that particular style of trading was just wrong.

"I would talk to the SEC about how I believed it was wrong, that rather than letting an order go to a major exchange, they would trade it on these regional exchanges, where nobody could interact with it. It was just done electronically; I buy it on the bid or sell it on the offer," Najarian explained.

"As they did that, they destroyed the ecology of the trading floor because there is no edge for the rest of us on the floor," he added. "The argument we would make to the SEC would fall on deaf ears: [Chairman] Arthur Levitt would hear the argument and say, 'You don't like Bernie because he is doing this and you're a competitor.'

"We would answer, 'Yes, we *are* competitors, but it's not a fair competition.' He has none of the overhead that we have as far as regulatory and all the rest, and, as it turns out, he had no regulatory oversight, it seems," Najarian said. "We thought it was unfair and would ultimately result in fewer participants in the market. The SEC never wanted to hear it."

Also to his advantage, Madoff was adept at both self-promotion and client relations. His corporate slogan, "The Owner's Name Is on the Door," would reinforce his managerial image, as well as provide his growing list of wealthy clients with a reassuring declaration—a personal acknowledgement of his fiduciary responsibility to them.

Madoff's seeming commitment to his clients is reflected in what can be interpreted as his mission statement (see Appendix A). The document was found by the authors on December 15, 2008, on BMIS's Web site, but was later removed by the U.S. government, which seized the site as part of the investigation into Madoff's Ponzi scheme.

While rambling and repetitive, with the odd bolding throughout of two words, *Madoff* and *security(ies)*, the document emphasized the firm's expertise, track record, integrity, and commitment to its clients—and in the wake of 9/11, concern for the security of their investments. That concern was reflected in Madoff's creation of a sophisticated "Disaster Recovery Facility," located near LaGuardia Airport in his home borough of Queens, which was described in detail on page three of BMIS's Web site. When read from the perspective of Madoff's giant scam and swindle, however, this document should be viewed as a cautionary tale concerning what the man was really about. While seeming to profess concern about the possibility of another 9/11, Madoff was apparently well into the process of perpetrating his $50 billion Ponzi scheme—a crime that could well go down in history as "12/11."

As Bernard Madoff began to avidly pursue his nefarious activities, he was soon rewarded with considerable financial gain, which he used to establish luxurious, although not ostentatious, homes: He spent $3.25 million on a Manhattan duplex in 1990 and also bought houses in Montauk, in Long Island's trendy Hamptons, and in Palm Beach, Florida, described as being worth $9.3 to $21 million. In addition to acquiring his three homes, Madoff had treated himself to a fifty-five-foot wooden fishing boat in 1977, which he purchased for $462,000. What did Madoff name his new toy? "Bull."

The Palm Beach place was located on the Intracoastal Waterway at 389 South Lake Drive, about one mile from the Palm Beach Country Club (where Madoff played golf with a 9.8 handicap), and was described by Lawrence Leamer as "a large house, a lovely house, maybe a mid-size mansion; not one of the mega-mansions. He didn't live the way he could have lived. But he lived extremely *well.*" Just one week before his arrest, Bernie Madoff enjoyed one of his $65 haircuts, as well as his customary $40 shave, $22 manicure, and $50 pedicure at the Everglades Barber Shop, just off Worth Avenue—his tab of $177 not even chump change for a billionaire.

In Manhattan, Bernie and Ruth enjoyed many meals at Primola, an eatery serving Italian food and located several blocks east of their cooperative building. The restaurant's manager, Tomas Romano, said that his billionaire client insisted on being seated at a front table, where he was invariably greeted by other well-heeled diners, many of whom were the very people he was defrauding

As for other trappings of achievement associated with the super-rich, Leamer observed that Madoff "didn't have a private jet—a sign of true Palm Beach wealth—although he could have afforded one."

From the vantage points of Manhattan, the Hamptons, and Palm Beach, Madoff observed his wealthy neighbors, joined their exclusive clubs, established their trust, and soon had them literally begging to be given the opportunity to invest in BMIS.

One of those exclusive gathering places frequented by Madoff was the Palm Beach Country Club. With its 300 member couples, Lawrence Leamer described the place as "the elite Jewish club—at least as elite as the two restricted WASP clubs: the Bath and Tennis and the Everglades. You have to give large amounts to charity; you have to have made your money in what is considered honorable professions," Leamer explained. "If you're a slumlord, you're not going to get into the Palm Beach Country Club. It's very exclusive and very insular. That's why a third to half of its members were hurt [by Madoff]."

One member of the club said that the Madoffs were not exactly social animals there, nor were they social climbers—members of the "blister pack," as another member put it, referring to the figurative abrasions suffered by those members preoccupied with making the right connections and ascending to the top rung of the social ladder. In fact, said one investor who did not want to be identified, Bernie Madoff was held in such high regard that "people were joining golf clubs just to get into his fund."

Madoff didn't accept just any investor, however, as Manhattan realtor Barbara S. Fox discovered. Fox, the president of the Fox Residential Group, who had sold Madoff's younger son, Andrew, his apartment at 10 Gracie Square, abutting East End Avenue, told the *New York Times* that she "literally begged" Madoff—in vain, it would turn out—to allow her to put money into BMIS.

Another Madoff wannabe, Robert Ivanhoe, chairman of the real estate practice of the law firm Greenberg Traurig, told the *Times* that he asked a Madoff client of many years' standing who had invested more than $50 million with BMIS to approach Madoff about the possibility of his investing. Bernie Madoff said no to that request, too, his refusal making the idea of investing with him even more desirable. "People chased to invest in him; he was turning people away all the time," said Ivanhoe.

As Madoff's enormous wealth accumulated, he reinvented himself as a pillar of philanthropy, becoming a member of the board of trustees at Yeshiva University, and with Ruth establishing the $19 million Madoff Family Foundation, which in 2007 donated to Kav Lachayim, a volunteer organization that works with Israeli schools and hospitals, as well as to a New York cultural institution, the Public Theater.

So generous were the Madoffs in their charitable giving that when Peter's son, Roger, died of leukemia in April 2006, the death notices pages of the *New York Times* and other publications were flooded with paid obituaries from major charitable organizations.

How do the Ponzi schemer's acquaintances account for his spectacular rise and precipitous fall?

It was Bernie Madoff's personality, ingenuity, innovativeness, and nerves of steel as he orchestrated con after con, they say, as well as his amazing amount of chutzpah as he robbed one trusting client to pay off another; and, most importantly, his total lack of moral core in his nearly fifty years of criminality. He was, simply, in the right places—Manhattan, the Hamptons, Palm Beach—at the right time: the money-mad era of greed.

It was also Madoff's clever merchandising, including adopting the reassuring slogan "The Owner's Name Is on the Door," as he brazenly denuded individual investors and Jewish philanthropic foundations and educational institutions of their portfolios.

As charming and reassuring as Madoff was to his clients, he was enigmatic to his employees in the Lipstick Building. There, he was rarely seen by his minions during the workday. Instead, he secluded himself in his inner sanctum, emerging only after hours, when he would look around the main work areas, noting messy desks and unevenly drawn window shades.

"This was a different type of person," Tara Pearl said. "This is not just a charming person, but one who can *make things happen.*"

Lawrence Leamer, who met Madoff "a bunch of times at Club Colette, a dining club," found him to be "just another pretty ordinary wealthy guy."

"In normal times—it's in bad times when these Ponzi schemes collapse—everybody is happy and only X percent of people are ever going to call for their money," former federal prosecutor Burns observed. "Madoff paid back people when they asked for it. But he didn't give them *their* money; he gave them *somebody else's* money. It just kept rolling and rolling and rolling, and it's almost impossible to figure out how much has been returned to people and how much is gone and how much he lost.

"In my opinion," Burns added, "the guy didn't lose fifty billion dollars, because even in the worst of the worst people are losing, by a rough estimate, thirty percent of their money. Unless I'm missing something—where there were ridiculous expenditures, like his buying hundreds of 747s—there is just no way that he spent fifty billion dollars. That's probably the gross figure. As I understand the case, it's a huge Ponzi scheme that finally blew up in bad economic times."

Many of Madoff's victims are amazed that his Ponzi scheme was not discovered long ago. There were anxious moments along the way, however.

In 1999 there was a probe of the BMIS operation, but investigators came up empty, and Madoff went on to score even greater financial coups.

Financial expert Harry Markopolos, a resident of Whitman, twenty miles south of Boston, is now regarded as an unheeded prophet in his nearly ten-year quest to expose Madoff's nefarious scheme to government regulators.

Back in 1999, Markopolos, then a forty-three-year-old with a strong moral sense and a willingness to challenge authority, became suspicious about Madoff: The figures just didn't add up.

He enlisted mathematicians, including Dan diBartolomeo, whose analysis of Madoff's methods confirmed his suspicions that a massive Ponzi scheme was being operated out of the offices of Bernard Madoff Investment Securities.

Markopolos repeatedly sounded his warning over the years, but to no avail. He hadn't wanted to talk about his experience until Madoff's scheme made headlines, although diBartolomeo always wanted to talk. He is highly critical of those regulators who ignored Markopolos's alerts over the years, saying, "People should have seen the writing on the wall." On December 31, 2008, the would-be whistle-blower Markopolos announced that he was ending his silence and that he would testify on Capitol Hill about his frustrating quest to unmask Madoff's scam on Monday, January 5, 2009. In the end Markopolos was not able to testify that day because he was ill.

Why did so many seemingly savvy individuals and institutional executives fail to grasp that it is impossible to achieve the high returns on investments delivered by Madoff?

Part of the answer may lie in Bernard Madoff's personality. As Tara Pearl observed "You have certain people, like a Bernie Madoff, who have type-A personalities, who have the ability to do things, who know they can do things, who know that they can walk in and take charge."

Leamer found Madoff "a little loud sometimes. But there's nothing to suggest this financial debacle which he created. Some people say he didn't promote; well, he promoted brilliantly, yet he seemed *not* to promote." Leamer explained, "That's how he got you into this. If you had invested five million dollars and wanted to take five hundred thousand dollars back, he would say, 'You have to take *everything;* you can't take out part.' That would scare you."

Victims' attorney Mark Mulholland said that Madoff "would tease his victims with just a small bit of information about how his strategy worked. He would release to his victims just enough information to entice them to believe that this really could be true;

that this man may have truly stumbled upon, or devised some ingenious method, for beating the market.

"The second thing he did was to turn away money," Mulholland said. It's a strategy he likens to "the velvet rope at a nightclub. Let's say that someone hears that their friend John has been getting ten percent or better year after year. Then they try to get in and they *can't*; Madoff spurns their money. Now their desire to get in is even *keener.*

"They talk about that in their circle of influence; they say to their country club friends and their business acquaintances, 'You know, my friend John has been getting ten percent with Madoff year after year and I tried to get in.' And everyone becomes like a moth drawn to the flame. People were vying for his attention to get into this Ponzi scheme."

"He was an incredibly shrewd man in understanding human psychology and human greed," Lawrence Leamer observed. "People thought they were being conservative by investing with him. When they would go to a dinner party, the person next to them had invested in a hedge fund and was getting twenty to twenty-five percent. Madoff's investors were making a consistent ten or eleven percent and thought it was just like a bond profit. It was very certain."

In an article written in 2001, *Barrons* reporter Erin E. Arvedlund questioned Madoff's stellar performance. When Arvedlund, who had talked with experts expressing skepticism over Madoff's claimed results, asked Madoff how he was able to produce compounded annual returns of fifteen percent for more than a decade, his less than candid reply was, "It's a proprietary strategy. I can't go into it in detail."

Especially striking about Arvedlund's findings is that even knowledgeable people do not comprehend Madoff's methodology.

As one investor told the reporter, "People who have all the trade confirms and statements still can't define it very well."

And one investment manager interviewed by Arvedlund said that he pulled his money out when Madoff "couldn't explain how [his investments] were up or down in a particular month."

So great was the need for Bernard Madoff's clients to believe in him that Laura Goldman, a Tel Aviv-based money manager, mailed copies of the *Barrons* articles, as well as one from *MAR/Hedge* to certain members of the Palm Beach Country Club, but received a hostile response.

As Goldman told the *Palm Beach Post*, "They said I was jealous. They said that the publications were anti-Semitic—that Jews have more faith in Bernie Madoff than they do in God."

One time in the 1990s, when Goldman lived in Palm Beach, she had a business meeting with Madoff at the Breakers. At that time, Madoff insisted that people were lucky to invest with him and urged Goldman to bring him *her* clients. He refused to talk about his investment strategy, however.

"This was my first clue that he was a little *off*," Goldman said. Then, she said, her uneasiness with Madoff increased when she spoke with several options traders, who informed her that they were not trading options for him, despite Madoff's having possessed a huge portfolio.

"I have this gut feeling that this Ponzi scheme was not designed purely to enrich Mr. Madoff—that it was really more of a function of his *ego*," said attorney and hedge fund expert Ron Gefner. "You have somebody who is high profile within the investment community, who took a lot of pride that he generated consistent returns. That was the driver. It wasn't a function of purely enriching himself economically; it was more a matter of *reputation*."

While Bernard Madoff was running his scam in New York, he kept an eye on Congress and the SEC. So much so that between 1997 and 2008, he spent $590,000 on lobbying efforts, almost all of it with Lent, Scrivner & Roth, a firm concerned with market regulation, security transactions fees, and stock exchange mergers.

And, as reported by The Center for Responsive Politics, since 1991 Madoff and his wife, Ruth, have donated $238,000 to candidates for federal office, political parties, and committees.

"There are some people who believe there will be no repercussions," Tara Pearl said.

When did Bernard Madoff actually descend into criminality?

"What I think happened to him is a logic-based, as opposed to an information-based, view," said Fred Adler. "Probably the guy did very well for a number of years; he probably made money for people for a while. And then, several years ago," Adler theorized, "he got hit and this so-called Ponzi scheme developed. It could have been during the dot-com period.

"You go through stages in life. My guess is that it became more ego than money at that point. I don't know much about his personality, but he reminds me of people whose ego takes charge," Adler said.

Does Bernard Madoff have a Jekyll and Hyde personality?

In an attempt to understand Madoff's behavior, the authors spoke with Dr. Andrew Twardon, the director of New York's St. Luke's-Roosevelt Hospital's Center for Intensive Treatment of Personality Disorders, who has treated quite a few accountants and financial service industry professionals who stole from their clients or companies.

"The first impression that anyone in my field would have is that Mr. Madoff has a personality disorder, which possibly revolves around what we now call antisocial personality traits or narcissistic personality traits, for they often overlap," Twardon said. "A person with an antisocial personality is someone who has disregard for others, who doesn't necessarily follow a moral code, who doesn't abide by the law, and who is very much focused on obtaining personal gratification," he explained.

"In general," Twardon continued, "we think that this disorder comes from very early childhood development that has to do with some sort of physical trauma and disregard for the integrity of the child by others in the child's environment, so the child never develops a positive attachment with parents or an attachment system that can facilitate compassion, empathy, and development of morality."

Twardon went on to say that Madoff may be a narcissist, a personality disorder that differs significantly from the antisocial pattern. "Whereas in the antisocial personality, the primary problem is disregard for norms and laws and the need to inflict suffering on others for personal satisfaction, the narcissistic personality is about self-aggrandizement—what you would call, in popular psychology, denial."

Noting that "the person begins to believe that things are different than they really are," he characterized the condition as "a powerful cognitive distortion of the perception of reality. All of his victims become more of a distant presence that almost doesn't exist at the level of a true human being. They are depersonalized; they are no longer *people*."

As Tara Pearl noted, "Just a short time ago, [Madoff] was quoted as saying that in this market 'you cannot commit SEC violations'…. Not only did Madoff know that the funds invested with him were not there; he knew towards the end that this [Ponzi scheme] would destroy people."

That did not stop Madoff from conning people, however. A potential client who approached Madoff only weeks before his confession and arrest said that Madoff agreed to handle his investment. That investor is now penniless.

"Let me tell you something about Madoff," venture capitalist Fred Adler said. "In mid-November a dentist in New York City met with him to discuss putting a large portion of his retirement funds into the Madoff fund. Madoff assured him that he is doing well, even in this terrible year for the market, and this very nice, bright, kind man gives Madoff his money. Madoff should go to jail for the rest of his life."

Regarding the ethical-religious aspects of Bernard Madoff's crimes, the authors spoke with noted Protestant, Catholic, and Jewish theologians.

"I don't think that one should expect anything less than resentment and hostility by the people who have been wiped out," said Dr. Donald Shriver, president emeritus of Union Theological Seminary, in New York City.

"My personal response to the Madoff scandal is that along with a large number of people on Wall Street and at other investment businesses, they have lost touch with elementary ethics. I have to underscore *elementary*," Shriver added. "No longer is it something to be assumed, or to go without saying, that one has to be honest about the pros and cons of anything dealing with money. The ordinary ethics of truth-telling and of being entrusted with other peoples' resources and being cautious about that responsibility, those are elementary.

"Having taught in business school, I feel that we haven't been strong enough in emphasizing 'Thou shalt not bear false witness.' If you don't practice that commandment in the economic realm, you undermine that realm. In the business world especially, on the banking and investment side today, there is this need to make money out of money rather than making money from producing concrete economic goods. Most of us who have been involved in institutions that are critically dependent on their endowment have been pushed more or less to trust our investment advisers. Sometimes that trust was justified; sometimes it certainly *wasn't*. The promise of a larger profit for oneself and for one's institution is certainly tempting.

"Forgiveness is one of the things Jews and Christians, based on the Bible, have to believe in." Shriver continued. "They also have to believe in accountability and some degree of punishment for one's sins. In the Bible, repentance and forgiveness go together. All just punishment should be tempered with forgiveness and empathy for the person being forgiven. But I don't expect to ever divorce forgiveness from repentance. The kind of repentance that is most appropriate to me is whatever the person can do to restore the damages he has inflicted.

"In Madoff's case, he probably does not have the capacity now to come up with the financial restoration that would come anywhere *close* to helping the people who have been impoverished or deeply damaged by those losses. I just don't want to think that forgiveness is something we just actually apply for and get, either from God or from other human beings."

Shriver said Madoff should be convicted of his crime. "I do think Mr. Madoff ought to go to jail. For how long, I can't say. But the disgrace of that is an important part, making clear to other people that when you do these kinds of things you are going to get punished by the society.

"There should also be a requirement that people like Madoff will finally come clean about the wrong they have done. He has done some of that by admitting to the Ponzi scheme. He is a thief, and giving the right words to these sins is important."

In Jewish tradition—as is likely in the traditions of most of the world's other religions—nothing is more important than one's good name. One can reach the heights of professional achievement, accumulate vast sums of money, and rise to positions of power and influence. For the sake of one's children and their children's children, however, what really matters is the quality of one's life, the regard of others for one's name.

The Reverend John Pawlikowski, professor of ethics at the Catholic Theological Union in Chicago, said, "When you place the Madoff scandal in the context of the wider economic turmoil, one of the biggest challenges we face is restoring peoples' confidence in the basic economic system."

In terms of Madoff himself, Pawlikowski said, "The general Roman Catholic view is that virtually anyone can be forgiven of virtually anything, provided that they seek forgiveness. But the added point would be sufficient restitution. What this possibly could entail boggles the mind.

"Obviously he is in no position to repay the amount of money that was stolen. So from the purely Catholic moral point of view, what would be partly required of him would be some kind of punishment. He may face a lengthy stay in prison."

As far as the victims are concerned, Pawlikowski suggested that "anger should not be the dominant emotion." In the short-term, the Reverend said, "anger needs to be expressed; but beyond that, anger ultimately corrupts the person who has been wronged. It doesn't repair anything or bring back the money.

"But the person who has been aggrieved has the right to demand that the responsible party be appropriately punished and to demand that, within the possibilities, some form of restitution or compensation be forthcoming."

Although Rabbi A. James Rudin, a senior adviser to the AJC, had never heard of Bernard Madoff until the middle of December

2008, when the Ponzi king was arrested in New York City, the rabbi said he was "quite familiar with his type of sociopathic personality.

"Madoff represents the quintessential 'smartest kid in the class,' who must continually prove to himself that he can outwit everyone else and game a system based upon ethical behavior and personal honesty.

"The 'smartest kids' of whatever age, religion, gender, or race, consider their classmates, friends, colleagues, and in Madoff's case, especially, his clients, as naive fools and targets of rapacious criminality.

"But Madoff's financial dishonesty is far more than mere trickery. It is a staggering, cruel act of personal treason, committed against both hapless, believing individuals and trusting foundations and institutions. Because Madoff's treason was carried out with perfect 'malice and forethought,' his crime is of a totally different type and magnitude than simply bad fiscal judgment or faulty financial actions.

"Treason means deliberately deceiving and systematically damaging the very people among whom you dwell and have your being. In that sense, the Jewish community that nurtured Madoff and treasured him as a gifted son was the primary, and first, victim of his treason. But that community was but the launching rocket that would place Madoff into his own personal orbit as the self-perceived greatest investment wizard in the entire world.

"In a sense, the Jewish community was akin to a retro rocket; something to be cast off as Madoff extended his treacherous reach into the global economic realm. Trapped in his carefully crafted money deception, Madoff required more and greater targets of opportunity to continually prove to himself that he was indeed 'the smartest kid' on the globe.

"Madoff, in his criminality, is much more than a giant, real-life version of Tom Wolfe's Master of the Universe, as portrayed in his novel *Bonfire of the Vanities.* Tragically, the venal Madoff is no work of fiction, and those he has fiscally raped are flesh-and-blood men, women, and children whose lives are forever shattered, even broken.

"Of course, Madoff is a Jew—a fact the media has repeatedly emphasized—and it is surely no surprise that centuries of collective persecution and prejudice forced many Jews to cringe in fear and shame when Madoff's evil actions were made public. However, I, for one, feel no personal Jewish shame at best or collective Jewish guilt or responsibility at worst for the actions of Bernard Madoff. He is what he *is,* and the rest of us are what *we* are.

"Madoff's treason was aided and abetted by a decades-long veneration, even worship, of investment brokers and bankers. Madoff was aided and abetted by generations of Americans, including my own, who grew up believing in the endless upward spiral of housing prices, aggressive hedge funds, lucrative monetary derivatives, a constantly expanding job market, rising incomes, and eternal gains in our personal portfolios. That widespread belief provided constant gratification and a sense of status and entitlement.

"Madoff was the culmination of those false and pernicious beliefs. His clients, both individual and institutional, conveniently looked the other way, or offered no questions, when they received their bogus fiscal statements from Madoff. 'Trust Bernie' was the deadly mantra that has destroyed so much and so many.

"The Jewish tradition teaches that *Shaaray Teshuva,* the 'Gates of Repentance,' are always open to those who truly atone for their sins, errors, misdeeds, deceit—and, yes, *treason.*

"I strongly believe in authentic, truer repentance. But in Madoff's case, he must first be judged under the American criminal laws he belittled and disobeyed. But because Madoff carried out his treason alone, and in secret, it is certain he will ultimately face those Gates of Repentance equally alone.

"No rabbi, spouse, child, sibling, or friend can join him at *that* moment. He will stand in judgment and wonder whether the gates will open a crack to allow a truly repentant Bernard Madoff to enter.

"But, of course," Rabbi Rudin concluded, "only *God* knows the answer."

CHAPTER FIVE

WHAT DO THE WIFE, THE SONS, AND THE BROTHER KNOW?

"In my heart of hearts, knowing as much as I do about the scope of the fraud, knowing as much as I do about how sophisticated the record keeping was and how clever the monthly statements and confirmations were, it defies logic and credulity to think that one man was sitting there, pumping out all this paper and making all this work."

—Mark Mulholland, victims' attorney

"I'll give you a Sherlock Holmes theory: Madoff sat down with his sons and said, 'Look, because of the economic climate, the recall rate on the money has escalated like crazy and this Ponzi thing is going to be brutal, like a house of cards.' Just theorizing, I think they came up with this idea that they somehow discovered it and they're turning him in. Honestly, I think it's a crock of shit."

—Douglas Burns, former federal prosecutor

Many bloggers are expressing their anger on the Internet about Madoff's enormous Ponzi scheme, focusing their ire on the extended Madoff family:

"...there is no way this guy operated alone, his family without a doubt had a hand in this."—Mottsman

"Madoff admits to the scam in order to protect those around him. He's likely decided that although prison is not a capstone to his career, the felony at his age, won't be stunting his career, as it would, in the case of a younger accomplice."—Canarsie

"You can't tell me there was no family involvement. Madoff will fall on his sword at the age of 70 plus after years of fraud. His family will walk."—Bob

"Well, well, well! More fraud among the privileged. This time the 'smart FBI Branch' office should arrest all Madoff family members and relatives until they discover what part of the $50 billion that was defrauded was taken as a financial adviser fee arrangement."—Gerry

"Wow! It's a crying shame that Bernard has created such a fiasco for his friends and family. What happened? It's hard to believe that none of his family members knew what was going on. He must have been really good to manage 50 billion all by his lonesome."
—Elmer Fudd

"There is no way this could have been done by himself. His family had to be in on it. That's why they 'turned in' their father—it was an agreement with their dad to save them from criminal charges."—Anonymous

"Investigators will eventually find that this organization will be similar to a Mafia's operation. Madoff was the head of this crime syndicate. He was too technologically illiterate, too finance and accounting illiterate to have perpetrated a scam of this size without any assistance. It almost seems that he

was the fall guy for this operation to save his sons,
brother, cousins and long-time associates jail time."

—Hammer

"There is no way he acted alone. The authorities need
to bring all accountable to justice."—G. girl

"Of course his sons, niece and brother were in on it. I
don't know exactly about the brother or the niece but
I do know his sons did not give him their money [they
knew it was a scam] so they didn't take it up the wazoo.
Not only do I believe the whole Madoff family knew
but also some govt. officials who had their 'palms
greased' to look the other way."—Fed Up

"I'm a data base programmer, among other things.
No way he did this alone. Printing hundreds
[or thousands] of statements that look good with
seemingly accurate data is not a trivial task."—Bob

"So does anyone not suspect that the Madoff sons
knew what was going on? All these years and they
were not aware of anything unseemly?"—SC

An enterprise as far-reaching as Bernard Madoff's—he
claims to have managed $17 billion in clients' funds—
would normally have required the labors of hundreds of
administrators, not those of one individual.

"If he had allegedly seventeen or twenty billion and it was
leveraged to the tune of three to one, then, of course, you get into
that fifty billion dollar number," Jon Najarian observed. "Certainly
the numbers I see cited in reputable sources like the *New York
Times* are supporting a larger number than I had thought of first—
I thought it was ten to twelve billion—but it seems more likely that
it's over twenty billion.

"Of course, he didn't really need leverage to do what he did because he really didn't do anything," Najarian added. "He took people's money and alleged to have invested it. I don't think he invested it and lost it, because there is not fraud in *losing* money; there is fraud running this Ponzi scheme."

In the ongoing investigation of how Madoff could possibly have pulled off the biggest Ponzi scheme ever, one question dominated: Were his sons or other close relatives abetting him as he sat in his inner sanctum, preparing meticulously detailed monthly statements, annual tax statements, and an almost constant stream of trade confirmation and bank transfers?

"One of the most important questions is whether he acted alone," Jon Najarian said. "How could he have done it without other people being involved, because what did all these people at Madoff Securities do on a daily basis? Did they show up for work every day, execute trades, not make any money, and then wonder why they were getting bonuses the way they were? If they weren't making money at Madoff Securities, how could they not be part of the deal? How could they justify what they were being paid? I don't believe they could have been making money *trading.*

"Just this summer," Najarian recalled, "one of my friends who had invested many millions with Madoff sat with me at a Chicago restaurant and asked me about Madoff: 'What do you know about Bernie?'

"I told him what I knew, which, of course, was everything, absent the fraud.

"He asked, 'How does he do what he does?'

"I responded, 'I have no idea; his strategy will not make double-digit returns. You can't buy an out-of-the-money put [whose strike price is lower than the market price of the underlying security] against the S&P 100 and sell an out-of-the-money call [whose strike price is higher than the market price of the underlying security] against it on a consistent basis and make more than five percent. It's just not *possible.'*

"So he said, 'How do you think he does it?'

"I said, 'I really don't know'—again, not accusing Madoff of fraud.

"He said, 'I talked to a mutual friend of ours, who is a billionaire trader and he does not know how he does it either.'

"I said, 'Well, that can be a red flag for you because if *he* can't tell you how this guy does it and *I* can't tell you how he does it, and we're both derivative experts, how the heck does *he* do it? Shouldn't that make you nervous?'

"We encouraged him to take at least all of his initial capital out. We said, 'If it's been a great run for you, wonderful. But at least take the initial stake out, so if you lose something going forward, you haven't cleaned yourself out.'

"I believe he did take seven million out of seventy million out. When this thing first blew up, he was the first person I thought of," Najarian said.

"I'm wondering what his family knew about it," said attorney Harry Taubenfeld. "Are they as totally innocent as they are trying to suggest at this point? It is hard to comprehend that they did not have any knowledge at all."

Lawrence Leamer said that while he knew nothing "specifically" about the sons, it did strike him as "highly unusual that the two sons were turning in their father; particularly when a week or so later the government would have got him anyway. It just seems there was a tendency to distance them from this scam."

Tara Pearl never met the Madoff sons. Did she believe that Andrew and Mark Madoff had known all along of their father's nefarious scheme?

"You know your father's fundamental values; you know the person's nature from a very young age," she said. "You know that if he turns around and talks about people and says, 'Fuck them,' that he really doesn't care about the other person."

"If I were a novelist," Lawrence Leamer said, "I would have Bernie falling on his sword and saying, 'I'm taking this for my two sons.'"

"Off the top of my head, there is no way that this guy did this alone; I just don't see how he could possibly have done all the logistics on his own," Douglas Burns said. "I also think there is a significant issue about his sons. To somebody like me, this whole point about their turning him in is very hokey. I was in a huge case where a guy about seventy took the fall for his sons. He got fifteen years and they walked free. This whole thing about their turning him in definitely needs some further examination."

Interestingly, Mary Shapiro, President Barack Obama's nominee to lead the SEC, in her capacity as the chief executive of the Financial Industry Regulatory Authority (FINRA), had in 2001 enlisted Bernard's son Mark Madoff to serve on the board of the National Adjudicatory Council as a reviewer of FINRA's disciplinary decisions.

Other family members besides Madoff's sons and brother were involved in the firm. Peter's nephew, Charles Weiner—a son of Peter's sister—joined BMIS in 1978, and in 1995, Peter's own daughter, Shana, an attorney, was hired as the firm's compliance lawyer. On December 11, the day of her Uncle Bernie's arrest, a panicky Shana telephoned her husband of a year, Eric Swanson, who for ten years had been a mid-level official at the SEC's Washington office, and told him that something was terribly amiss. It seems that officials from the SEC and the Justice Department had arrived at BMIS, and were at that very moment seizing records and asking very pointed questions.

Swanson was actually quite familiar with the Madoff operation, having occasionally worked on issues related to the firm long before becoming romantically involved with Shana Madoff.

As the investigation progressed, Swanson was being pilloried in the press, as well as by certain bloggers, who suggested that he played a role some years ago in convincing the SEC to drop its inquiry as to whether the Madoff operation was really an enormous Ponzi scheme. Swanson said that he would cooperate fully with the current investigation. As to whether Mark and Andrew Madoff were in on the scam, agreeing with their father's scheme of taking the blame, only time will tell.

Evidence exists on both sides of the argument. In the complicity scenario, it was pointed out that Bernie Madoff could not possibly have handled all the required paperwork—that he would have required the assistance of confederates on the 17th floor.

"Obviously, the money trail is the one that most people are concerned about right now. The exposure of this fraud shocks people," said Jon Najarian. "His ability to hide the money will be tested. I have met the guy several times and I don't believe he is shrewd enough to have hidden this much money very effectively.

"A lot of the money went to the older investors who had been in the fund longest. That's the nature, of course, of a Ponzi scheme," Najarian noted. "The last ones in are the ones that get fleeced the most. He probably squirreled away a fair amount of money, and the question going forward will be how involved other members of his family and/or of his firm were."

On the other side of the debate is the fact that Mark and Andrew had refused to speak to their father since the evening of Wednesday, December 10.

Is that evidence that they were enraged beyond forgiveness?

Is the fact that each son had lost much of his own fortune of millions of dollars proof that neither Mark nor Andrew would have agreed to participate in such a risky scheme?

Significantly, perhaps, in light of the question of whether Madoff's brother, Peter—he graduated from Fordham Law School in 1967 and joined BMIS three years later—and Mark and Andrew were in on the scam, Peter was mentioned on page four of the BMIS mission statement as having been "deeply involved' in the firm's activities, while Mark and Andrew's names weren't even mentioned.

Whether or not Mark and Andrew were involved, they certainly spent enough time together to share family secrets.

As Mark Madoff told the *Wall Street & Technology* magazine almost a decade ago, in August 2000, "What makes it fun for all of us is to walk into the office in the morning and see the rest of your family sitting there."

As the investigation of Bernard Madoff's evildoing progresses, the money managers and banking institutions that steered clients to BMIS and who profited so handsomely from their dealings with him by charging hefty fees for their middleman services are scrambling to distance themselves from the scheme by declaring that they, too, are among the Ponzi schemer's victims. The question remains, however, as to why so many of these savvy professionals signed on with Madoff without performing the due diligence that would have revealed some glaring holes in BMIS's operation.

For starters, there is the matter of the name of the accounting firm affixed to BMIS statements. Wouldn't a major client expect that the BMIS books be audited by a major Manhattan firm?

"Madoff's reliance on an unknown accounting firm could have been dismissed by people suggesting that Bernard Madoff was well known on the Street, had been doing this for thirty to forty years, was not operating from his home or from a one-person office, and was surrounded—whether they directly impacted his business or not—by hundreds of other employees. So it was a verifiable business," said attorney Ron Gefner, an expert on hedge funds.

In fact, Madoff's accountancy firm, Friehling & Horowitz, consisted solely of forty-nine-year-old David Friehling, the only active person in the firm. The immediate past president of the Rockland County chapter of the New York State Society of Certified Public Accountants, Friehling works out of a thirteen-by-eighteen-foot office in a small plaza located at 337 North Main Street, in the town of New City, in Rockland County, New York, approximately thirty-four miles northwest of Manhattan. The building also houses at least six other accounting firms, as well as medical offices and the Rockland County Bar Association.

Shouldn't clients have wondered: Is there something not so up-and-up about BMIS's dealings? Did Bernard Madoff know that his paperwork would never pass muster with a major accounting firm?

Then there is the broader issue of how BMIS could possibly have produced such high yields on clients' investments when other highly experienced and regarded financial services firms could not.

"I was on the board of the Chicago Board Option Exchange [CBOE] and we had an asset on our books, the Cincinnati stock exchange," Jon Najarian recalled. "Bernie was very instrumental in building up that exchange from just a little tiny regional exchange to seeking to make it more like a mini NASDAQ—that is, an electronic stock exchange with no trading floor necessary. To do that, though, he didn't have the expertise himself, nor did he have the regulatory cover.

"We met in one of his New York trading rooms, and in hindsight I find it strange, because that trading room had no traders in it, just lots of desks, lots of computers, and workstations. I suspect he may have been doing a little Enron of his own—Enron had all those work areas where they were going to trade weather futures, and electricity, and they more or less put traders in those rooms to dummy it up to make it look like they were doing something.

"They trotted this out and duped investors to think that they had a large energy trading operation, which they didn't. Bernie may have been doing the same thing a decade or at least five years earlier. If I came by every day and saw a room like that," Najarian said, "I would become suspicious. As it was, he told me it was an expansion area—that they were getting ready for additional business. I took him at his word. Why *wouldn't* I?"

Those gullible investors who so readily entrusted their funds to their friend, good old Bernie Madoff, must now have been pondering this question over and over again. And they would likely continue to do so for months, if not years to come, as the investigation of this latter-day Ponzi scheme proceeded.

Will the truth about whether Bernard Madoff had accomplices in the 17th floor of the Lipstick Building eventually come out?

After all, the biggest Ponzi schemer ever left an enormous paper trail in his inner sanctum on December 10, 2008, when he brought his close relatives home and confessed.

There must be very revealing fingerprints on all those documents.

Part Three

Absorbing the Shock and Dealing with the Consequences

CHAPTER SIX

THE PROFOUND SENSE OF LOSS

"In synagogues and community centers, on blogs and in countless conversations, many Jews are beating their chests—not out of contrition, as they do on Yom Kippur, the Day of Atonement, but because they say Mr. Madoff has brought shame on their people in addition to financial ruin and shaken the bonds of trust that bind Jewish communities."

—Robin Pogrebin, *New York Times* reporter

"The fact that he stole from Jewish charities puts him in a special circle of hell. He really undermined the fabric of the Jewish community because it's built on trust."

—Rabbi Burton L. Visotsky, professor,
Jewish Theological Seminary

Blogs proved to be an effective way for many of Madoff's victims to express their sense of loss.

"Why did he do this to us at the country club? We all loved him and respected his family. He is as bad as the Germans were to my family."—Sal Milstein

"I have lost several million bucks that I entrusted to Big Bernie... So please add my name to the list of Destitute Dealmakers and please cut me a fat check when restitution is made."—doggerell3000

"Not everyone who trusted that scum Madoff was a 'rich' person. My husband and I worked for more than 30 years and now we are too old to recover...and there's a lot of other folks like us who were taken. We trusted the SEC and other regulatory agencies and now we're broke."—Marilyn

"Just to set the record straight, and so everyone understands, not all of Bernie's investors were multi-millionaires. My family was invested in a partnership where hundreds of us banded together to invest in one of Bernie's clients. We invested pensions, IRA rollovers, life insurance money. I live in a trailer, work a full-time job, drive a 100,000+ mile Mazda from '95, and struggle to make ends meet every month. My mother, because of this theft, is going to have to go back to work full-time at age 63. My uncles, who worked, collectively, for almost 90 years in a paper mill lost their life savings. We are ordinary people who just plain got screwed."—Melanie

"I was an early investor, courtesy of a modest account opened by my grandfather-friend of Madoff's in 1975. I received regular statements, records of stock trades showing BOT and SLD every quarter for 32 years. The stocks were a conservative low risk blend—like my own 401K—and seemingly owned in my name. It appears that these statements could be nothing more than a fantasy. The media suggests that investors were victims of greed and fell for a scam that was too good to be true; many investors don't fit that mold. I am left to wonder at what point did an honest investment house become corrupt? Was it ever an honest operation? Madoff was investigated years ago and regulators found no irregularities. I don't feel swindled or charmed out of my investment, I feel flat out robbed—a subtle difference but one I suspect many other investors can relate to."—EC

In the organized Jewish community, as wounds were licked, steps were being taken to make sure that there could never again be a financial scandal to equal that engendered by Bernard Madoff. To that end, the Jewish Funders Network (JFN), on December 23, 2008, convened an emergency meeting in New York. Attending were representatives of thirty-five of the largest Jewish foundations in the United States.

An international organization dedicated to advancing the quality and growth of Jewish philanthropy, the JFN is open to both individuals and foundations that give away at least twenty-five thousand philanthropic dollars and do so through the "lens of Jewish values, no matter that the funds go to a specifically Jewish cause or to a cause more broadly defined."

In conjunction with its meeting on December 23, the JFN, which estimated Madoff-driven losses in the Jewish world to total $2.5 billion, said that "taking action" was the meeting's goal, and in announcing the gathering, stated:

> "We are all shaken in the wake of the economic crisis and the recent Madoff scandal, which has disproportionately affected the Jewish funding community and, in turn, dozens of Jewish nonprofit organizations in the U.S., Israel, and the former Soviet Union. Some foundations and funders have seen their assets evaporate overnight, and grantees are struggling to determine where the funds will come from to support their essential programming."

Among the issues discussed by the organizational representatives during the three-hour meeting was strategy, including the creation of an information hub that will list financial commitments to nonprofits made by foundations that were hit by Madoff and could no longer meet their obligations, as well as the establishment of a clearinghouse, enabling nonprofits to share resources, to publicize their needs, and, if in danger, to "sound the alarm."

On December 15, 2008, the Jewish Community Foundation of Los Angeles disclosed that it had invested $18 million—approximately five percent of its total assets—with BMIS. Only days later, the foundation announced the formation of a special committee whose mandate was "to pursue the recovery of the defrauded assets and to conduct a comprehensive evaluation of the Foundation's investment processes."

While one has to admire the organization's pledge of "transparency" with respect to Madoff-related issues, the fact that even a relatively small portion of its assets were placed with BMIS raises questions about the foundation's fiscal judgment and governance. The formation of the special committee offered hope that the Los Angeles Jewish community will recover from its experience with the king of the Ponzi schemers.

In Upper Manhattan, meanwhile, as more and more details concerning the enormity of the biggest Ponzi Scheme ever were revealed to the public, not only were the trustees of Yeshiva University feeling the enormous financial loss, but the fifteen students in that institution's graduate seminar on Jewish Social Philosophy were grappling with the moral issues arising over the commission by Bernard Madoff, a once esteemed and trusted trustee, of the onerous crime of stealing from his own people.

According to the *New York Times*, Rabbi Norman Linzer's students in the seminar debated whether Madoff's crimes are really sins and the significance, if any, of his being a Jew. While some said that Madoff's religion is not relevant, others are concerned that his Jewishness may redound negatively on that community.

Madoff's crimes were especially troubling to the professors and 7,000-member student body. They resented Madoff for the damage he had inflicted on individuals and institutions; they feared the revival of the ugly stereotypes of yesteryear; and were uncertain as to how Jewish institutions should in the future select their role models. Elsewhere on the university campus, undergraduate students in Intermediate Accounting I were analyzing how Madoff was able to succeed in fooling the SEC for so long; and in Rabbi Benjamin Bleich's Philosophy of Jewish Law course, others discussed whether Jewish values had been skewed in rewarding material success.

Rabbi Bleich, who has taught at Yeshiva University for forty-two years, viewed the current debate as "An opportunity to convey to students that ritual alone is not the sole determinant of our Judaism, that it must be combined with humanity, with ethical behavior, with proper values, and, most important of all, with regard to our relationship with other human beings."

It may be an uphill struggle. As Josh Harrison, a graduate student in Jewish philosophy, put it, "There's no such thing as wanting to be a professor in this community. All my friends who are intelligent and interesting and asking questions are pre-med and beginning law school."

"In elevating to a level of demi-worship people with big bucks, we have been destroying the values of our future generation," Rabbi Bleich said. "We need a total rethinking of who the heroes are, who the role models are, who we should be honoring."

Individuals throughout the country, who are also beginning the healing process, are giving voice to their feelings about those who are critical of Madoff's investors for not questioning their inordinately high yields.

"I thought I was a millionaire; now I don't know how I am going to pay my bills," Ronnie Sue Ambrosino told the authors on December 31, 2008. Originally a resident of Long Island, New York, she would later travel the country with her husband in a motor home. "I believe it was twenty-eight years ago when I first started with Madoff. I'm fifty-five years old and my husband, Dominic, is forty-eight. When he retired four years ago because we had security from our Madoff investments, we sold our house in New York and moved into a motor home and decided we wanted to travel for as long as we wanted to. We loved every second of it—until December 11th.

"Needless to say, all of our money was invested with Madoff, so we are penniless and are no longer retired because we have no income other than a small pension for my husband, that doesn't pay the bills and doesn't cover our motor home payment, so we had to go back to work.

"We are *devastated.* But we are strong and we have an incredible support system of friends and relatives, and we will endure. We thought we were headed down one road and, as my husband says, the road is now different."

Blaming the SEC in part for her predicament, Ambrosino said that "[SEC chairman] Christopher Cox admits that. The SIPC is also at fault," she said, "because it is going to be almost a month since this happened before it gets claim forms out to the victims. There are people that are selling things that are very near and dear to them, including their homes, in order to survive, yet SIPC is dragging its heels."

Noting that "the government has appropriated $28.1 million to go for paperwork of a business they tell me has no assets," Ambrosino exclaimed, "We have been raped once and now we are getting raped a second time!

"There is something wrong here," she insisted, "because the insurance company the government put in place to help investors is not doing that. Madoff was a scam, but so are the SEC and the SIPC, so I've been defrauded *twice*! This is the biggest financial devastation the country has ever seen. It has ramifications that are absolutely phenomenal, and we haven't seen all of them yet. In this situation, the government cannot just think inside the box; it has to think *outside* the box."

Ambrosino said that she has "written to many U.S. senators, and they respond that they can only respond to e-mails sent from constituents in their state. But this is not an individual state problem. The government is not responsive to the people."

As to how Ambrosino did not realize at first that she was being scammed, she said, "I would get confirmations of stock trades. At the end of the month, I would receive a statement, and I also received quarterly statements. I used to work in the computer business and I understand bookkeeping; everything was totaled *to the penny*.

"I want to know: Do I own the stocks? Did I ever own them? There is a paper trail. Why can't somebody tell us if we owned the stocks? As far as I'm concerned, I still have $1.66 million because I haven't had one person notify me that Ronnie Sue Ambrosino does *not* have that money with Madoff.

"The head of the SIPC has said that his people went into Madoff's office and found that the paperwork was in a state of total disarray. My question to him would be: How can somebody who has his books in a total state of disarray send out meticulous statements?"

Ambrosino said, "I've been in touch with many of Madoff's victims, and everyone has reported that their statements were meticulous. How did somebody in a state of disarray get those statements out?

"I called Madoff's office yesterday [on December 30, 2008] and they answered the phone. There is something *wrong* here. Can someone tell me why Madoff's staff is still being paid?"

Ambrosino continued: "I called Madoff's office the first morning after I found out, and I got Eleanor, who said she was Madoff's secretary, and she sounded as shaken up as I was. I asked her if she could tell me what was going on, and she said, 'No.' Then I heard her say, 'Peter, we need toner for the copier.' I don't know if that was Peter Madoff or Peter the *flunky*. Maybe they were making copies for the FBI."

Ambrosino's former husband, Larry Leif, a retired entrepreneur, of Delray Beach, Florida, lost his entire $8 million retirement account.

He, like his former wife, had a positive attitude. As he told *Time* magazine, "I'm blessed, I'm healthy, I have great friends, and I have a new focus in my life [abolishment of the SEC], one I didn't expect three weeks ago. We can make this system better for everyone. This is now my mission."

It really bothered Bette Greenfield when she heard that "People did it for greed. I may be naive," she says, "but I believe that [Madoff's] reputation was so good that people felt that their money was secure and they were going to make a nice income, and it's terrible to criticize people now and say, 'How could you have been so stupid?' It was such a setup that there was no way that you could doubt it. The SEC should have known something, should have seen something, should have reported something. It was left to each individual.

"Now my father didn't go over to Steven Spielberg and say, 'What do your reports look like?' He only saw his own. We kept getting reports on a regular basis. We kept getting confirmations of sales. We even got a check in September when we asked for it.

"One of the things I really get upset about—I just saw something on television—they said people should not have put all their eggs in one basket. That's not what many very wealthy people did. To me, when you have wealth, you diversify your funds. But the little people like us did not have enough money to diversify at all.

"When we wanted money in September," Greenfield said, "my brother called and then wrote a backup letter or an e-mail and the money came right away. There was absolutely no doubt at any time; when he called them he always felt like he was dealing with people who knew what they were doing. One of my brothers is an attorney; one is an accountant; and I'm an educated person—I worked for Merrill Lynch. We are not stupid, and yet it just looked *so real.*"

Today, Bette Greenfield is left nearly penniless. "Other than social security I have no income," she said. "You can't live in Florida with only social security and eat dog food. I'm going to put myself into a business making homemade jewelry. I never intended to be rich. None of us did. We just thought we were going to be *secure.*"

CHAPTER SEVEN

THE ANTI-SEMITIC VOX POPULI SPEAKS

"The greed and corruption of the Jews has brought the financial system and the American economy low."

—Jean, portfolio.com

"Ho hum, another Crooked Wall Street Jew. Find a Jew who isn't crooked. Now that would be a story."

—Anonymous, dealbreaker.com

"One jew [sic] thief robs another bunch of jew thieves—I suppose that's what you'd call a victimless crime. I suppose if he'd not screwed his fellow Jews—and robbed us poor gentiles it would have been absolutely kosher, eh?"

—XDFXDFXDF, nymag.com

"Nice he could have managed to send money to Isreal [sic] and pass the losses on to US investors."

—Cbmiked, forbes.com

"Do the right thing, Madoff and blow your brains out."

—Avengers, nypost.com

These were but a few of the thousands of comments made in cyberspace, on popular, mainstream Web sites by anti-Semites as they exercise their First Amendment right of free speech in the wake of the exposure of Bernard Madoff's Ponzi scheme.

"I had thought that anti-Semitism was gone from America, and, basically, from the world," said Lawrence Leamer. "But if you look at the comments on some of these blogs, it's just amazing. These people find a way to blame Jews for everything. It's a very scary time."

"It's very sad that this *one* sociopath has hurt so many of the people of his own upbringing," said Tara Pearl, speaking of the cyber prejudice that now inundated the Internet.

This prejudice was not being committed solely by white supremacists and other radical groups. Rather, it is being perpetrated by your garden-variety bigot.

Abraham Foxman, national director of the Anti-Defamation League (ADL), which monitors all manner of anti-Semitism in the U.S. and abroad, believes that "The fact that so many of the defrauded investors are Jewish has created a perfect storm for the anti-Semites."

Foxman's very troubling conclusion was based on evidence compiled by the ADL of the virulent hatred being unleashed against the Jewish community, and by extension, the nation and people of Israel, on many thousands of Web sites.

Major news sources in New York and Florida, the epicenters of the Madoff scandal, were experiencing a flood of anti-Semitic postings on their Web pages. In fact, the comment section of the *Palm Beach Post* had received so many anti-Semitic messages that the site's administrators decided to remove them.

One of the particularly offensive of the deleted items, signed "Adolf," focused on the stereotypical "devious money-mad Jew" canard, and read: "Just another jew [sic] money changer thief. It's been happening for 3,000 years. Trust a Jew and this is what will happen. History has proven it over and over. Jews have only one god—money."

Elsewhere on the Internet, posters identifying themselves as "Thieving Bastards" called Madoff "another Jew banker" on the site of the *South Florida Sun-Sentinel,* and referred to "Jewish gatekeepers who routinely turn a blind eye to Jewish financial bandits."

The comment-enabled sites of other publications that received anti-Semitic hits included *Forbes, New York* magazine, the *New York Post,* and Israeli sites such as *Haaretz* and *The Jerusalem Post,* as well as popular blogs.

For example, Patriot II writes on huffingtonpost.com: "What's more shameful are the charities that Madoff and peers fund. Since the uncovering of Madoff scheme, a whole underworld is now exposed. It's funny how a club can freely be called Jewish and exclusive. If it was any other way it would be again considered racist."

Expanding on that theme, Anonymous wrote on dealbreaker.com: "Race, religion, party. None of that bullshit matters to me. People are people in my book. BUT—IT MATTERS TO THEM. From early childhood they are taught to look at the world in terms of 'Jew' or 'Other.' Thus there will never be peace in Palestine, or anyplace to which they lay claim. In my experience, the worse thing you can assert to a hardnose JEW is that 'everyone is equal.'"

Regarding Israel, a hatemonger with a rather long handle, "Guppyinthecesspooloflife," wrote in a punctuation and spelling-challenged message on huffingtonpost.com, "Money heaven hmm, let me think, that'd be an underground vault somewhere in the Negev Desert in Palestine [isr-eal]."

A blogger identified as Chris posted a message on haaretz.com: "Well, now we know how Israeli banks have emerged unscathed as the rest of the world's economy went into freefall."

And Internet discussion groups on finance, blogging on Yahoo! and Google, are posting alarming comments.

On Yahoo!, for example, one can read such offensive comments as "This is what happens when you let Jews run amok in a country for too long"; "You are guaranteed to get screwed when trusting a JEW"; "He [Madoff] is a jew [sic]. Remember GOD'S CHOSEN PEOPLE, so he gets away with shit cuz the fukking dumb evangelicals are totally brainwashed"; "Jews should be banned from working on Wall Street. All they do is steal our money"; "Wall Street crooks are about 95% Jewish with a lot of influence from the Russian Jewish mafia."

Anyone logging on to Google's finance discussion site can read the following: "Notice how the jew [sic] owned media 'ignore' this news about this corrupt criminal Jew" and "jews NEVER lose on the stock market scams. THET [sic] RUN THEM."

And in yet another Google posting, "Winning Man" wrote "'WORLD'S MOST SUCCESSFUL THIEVES' Latest ranking...by name, wealth in billions of dollars and the source of their stealing." Madoff is at the top of that list, which includes such respectable entrepreneurs as Microsoft's Paul Allen and Steven Ballmer, Dell's Michael Dell, and Oracle's Lawrence Ellison.

PART FOUR
The Shakeout

CHAPTER EIGHT

WHERE DO WE GO FROM HERE?

"You folks around the country probably know this, but here in New York City, it's freezing cold. It's so cold today that Bernie Madoff is actually looking forward to burning in hell."

—David Letterman, late-night
television personality

"It will be three to five years before Bernard Madoff will come to trial—that is, if he doesn't in the meantime cop a plea and go to prison immediately. If he pleads guilty, he is going to prison for twenty to thirty years. You could go to trial because he could say to the jury, 'I'm old,' and he could appear to be emotionally unstable and they would be sympathetic. Sometimes you can get an acquittal."

—Barry Slotnick, victims' attorney

It could take months, even years, before Bernard Madoff is brought to justice. Lead attorney Ira Sorkin said, "I can't answer when this case will be adjudicated, not because I'm hiding something, or I'm not permitted to talk about it; there is no way to know when this is going to be resolved."

Would Sorkin's client face additional charges? "I cannot speculate as to whether there will be additional charges," Sorkin said. Let me put it to you this way: he has not been charged. He was arrested on a *complaint*. The only action the complaint permitted the government to do was to arrest him."

"In federal court, a complaint is just a triggering charge; it's not a *formal* charge. The person doesn't have to plead guilty or not guilty. You are not even arraigned. It's just a charge that triggers the process," former federal prosecutor Burns explained.

"The government then has thirty days to bring a formal charge. This can be extended, as often happens. The government will claim he devised a scheme to raise money by virtue of misrepresentation. He will likely be charged with mail fraud and wire fraud, and they could charge him with money laundering."

How would Bernard Madoff and his family survive financially as they awaited further developments?

It appeared likely, given Bernard Madoff's track record, financial smarts, and criminal sophistication that he could have hidden ample funds, whether in numbered bank accounts or offshore accounts. But then the government could discover and seize those funds, rendering Madoff virtually penniless.

In that event, Madoff would be forced to seek relief from the court. Would it be granted? "As a general rule, if it is consented to by the government, the court will go along with it," Sorkin said.

Is there a possibility, given Madoff's guile and possible hidden resources that he could be smuggled out of 133 East 64th Street in the middle of the night, be rushed to some rural airfield, and be spirited away to a villa on some remote island?

"While the idea of his running may seem sexy, it is virtually impossible to do this in today's technologically advanced and interconnected world," said Douglas Burns, "coupled with the fact Madoff has intense family relationships and owns all kinds of properties."

Should Ira Lee Sorkin advise his client against copping a plea, Bernard Madoff will eventually be brought to trial. One can only wonder what sort of defense his legal team will mount, given Madoff's own confession—albeit eminently recantable—as well as the enormous paper trail that at the moment forensic accountants and other investigators were poring over in Madoff's former 17th floor inner sanctum in the Lipstick Building.

"If I were defending him, I would have a laundry list of options," Douglas Burns said. "Option number one, obviously, would be to throw our hands up and tell the government, 'Mea culpa. This guy will sit down with you and do everything he can to sort the mess out.'

"The next option would be some kind of psychiatric defense, but I think this would be pretty weak. If you think about it, this was a sophisticated person, highly functioning, multiple homes and country clubs. Everybody loved him. Also, remember that a psychiatric defense would be better for an isolated incident rather than for conduct over a long period of time."

Former prosecutor Burns predicts that "there will be a slew of civil suits. Victims are going to sue intermediary brokers and then Madoff himself. Then you may have a bankruptcy with a court-appointed receiver. The simple answer to be arrived at is: Where is the goddamn money? How much of it was lost? Where is the *rest* of it?"

"We filed the first proposed class action on behalf of Irwin Kellner, a Long Island resident, a well-known economist and a victim," victims' attorney Mulholland reported. "One of the first events in the Southern District proceeding filed by the SEC was that an order was issued staying all litigation against Madoff, so no one on earth can directly sue Madoff, or the owners of Madoff Securities, LLC right now.

"We are also examining a series of class actions that we believe can be filed against the hedge funds which invested in Madoff without conducting sufficient due diligence," Mulholland added: "Those litigations are not stayed at this time."

Drawing from experience gleaned during investigations of such cases as the Enron swindle, federal prosecutors have now begun the complex process of investigating what role, if any, offshore operations may have played in Bernard Madoff's Ponzi scheme.

Did Madoff and certain of his investors use such funds to evade U.S. taxes?

Did Madoff improperly allow donors to charities whose accounts were managed by BMIS to place their funds in such accounts?

Did offshore banks fail to withhold taxes due to the U.S. Internal Revenue Service, as required by the tax collecting agency?

According to information contained in certain regulatory filings, it appears that BMIS was involved with at least a dozen such banks. Among the U.S. firms mentioned in that context are the Fairfield Greenwich Group, which operates in such offshore havens as the Cayman Islands; Tremont Group Holdings; and a number of Swiss banks, including Union Bancaire Privée and Banc Benedict Hentsch & Cie.

One of the most controversial aspects of the case against Bernard Madoff is the role played by regulatory agencies, particularly the SEC, in examining complaints lodged against the BMIS.

"When I was at the SEC we would take turns responding to investor complaints," attorney Ron Gefner recalled. "You can imagine that in the last year or two, complaint phone calls or letters have gone through the roof.

"In balancing the complaints out, if you had complaints against Merrill Lynch and one against Joe's Bargain Basement, you might take the one against Joe's Bargain Basement as requiring greater attention because you presume that Merrill Lynch has compliance policies and procedures.

"So if there is a real problem they would deal with it internally," Gefner added, explaining that "the SEC has limited resources and prioritizes complaints. So a complaint against Madoff, although it would have received some form of attention, may not have gone too far because of his *reputation.*"

The *Wall Street Journal* reported that regulators, following up on tips describing Madoff's business practices as "highly unusual," had investigated BMIS at least eight times in a period of sixteen years. In the first of those investigations, which took place in 1999, the SEC began a limited examination into the trading practices of BMIS and two other firms, finding violations in trade executions, which Madoff promised to address.

Five years later, in 2004, the SEC began a limited examination into the possibility that Madoff was engaging in the "front-running" of his market trades in order to benefit his hedge fund clients. No violations were discovered, however.

Then in 2005, the SEC's New York office began a limited examination concerning Madoff's consistent returns. As a result, the agency would issue a delinquency letter citing execution and trading violations. In November of that year, SEC investigators in New York met with whistle-blower Harry Markopolos, who had suggested in a letter to the agency that Madoff was running a Ponzi scheme.

Finally, in 2006, the SEC's New York staff began an enforcement investigation, in which it was found that Madoff and one of his clients had in the past misled the agency, as well as investors, concerning its money management business.

As a result of that finding, Madoff agreed to register as an "adviser." The SEC would end that investigation twenty-two months later.

One of the most intriguing questions concerning the U.S. government's involvement with BMIS is: What did the SEC know, and when did the regulatory body know it? After the scandal broke, the *New York Times'* Dealbook reported that the agency's current chairman, Christopher Cox, acknowledged that "our initial findings have been deeply troubling," in announcing that the SEC had ignored specific, credible evidence of problems going back at least to 1999.

Only a day later, Cox backtracked, telling reporters, "I want to emphasize that there is no evidence that anyone is aware of at this point that any personnel did anything wrong."

Whatever Cox's position may have been on a given day in 2008, there is a significant body of evidence to indicate that the SEC had been warned in the 1990s that BMIS's practices should be scrutinized.

The agency's chairman at that time, Arthur Levitt Jr., was ambivalent regarding Madoff. In a speech to the Security Industry Association in 1999, Levitt criticized Madoff for having compensated financial institutions that had directed trades to his firm. On other occasions, however, Levitt sought Madoff's advice concerning how the markets work, and appointed him to an advisory commission charged with exploring the changing structure of the financial markets.

Perhaps the most striking example of the SEC's malfeasance regarding Madoff was its refusal to take seriously the claims of Harry Markopolos, a well-respected figure in the financial world, who for nine years had tried to persuade the agency to respond to his charge that Madoff was a fraud.

In Markopolos's view, Madoff's strategy could not possibly, in mathematical terms, have been yielding the results reported by BMIS. In a seventeen-page letter sent by Markopolos to the SEC in November 2005, in which he wrote of what he described as a "highly likely" scenario, the would-be whistle-blower stated that "Madoff Securities is the world's largest Ponzi scheme."

And in an article published in the January 4, 2009, edition of the *New York Times*, the financial experts Michael Lewis and David Einhorn recommended that President-elect Barack Obama appoint Markopolos to the post of the SEC's chief of enforcement.

While the SEC did launch eight investigations into BMIS's dealings and practices over the years, many bloggers responding to the scandal have nothing good to write about the regulatory agency, taking it severely to fault for failing for years to detect Madoff's Ponzi scheme:

> "The whole situation is unbelievable! To think that the SEC the entity that is supposed to protect investors from exactly this type of scandal, did not take seriously the earlier allegations and red flags directed towards Madoff, are truly horrendous."—Oxford Thunder

> "Many people might accuse me of naivety but it seems obvious that if the S.E.C. failed in its duty to the investing public; it is that organization which has to be culpable and ultimately responsible for compensating the losers in this fiasco, having first gathered what it can from Madoff's companies. There is not any point in having a regulatory body, which is not answerable in law for its lack of due diligence and duty of care. Confidence in the system has to be maintained. There is also very little point in placing trust in the system if it is full of 'Buck Passers'. In the words of the infamous film, 'Who is monitoring the monitors?'"—Paddy

"Is it surprising to anybody that SEC auditors could look at bogus books and see nothing wrong with them? Many who work at the Commission are simply looking for an opportunity to put 'Securities and Exchange Commission' on their resume and few have any real commitment to the public service sector or in actually performing at any kind of significant level."

—Dave

"This is absurd! Clearly this guy has paid off high officials in politics and in the SEC."—Hanan

In the meantime, each day brings a slew of developments:

On Tuesday, December 23, 2008, the trustee in charge of BMIS won court approval to use $28.1 billion of the firm's funds to pay for its liquidation costs.

Then, at 1:45 p.m. on Monday, January 5, 2009, the cable channel Fox interrupted a news feature to report that Bernard Madoff was at that moment on his way downtown to a court appearance regarding his bail arrangements.

The case took a strange turn: The government asked U.S. Magistrate Judge Ronald Ellis to revoke Bernard Madoff's bail, arguing that the failed financier had violated his bail agreement by mailing packages containing what U.S. Attorney Mark O. Litt described as "at least a million dollars worth of jewelry" to family members and close friends.

When Madoff's sons received three packages, the contents of which, according to the *New York Times,* included "valuable jewelry and watches, as well as inexpensive items, like cuff links and mittens," they contacted their attorneys, who in turn informed the U.S. Attorney's Office. At the court hearing, Bernard Madoff's attorney, Ira Sorkin, claimed that the items are inexpensive and not of genuine value.

Judge Ellis, who reserved decision on the government's motion, ordered the parties to present briefs within two days.

What puzzled the growing army of Madoff-ologists is whether Madoff had merely sent sentimental trinkets to those nearest and dearest to him or whether his intent was to ask the gifts' recipients to sell them and then give him the proceeds.

Also puzzling was the government's contention that by sending the packages, Madoff was now a flight risk.

According to Litt, "The case against the defendant is strong, and continuing to grow stronger as the government's investigation continues. Given the defendant's age, the length of the likely sentence, the strength of the proof against the defendant, including his own confession, these facts present a clear risk of flight."

How might Madoff slip past the private security guards mandated in his bail agreement, and paid for by his wife?

And where would Madoff flee to?

After all, as his photograph has appeared in publications throughout the world, where on earth could he go, sans passport?

Those questions were not answered by Litt in his presentation to the court.

On a much lighter note, eBay, capitalizing on Bernard Madoff's notoriety, was now offering the following items—BMIS promotional giveaways emblazoned with the firm's name and offered to well-heeled clients and prospective investors—for sale: flashlights, beach tote bags, beach chairs, backpacks, golf caps, Corporate Challenge T-shirts, fleece blankets, and desktop cigar humidors.

And, the pièce de résistance: a disaster recovery bag given by Bernard Madoff to all employees and replete with New York City bus and subway maps, air-filter mask, whistle, emergency blanket, sanitary wipes, and a water pack.

One can only wonder: Was the Ponzi King anticipating that his gift to employees would one day come in handy? Was he thinking: When everything falls apart, they'll be able to use the maps to escape from the Lipstick Building before the Feds get here.

In the meantime, they can protect themselves from the hot air emanating from the 17th floor by using their masks; if so disposed, they can use their whistles to become whistle-blowers; if they find themselves out on the street when they discover that there's no money left in the till to pay their salaries or to allow them to redeem their own small investments in BMIS, they can always shelter atop the subway grate on East 53rd Street, using their fleece blankets for extra warmth, and washing off daily with their sanitary wipes. And, last but not least, they can sustain themselves with fluids from their water packs.

CHAPTER NINE

AND THE NEWS KEEPS ROLLING IN

"Please accept my profound apologies for the terrible inconvenience that I have caused over the past weeks. Ruth and I appreciate the support we have received."
—Bernard Madoff, in a letter distributed to fellow owners at his apartment building on December 22, 2008, expressing his concern over the chaos caused by all the media attention

"My family's a victim, more so than anybody else. It's very painful."
—David Wiener, son of Sondra Madoff Wiener, Bernard Madoff's sister, speaking in January 2009 of his parents' having been scammed out of an estimated $3 million

"Because the Government has failed to meet its legal burden, the motion is denied."
—Judge Ronald Ellis, on Monday, January 12, 2009, in his Opinion and Order that he will not revoke Bernard Madoff's bail

"The decision speaks for itself and we intend to comply with the judge's order."
—Ira Lee Sorkin, Bernard Madoff's lead attorney, responding to the authors' request for comment immediately following the announcement of Judge Ellis's decision

Today is Monday, January 12, 2009, one month and two days since Bernard Madoff confessed to his sons and his brother in the seclusion of Apartment 12A that he had for years perpetrated an enormous scam on banks and hedge funds, charitable foundations, day schools, institutions of higher learning, and individual investors.

Each day of the new year has brought headlines and news flashes: Another newly-destitute victim coming forward, the possible addition of new names to the list of plaintiffs in the first class action suit to be launched against Madoff, and the most riveting news story of them all: whether the judge will decide to revoke his bail and jail him immediately, in response to the Ponzi schemer's latest outrage, the mailing of more than $1 million of his assets to his nearest and dearest.

As for the latest of Bernard Madoff's victims to come forward, or to be revealed, they range from individuals such as Allan Goldstein and Edith and Thomas Liccardi to the flamboyant, titian-haired Sonja Kohn, the founder and seventy-five-percent owner of Italy's Bank Medici, who is reported to have solicited many investors for her good friend Bernie Madoff, to Madoff's own sister, seventy-four-year-old Sondra Wiener, and her husband, Marvin.

Goldstein, a retired fabrics distributor from New York who had an IRA retirement account with BMIS, testified on January 5 before the House Financial Services Committee: "Everything I worked for over a fifty-year career is gone. Somewhere inside of me was the thought that this was a regulated industry. It wasn't. The warning flags were just pushed aside."

On January 9, as Bernard Madoff remained under house arrest in his luxurious duplex, awaiting Judge Ellis's decision on whether or not to revoke his bail, we wondered: Was the Ponzi King passing the time by reading that morning's *New York Times?*

If so, did he peruse James Barron's story on page twenty-four about the difficulties now being faced by an elderly couple, Edith and Thomas V. Liccardi, two of the many "little people" he had swindled over the years?

While an average reader would probably perceive Barron's account of the Liccardis' plight to be a stark lesson on the destructive effects of Bernard Madoff's scam on the not-so-wealthy of this world, given Madoff's penchant for demonstrating just how abnormal—and likely sociopathic—he is, it may very well be that the Ponzi King just doesn't *get* it.

As of this moment, Edith and Thomas V. Liccardi, remain secluded in their small room at Fountains at RiverVue, a senior citizens' facility located in Tuckahoe, New York. There they pass the time of day wondering where they will spend the rest of their lives.

If indeed he did take the trouble to read the *Times* article, Bernard Madoff may have recalled that in the late 1990s, Mr. Liccardi, an accountant specializing in estate tax returns, had invested $400,000 in BMIS after preparing a tax return for a client who invested with Madoff's firm.

Liccardi was intrigued with the return on his client's investment and visited the BMIS offices, where he met with Madoff. As he recalled, "He impressed me very much, as he did everyone else, and there were banks of computers and people running all over the place. I thought this had to be legitimate."

Taking Liccardi's money, Madoff would generate statements eventually showing the growth of that initial investment to $2.7 million. Thus, despite having suffered two heart attacks and a stroke, the eighty-six-year-old Thomas Liccardi maintained his positive attitude about life, convinced as he was that he had no financial worries.

That is, until the moment he learned of Bernard Madoff's fraud, and his sense of well-being vanished. Recalling that moment,

Liccardi says, "I just about fell to the floor. It was impossible. I had so much faith."

Now the Liccardis can only hope that when their remaining money runs out, the management of Fountains at RiverVue will enter into an arrangement with them to lower their monthly charges, and that Medicaid will cover the cost of their home health aides.

Sonja Kohn, the sixty-year-old, well-traveled founder of Bank Medici—who spends a good deal of time in Milan, Zurich, London, New York, and Israel—has been described as "Austria's Woman on Wall Street." On January 7, it was revealed by the *New York Times* that she had gone missing. Is she merely too ashamed of her mistake in having invested so many of Medici's assets with Madoff? Or is the Viennese banker running from what the *Times* characterizes as "some particularly displeased investors"—namely Russian oligarchs, $2.1 billion of whose assets, thought to have been invested with Bank Medici, were instead entrusted by Kohn to BMIS.

Whichever of the two scenarios is the case, Bank Medici scrambled to do damage control. In a statement issued by that financial institution, Nicole Back-Knapp, a public relations official with the Viennese firm Ecker & Partner, stated that Kohn "...is a victim and the Bank Medici as well."

As for Bernard Madoff's own kin, Sondra and Marvin Wiener were reported to be in such dire financial straits that they were forced to put their large home in one of Palm Beach's gated enclaves up for sale.

During the first week of January, several of the major players in the Madoff scandal were deciding on their next moves.

Carl Shapiro hired the experienced litigator Stephen F. Molo of Shearman & Sterling. Shapiro's spokesman, Elliot Sloane, who also represents Shapiro's son-in-law, Robert Jaffe, explained, "They're evaluating and reviewing their legal options right now."

Just what those options might be is difficult to assess, as it is highly unlikely that Carl Shapiro will be able to recoup a significant portion of the hundreds of millions of dollars he and his foundation had entrusted to Bernard Madoff. Indeed, the noted Boston philanthropist may be forced to settle with SIPA for what he would regard as mere chump change.

Meanwhile, the fifty-two-year-old Harry Markopolos, now regarded as nothing short of heroic for attempting for so many years to expose Bernard Madoff's fraud, was at home in Whitman, Massachusetts, fighting off a nasty cold as he sifted through offers from authors and film producers eager to capitalize on his newfound fame.

According to *Time* magazine, one of those producers, Steven Pearl, envisions "a remarkably compelling story about a guy who didn't want to be in the middle of this. It's like Cary Grant in *North by Northwest*, where he's thrown into a case of subterfuge and espionage because of a random phone call." With all due respect to Pearl's vision, Harry Markopolos's warnings were hardly "random" acts, but rather his determined effort to convince unbelieving regulators that Madoff is a crook who must be stopped.

As for whom Markopolos may select to bring his saga to the screen, the whistle-blower is concerned that his privacy may be violated; he fears that in a Hollywood treatment of his long effort to stop Bernard Madoff's nefarious activities, a screenwriter would "just add sex and violence" to beef up the scenario.

On January 4, the roster of Bernard Madoff's victims in the financial institutional world grew with the announcement that Harley International Ltd., a hedge fund operated by Euro-Dutch Management Ltd. and based in the Cayman Islands, had invested all of its assets—$2.76 billion as of October 31, 2008—with BMIS. A spokesman for Euro-Dutch declined Bloomberg News's request for comment.

And J. Ezra Merkin's troubles continued to accumulate, when on January 6, New York State Supreme Court Justice Richard Lowe extended a December 24, 2008, order barring the embattled financier from either shutting down or withdrawing money from his Madoff-tainted bodies, Ariel Fund Limited and Gabriel Capital Corporation. Judge Lowe arrived at his decision in response to a lawsuit filed against Merkin by New York University (NYU), the nation's largest institution of higher learning in terms of its enrollment. In the suit, it is claimed that NYU lost $24 million when funds under Merkin's control were invested with BMIS without the university's consent.

In an affidavit filed with the State Supreme Court, Maurice Maertens, the university's chief investment officer, claimed that "Until December 12, 2008, we had no knowledge that NYU's funds were instead being managed by Bernard Madoff. None of the documents we received throughout the years from Gabriel or Ariel ever stated that Mr. Madoff was managing NYU's assets."

In response, Merkin's attorney, Andrew Levander, said that his client "has always acted in good faith and did not deceive NYU or any other investors."

Adding to Merkin's woes is the fact that he has, apparently, lost tens of millions of his own dollars by having invested with Madoff.

One can only wonder why NYU's administrative staff or its board of trustees failed to carefully examine the operations of the two Merkin-run entities.

Were they, perhaps, counting too heavily on the Merkin family's reputation—established by J. Ezra's late father, Hermann, a man known both for his financial acumen and for his probity?

As the Madoff scandal continued to unfold, many questions were being asked as to why so many individual investors placed most, if not all, of their assets in his hands. In an article published in the *Washington Post*, Michael Rosenwald wrote: "In over-allocating money to one position, investors are typically prone to several shortcuts that get them into trouble. One primary mistake is uniquely intertwined with Madoff's alleged scheme—the allure of consistent small gains," and an accompanying chart, depicting Madoff's purported returns, showed a line going steadily up one or two percent, month after month.

In his article, Rosenwald quoted Richard Peterson, a psychiatrist who cofounded the psychological and financial consulting group MarketPsych: "It's like a slot machine that pays you a little each time. Over time you kind of fall in love with that machine. You'll actually have the hormones and strong attachment and bonding. You trust it. You want more satisfaction from these gains."

In addition, according to Rosenwald, "The Madoff trap also exposed a persistent problem among all investors: the failure to do timely rebalancing of their portfolios."

The writer described a "remarkable" survey of 1,000 investors conducted by AllianceBernstein, in which it was shown that nearly forty percent of those investors without advisers lack strategies for the allocation and rebalancing of their investments.

Rosenwald also cited the "strange sort of competition" engendered by friends talking among themselves about their investments and described their fear of losing out on the big one— "the fear of being inferior; that the other guy is going to do better." Apparently that dynamic was at work in the country clubs, fine restaurants, and private homes where Madoff's go-betweens and investors boasted about how much they were salting away through their relationships with him.

There were several bits of good news for victims of Bernard Madoff's Ponzi scheme. In the first instance, on January 2, SIPC—seven days ahead of its previously announced schedule—mailed claim forms to 8,000 of Bernard Madoff's clients. SIPC spokeswoman Allis Aaron Wolf explained that the list had been developed using BMIS records, as well as telephone inquiries.

While claims cannot be filed electronically, and SIPC cannot determine exactly when eligible investors will receive compensation provided according to its regulations, investors can download claim forms, which are due by March 4, from the SPIC Web site. In addition, the agency placed notices directed at customers and creditors in major newspapers, including the *New York Times, Wall Street Journal, Financial Times*, and *USA Today*.

Then five days later, on January 7, SIPC announced that investors may begin to recover funds as early as February or March, while others may have to wait months for recovery.

Stephen Harbeck, who heads the agency, explained that determining an individual's compensation is "like unscrambling an egg." He added that the Madoff case is "of a completely different order of magnitude" from anything the agency has had to deal with in the past.

On that same day, Lynnley Browning reported in the *New York Times* that, according to "experts" on American tax law, investors may receive some relief by claiming that the taxes they paid on profits from their investments with BMIS "were illusory."

"At the center of the tax question is a commonly used provision known as the theft-loss deduction, which enables investors to increase their taxable losses and possibly claim refunds for taxes paid on income that turned out to be fictitious," Browning noted.

"Under this provision," he explained, "investors typically file amended tax returns going back three years from the date they discover the fraud. They then claim on their current federal returns a theft-loss reduction equal to the lost principal. Deductions for such losses generally can be carried back three years or forward for twenty years."

An Internal Revenue Service (IRS) spokesman would not comment on the implication of Madoff's fraud for taxpayer relief. According to tax expert Harold Levine, chairman of the tax department at the New York firm Herrick, Feinstein, such relief could cost federal, state, and local governments as much as $20 billion.

Interestingly, the IRS had addressed the specific issue of tax relief for Ponzi fraud victims in a memorandum in 2004, in which it is suggested that those investors should neither file amended tax returns nor seek refunds. Rather, they should claim theft loss deductions equal to their original investments.

According to Solomon L. Warhaftig, a senior tax partner at Proskauer Rose in New York, who was quoted in the *Times* article, the steps suggested in the IRS memorandum "dramatically increase the theft-loss deduction," as they allow the taxpayer to include, in addition to the principal, accrued phantom interest and income.

Given the need of many of Madoff's victims for tax relief, accountants, tax attorneys, and other financial industry experts should expect a dramatic increase in their client lists in the next months and years.

Indeed, some law firms have already set up special divisions to deal with the legal issues devolving from the scandal.

One of those firms that has established a Madoff Securities task force is Carter, Ledyard & Milburn LLP, where U.S. District Court Judge Louis L. Stanton—the very judge who presided over the initial SEC filings against Madoff—was a partner before being appointed to the bench by President Reagan.

On the firm's Web site, the task force is described as "an interdisciplinary team with significant experience in SEC, FINRA, and SIPC regulatory matters, government investigation, civil and criminal litigation, tax, bankruptcy, and finance to help clients address the myriad of issues arising from the Madoff debacle."

During the first week in January, during a brief telephone conversation—so brief that it can hardly qualify as an interview—with the task force's head, former SEC securities investigator Steven J. Glusband, the authors asked whether a conflict of interest is now in play, given Judge Stanton's former service as a partner in Carter Ledyard. Glusband told the authors that the judge's participation does not pose a conflict of interest.

Regarding the class action suit (see Appendix F) filed by noted economist Irwin Kellner on December 12, 2008, the day following Madoff's arrest, Kellner has been joined in his action by other victims of Madoff's fraud.

As explained by Kellner's attorneys, Mark S. Mulholland and Kimberly B. Malerba of the firm Ruskin Moscou Faltischek:

> *A class action is superior to other available methods for the fair and efficient adjudication of this controversy. Individual damages to any one investor may be relatively small, making the expense of non-class litigation prohibitive or impractical for class members. Moreover, in light of the disclosures of the SEC investigation and pending criminal charges, additional lawsuits are likely to be filed. An overall resolution, fairly apportioned among all defendants, is preferable to the result of inconsistent litigations dealing with individual investors.*

As the rush by Bernard Madoff's individual and institutional victims to initiate legal action accelerated, Kingate funds, whose investment in BMIS totals $2.7 billion, was wavering: Should the fund join a class action suit or pursue its own class action or file a separate civil suit, as the only plaintiff?

In a letter sent by Kingate to its investors, a copy of which was obtained by MarketWatch, the funds' officials wrote: "We can certainly commence a lawsuit on behalf of the funds, but we caution against that at this early stage because not only is that a costly step but it puts the Kingate Funds and potentially all of the investors' identities in the limelight. We lose nothing by waiting and we gain the ability to watch as the facts unfold."

Kingate's dilemma is shared by many of Bernard Madoff's other victims whose losses exceed $500,000. Due to the scope of the unprecedented fraud, the complexity of uncovering all pertinent facts, the probability that the case will take new and unexpected turns, it is likely that only a small fraction of the dollar loss will be recoverable, despite the best strategies implemented by the best legal minds.

Nonetheless Kingate, in an action that will likely be emulated by other Madoff victims, is conducting its own investigation in order to determine whether others share responsibility for the fraud. Thus the funds' attorneys are "...seeking to identify other entities which provided services to or on behalf of Madoff's entities that may have had knowledge of, aided or abetted his fraud."

Whatever Kingate and other victims decide to do, it is obvious that the Madoff affair has severely shaken the already tottering financial landscape. The exposure of his fraud comes as the nation prepares for a new administration, one facing the most difficult economic crisis since Franklin Roosevelt assumed the presidency in March 1933, at the height of the Great Depression.

To be sure, even if final losses should amount to fifty billion dollars, a figure that increasingly appears to be somewhat inflated, that figure is dwarfed by the sums lost in the failure of both Bear Stearns and Lehman Brothers, as well as by the huge amounts of money swept off the table due to the falling stock markets.

The approximately 8,000 people holding accounts directly with BMIS, along with thousands of others who have lost money because their funds were shuttled off to a partner entity, are but a fraction of those who have been ripped off in the last few years due to the chicanery, malfeasance, or downright thievery committed by satellite financial institutions. Bernard Madoff's victims are now emerging as symbols of just how rotten the system has become.

Following his inauguration on January 20, 2009, as the forty-fourth president of the United States, Barack Obama, along with his chief financial officers and members of the new Congress— whose predecessors signed off on the costliest federal bailout in U.S. history—will need to address the systematic flaws that not only allowed for the near collapse of Wall Street, but fostered the conditions under which Bernard Madoff was able to operate with impunity for so long.

On January 5, at about the time Madoff was arriving at his bail revocation hearing, the Financial Services Committee of the U.S. House of Representatives, convening the day before the new Congress was to be sworn in, held a hearing focusing on the SEC's method of operation.

David Kotz, the SEC's inspector general, told the committee that he is planning to expand the inquiry called for in late December by the agency's chairman, Christopher Cox.

Kotz said that he will examine the SEC's methods and offer recommendations concerning its enforcement and inspection divisions, and added that he will also look into the relationship between Bernard Madoff's niece Shana and her husband, Eric Swanson, prior to their romantic relationship, when, as an attorney with the SEC, Swanson had participated in the agency's examinations of BMIS in 1999 and 2004.

However decent Kotz's intention, it is disturbing to note that when the SEC official was asked by Representative Gary Ackerman of New York to disclose the location of Madoff's assets, the SEC official replied, "We don't have that information." Kotz must surely have known that just five days earlier, on the evening of December 31, 2008, the SEC had confirmed receipt of the Madoffs' list of assets.

A number of the Financial Services Committee's members—Democrats and Republicans alike—were skeptical about the SEC's capacity for change within its system. They were concerned that Congress, in the wake of the SEC's apparent lapses in its investigation of the activities of BMIS, could pass new regulatory measures.

Among the Democrats, Representative Paul Kanjorski of Pennsylvania, who was presiding over the session, stated, "Clearly, our regulatory system failed miserably, and we need to rebuild it anew," while Ron Paul, a Republican from Texas—he was a candidate in the 2008 presidential campaign—urged that the SEC either be "scaled back or eliminated." According to another Republican, Spencer Burns of Alabama, "What we have in the Madoff case is not necessarily a lack of enforcement and oversight tools, but the failure to use them."

The Committee's chairman, Democrat Barney Frank of Massachusetts, said in an interview with Bloomberg News that the

SEC should be given additional resources, adding that both the SEC and the Commodity Future Trading Commission "both have to beefed up as market integrity regulator and investor protector [respectively]."

A more skeptical view was expressed by business columnist Allan Stone, who wrote in the *Washington Post*:

> *Not to prejudice the SEC's investigation of itself, but I'll bet the answer will turn out to be that things have always been this way and probably always will. If the commission enforcers get a bigger budget and are treated with respect rather than being dissed— including, I'll bet, by some of Madoff's victims—as an obstacle to free markets, things may improve. But don't expect a fraud-free era to ensue.*

In hindsight, Bernard Madoff's investors should have welcomed and supported any SEC efforts to meticulously investigate BMIS. As many of those investors were delighted with their yields, however, they would likely have been distressed to learn of major enforcement measures, let alone public criticism, of their seeming financial wizard's firm.

From Bernard Madoff's perspective, his clients' loyalty, as well as their need for his continued efforts on their behalf without major government interference, likely reinforced his belief that, given the SEC's poor management—top-heavy bureaucracy functioning with a budget in excess of $900 million and a staff of more than 3,500—he could operate his scam with impunity.

Whether the congressional hearing held on January 5 was but the first step in the reformation of the SEC or simply a means for congressional posturing will likely become evident when the Obama administration takes office.

It is anticipated that the new president will recommend that the SEC merge with the Commodities Futures Trading Commission—an action that would make Mary Shapiro, the SEC's new chair, one of the most powerful financial regulators since the SEC's creation in 1934. Yet the shell-shocked public may not take well to Shapiro's former dealings with Mark Madoff: While she was chief executive of the Financial Industry Regulatory Authority (FINRA), she appointed Mark Madoff in 2001 to that agency's National Adjudicatory Council, a body for review of FINRA's disciplinary decisions.

In what, in retrospect, turns out to have been a prescient observation, Shapiro stated in an address she delivered in 2007:

> There is no question that the future can be intimidating. But as a famous scientist once said, "The best way to predict the future is to invent it." Right now, we have an unprecedented opportunity to invent the most effective and efficient regulatory approach—one that will better protect investors, and help investors to reach their dreams and give them the tools to invent their own financial futures.

Whatever Shapiro's good intentions and however impressive her résumé may be, it is disquieting to think that she could have appointed Mark Madoff, an executive of a firm that had come under scrutiny in the 1990s, to a position involving, of all things, review of FINRA's disciplinary decisions.

Is there, then, a relationship between government regulators and the financial industry firms and leaders they are charged with regulating?

As compelling as the above noted happenings were, the story that kept viewers glued to their television and computer screens on the afternoon of Thursday, January 8, was but the latest chapter in the cliff-hanger: Would Bernard Madoff's bail be revoked, requiring that he be jailed immediately?

Madoff flouted the terms of his bail agreement when he mailed five packages containing valuable watches and jewelry to family and friends, perhaps in an attempt to dispose of assets in order to raise cash. Having coolly defied every ethic of his profession in perpetrating his $50 billion swindle, Madoff was once again playing with fire—in effect shouting from the rooftop of Apartment 12A, "Try to jail me if you can!"

Was the seventy-year-old alleged Ponzi schemer attempting to relive the way he defied nature nearly a half century ago, when as a lifeguard he plunged into the waves at the Silver Point Beach Club? Did he not realize that there is an enormous difference between defying nature to save lives and flouting ethical standards to ruin lives?

Then the question arose: Was Bernie Madoff's latest stunt part of an elaborate scheme to plant the seeds of an insanity defense? Or was he fully aware of what he was doing and simply short on cash to support his house-arrest lifestyle?

While Bernard Madoff may have filed a statement of his assets on December 31, 2008, as required, it is quite likely that, in addition to whatever assets he listed, he may have hidden away a significant amount of cash and other valuables.

Addressing the issue, former Madoff investor Robert Chew wrote in *Time* magazine that he speculated that Madoff may have put money into bearer bonds, which can be made out for any amount and without record of purchase—"instruments that can be presented to banks by anyone bearing them—no questions asked."

Regarding the difficulty of uncovering Madoff's money trail, Chew quoted an unnamed, former Los Angeles-based Treasury

Department special agent: "You'll see an amazing loss of memory and material in the months ahead. Computers will be lost, fires will be started, records and books destroyed. It always happens."

Chew also quoted Christopher Reich, a best-selling author of financial thrillers, as saying, "There is no way investigators will ever find all the Madoff money. There just isn't enough manpower to go through all the legal hurdles to track it down." According to the *Time* correspondent, Reich believes that perhaps $40 to $80 million has been hidden away by Bernard Madoff.

Reich's suggestion prompted the authors to recall that whether for business or for pleasure, Bernard Madoff has traveled the world for many years. Thus there is a strong possibility that he may have stashed cash, bearer bonds, negotiable securities, precious metals and other fungible assets in any number of secret locations.

Could the king of the Ponzi schemers have secreted his assets beneath his home in the south of France or in the storage space of his Manhattan cooperative apartment building or in one of a zillion bank safe deposit boxes, either in the U.S. or abroad?

Whatever the answers to all these questions, Bernard Madoff managed to dominate the headlines on a day when war raged in Gaza; President-elect Obama, newly arrived in Washington, met with the Congressional leadership to discuss crucial economic issues; and Obama's naming of Leon Panetta as director of the CIA sparked controversy within the Democratic Party.

More controversy and confusion arose on January 5 over whether Madoff was cooperating with investigators as they sifted through mounds of documents and other evidence in their attempt to discover the extent of his crimes. In a bizarre sequence of confirmation, denial, fudging, and then reconfirmation, one of Madoff's lawyers, Dan Horwitz, told Reuters, "We are cooperating with the government investigations," while lead attorney Ira Sorkin said that they were not doing so, according to the *New York Times.*

Sorkin appeared to be contradicting his colleague, saying, "No one said that he is cooperating with the government"—this despite the fact that Sorkin had previously stated that "we" were assisting FBI and SEC investigators.

In attempting to clarify his first statement, Sorkin said that he had meant to say that BMIS is cooperating with the investigators.

Is it "we," "they," or "BMIS"?

Confusing? You bet!

Sorkin later confirmed that his client is cooperating with the authorities, raising concern among certain of Madoff's go-betweens, who fear that in an effort to reduce his potential prison sentence, he might implicate them in his scam.

Knowing of Madoff's track record for prevarication, isn't it possible that he may falsely accuse family members and erstwhile close friends, who, if found to be complicit in Madoff's fencing scheme, could face serious consequences?

According to legal experts, if it can be proven that certain of Madoff's go-betweens are, in fact, involved in his latest attempt at defrauding his investors by trying to raise cash by fencing assets, those individuals would be considered guilty parties in the scam. And even if the go-betweens were to escape criminal prosecution, they would likely face civil suits brought by investors who were persuaded by them to entrust their assets to Madoff—a particular concern as civil charges are easier to prove than criminal ones, and plaintiffs in such actions would not have to prove fraud, only breach of fiduciary duty. It is anticipated that such litigation will likely be brought either individually or in class actions.

On January 8, Bloomberg reported that although one month had passed since Bernard Madoff's arrest, personnel from the FBI, SEC, and the U.S. Attorney's office in Manhattan were examining a growing mass of information in order to learn how Madoff directed his Ponzi scheme and how widespread it may be.

Daniel Richman, a professor at Columbia University and a former federal prosecutor, told Bloomberg's correspondent, Patricia Hurtado: "This is like an explosion that ripped a hole which the investors are pouring through and it probably doesn't relate to Madoff alone."

The professor estimated that it will take months for the investigators to complete their work. "These kinds of investigations are incredibly resource-intensive because of the paper trail and the level of sophistication needed to go through the paperwork," he said.

Given Bernard Madoff's duplicitous nature, it is likely that the paper trail emanating from the Lipstick Building may eventually run cold. If, as many believe, the Ponzi King has indeed hidden some of his assets, then he must have also hidden crucial documents.

Did he have secret loose-leaf notebooks where key transactions were recorded? Is there a CD or other electronic file containing important data that is currently well out of reach for the most meticulous and dedicated investigators? And are there collaborators who did not work for BMIS, who were not known to Bernard Madoff's family and associates, and thus must now be reposing completely under the radar?

If so, those individuals could even be hiding in plain sight, in New York, London or Tokyo. Perhaps they are even at work, hunched over computers in any one of a thousand offices, homes, or apartments anywhere in the world.

Are we assuming that Bernard Madoff was truly the evil genius he appears to be? Could he instead have been acting as a front man for the Mafia, a foreign government, or a private individual? Will investigators discover a small cadre of Bernard Madoff's operatives working underground, perhaps, if one is allowed a flight of fancy, in the dark recesses of the subway tracks adjacent to the East 63rd Street subway station?

And did Bernard Madoff have a life away from BMIS? Considering that the Ponzi King spent forty-eight years at one company, albeit his own, did stealing from the rich and the less rich ever become a real bore? Did the country club denizen eventually tire of one more golf date or business lunch with a prospective client?

Was Bernard Madoff beginning to find the glad-handing of potential investors just a tedious chore as he searched for more and more cash? Or did the Ponzi King experience an adrenaline rush each time he seized his perverted opportunity to make marks out of old friends?

As Bernard Madoff stole from the mega-rich—people like Carl Shapiro, Jerome Fisher, Fred Wilpon, and Mort Zuckerman— did the former sprinkler installer experience a surge of accomplishment?

When he enticed hedge funds to place hundreds of millions, and in some instances, billions of dollars in his care, did Bernard Madoff feel superior to both the careless people who ran the funds and the suckers who never bothered to learn how their money was being handled?

Did the Ponzi King get a special kick out of scamming a charity or a foundation, and did he salivate in anticipation when he was about to receive the life savings of a moderately affluent professional or wage earner?

Did the kid from Laurelton take satisfaction in his ability to steal in pound sterling, euros, Swiss francs, rubles, and yen as well as U.S. dollars?

Did Bernard Madoff ever experience a single moment of remorse or a tinge of regret?

Or was he incapable of such normal human feelings?

As Bernard Madoff observed the market beginning to crash, did he anticipate how quickly his carefully constructed house of cards could collapse?

Was there a point, even a few years ago, when the Ponzi King could have pulled the plug on his fraud? Or did perpetrating his scam feed Bernard Madoff's outsized ego, thus preventing him from calling it quits when he still could?

Many other questions remain about what makes Bernard Madoff tick.

Did he hide his scam from Ruth, his long-ago schoolmate and his wife of many years? If so, how did Ruth react when she found out the truth about her mate of forty-five years and realized that their lives were forever changed?

One can only marvel at Bernard Madoff's self-confidence and self-control until almost the very end.

Was there never a moment when he wanted to blurt out the truth, whether out of a compulsive fit of conscience or because he needed to brag about his exploits?

Did he ever sit next to someone on an airplane and struggle with the temptation to hint about how smart he is—and why?

Did the Ponzi King ever seek the advice of a member of the clergy or a psychologist or a psychiatrist?

Did Bernard Madoff ever embark on a systematic study of Ponzi schemes, particularly those perpetrated in recent years? For instance, the activities of Scientology minister Reed Slatkin, who raised $600 million from 500 wealthy investors until the SEC found him out, or those of the Foundation for New Era Philanthropy, whose assets were frozen by Pennsylvania's attorney general after the organization had raised $500 million from more than 1,000 donors, including the Red Cross?

And was Bernard Madoff aware of Ponzi schemes that were uncovered in Albania, Costa Rica, Haiti, Malaysia, Pakistan, and the Philippines? Did he research the work of William Miller, and, specifically, the notorious Charles Ponzi?

Or in his arrogance and conceit did Bernard Madoff imagine that it was he who had invented the Ponzi wheel?

In the days immediately following Bernard Madoff's arrest, financial pundits were speculating as to when he likely began his Ponzi scheme: Was it in the 1990s or following the turn of the new century? Was Madoff's descent into criminality his attempt at stemming major losses suffered in his trading operations?

After all, Bernard Madoff may be totally corrupt and even amoral, but he isn't stupid. He, like anyone else with access to news reports during the second half of 2008, could see that the Dow was falling faster than the thermometer in a Texas blue norther.

Thus his panic may date from even before Thanksgiving of that year. At that time, Madoff attempted, but failed, to con the seasoned investor Kenneth Langone—he was told that Madoff was putting together a new fund and received a nineteen-page pitch book before meeting with the Ponzi King in his offices at the Lipstick Building—and his business partner, Steve Holzman, out of between $500 million and $1 billion.

But even if Bernard Madoff had succeeded in secreting millions of dollars, as well as other assets, and even if every hidden asset can be found, that amount would still be but a drop in the ocean of loss sustained by his many victims.

During the first week of 2009, however, certain financial experts were suggesting that Madoff may have begun to perpetrate his enormous fraud as early as the 1970s. If that should prove to be the case, it is likely that Madoff's fraud was intentional rather than a response to difficult financial circumstances, thus reflecting his criminal proclivities.

Should anyone doubt that Bernard Madoff's crimes were likely rooted in an innately criminal nature, rather than resulting from financial need, consider that merely weeks before his confession, he was still soliciting money from wealthy investors and "little people" alike.

Take, for instance, the sad story of Martin Rosenbaum, the president of a fuel company located in the Bronx, from whom Madoff accepted $10 million as late as December 5. In yet another instance of Madoff's criminality, an unnamed Los Angeles couple also invested heavily, doing so in mid-November 2008.

Most starling of all is that just ten days before his arrest, Madoff, in a desperate attempt to prevent his Ponzi scheme's collapse, took—either as a loan or as an investment—$250 million from the ninety-five-year-old philanthropist Carl Shapiro, the very person who in 1960 had given him tens of thousands of dollars toward getting BMIS up and running.

That $250 million, which obviously has never been repaid, is part of the estimated $400 million that Shapiro entrusted to Madoff over the years. The word *betrayal* doesn't begin to suggest the magnitude of Bernard Madoff's crime against his very close friend and mentor.

What kind of a person would be capable of such egregious behavior? How can one lie to friends and colleagues time and time again?

Let us examine Bernard Madoff's persona: In a society where money is almost everything, he was until now lionized by the very affluent people he had been scamming for years. It is not simply that he made more money for the already affluent. Because of the mystique surrounding his moneymaking, he was able to attract so many devotees before his precipitous fall from grace on December 11, 2008. The fact that he refused to reveal the secrets of his operation only encouraged his investors to believe that of all the extant investment advisers, he and he alone possessed the right stuff.

Thus, for many highly intelligent, successful people, investing with Bernard Madoff became a badge of honor and pride. By placing their assets with him, they became members of a very exclusive club, one far more prestigious than even the most desirable ones in South Florida or Westchester or Long Island.

As his reputation grew, Bernard Madoff hobnobbed with the rich and famous, befriended some of the world's most successful entrepreneurs, advised major financial entities and government agencies, and attempted to influence the legislative process.

Even at his New York cooperative apartment building he was king, presiding over its board and thus becoming privy to the financial status of prospective buyers. One can imagine Bernard Madoff poring over a would-be buyer's tax returns and other financial data, including pay stubs, alimony agreements, and prenuptial agreements, as well as examining that individual's real assets and liabilities—people who most likely have earned those assets honestly.

As the second week of 2009 began, the Associated Press (AP) reported that hundreds, perhaps thousands of BMIS's clients, who have for years been drawing money from those accounts, were being warned by their attorneys to "do the math" before applying for SIPC funds, as the profits from their investments were likely generated from funds stolen by Bernard Madoff from other clients. In turn, those investors may face the possibility that they will have to forfeit some of their enormous gains.

In many instances, BMIS clients have taken out more than their principal investment. As AP correspondent David Caruso explained, "many of Madoff's long-term investors have, over time, cashed out millions of dollars of their supposed profits, which routinely amount annually from eleven to fifteen percent."

Jonathan Levitt, an attorney representing several of Madoff's clients, told the Associated Press that he had heard from someone who had invested $1.8 million more than a decade ago, then cashed out nearly $3 million worth of profits as the years went by.

And the *New York Times* revealed that those candidates seeking nomination to the U.S. Senate seat being vacated by incoming Secretary of State Hillary Clinton are required to submit a form to New York's governor, David A. Paterson, in which they must state—in addition to whether they have ever hired illegal immigrants, written controversial blogs, or failed to file tax returns—whether they have ever participated "in any investment program run by Bernard Madoff Investment Securities."

Just why one's investment history with Madoff could dash the aspirations of a Senate candidate is not readily clear. Many of his victims are surely as well qualified as any of the people currently serving in that august body. Governor Paterson may be thinking that someone who has invested with Madoff and likely lost significant sums of money would find it difficult to cough up the estimated $40 million it will take to run in a special election in 2010 for the seat, and in 2012 in the regularly scheduled contest.

A growing sense of uneasiness, if not despair, now pervades the not-for-profit world, as officials of U.S. charitable organizations that have been recipients of grants from some of the many foundations affected by Bernard Madoff's villainy, amounting to $73 million in 2007, reexamine their 2009 budgets and income forecasts. In many instances it is impossible to estimate the shortfall that will ensue as a result of their Madoff-generated losses.

Also in question is what will happen to the millions of dollars on deposit in the bank accounts of foundations run by Bernard and Ruth Madoff, as well as those held individually by their sons, Mark and Andrew.

While it is likely that the assets of the Bernard L. and Ruth Madoff Foundation will be seized, it is not yet clear whether the federal government will also attach funds from Andrew and Mark's foundations.

On January 8, responding to the Madoff scandal, the British Serious Fraud Office opened an investigation as to whether Madoff, who operated in the United Kingdom under the name Madoff Securities International, engaged in criminal activity. That agency's director, Richard Alderman, is asking clients and former employees to help with the investigation in order to "discover the truth behind the collapse of these huge financial structures."

Intriguingly, the *New York Times* reported on January 9 that one of Madoff's indirect victims is none other than Marc Rich, the fugitive financier who either purchased or won himself a highly questionable pardon in the last hours of the Clinton presidency. Over the years Rich invested some of his assets, including between $10 and $15 million, with BMIS.

While Rich is not an acquaintance of Madoff's, he does know J. Ezra Merkin, having once been a member of the Manhattan synagogue where Merkin served as president. The article's author, Alison Leigh Cowan, raised the question as to whether Rich, who fled the United States years ago following his indictment on more than 100 federal charges, will seek recourse through U.S. courts. Gerald B. Lefcourt, one of the nation's premier criminal defense attorneys, told Cowan, "He'd never appear for discovery proceedings that will be required, and he's not going to be sympathetic to any party, including the courts, after his failure to appear, notwithstanding the fact that he was pardoned." It seems Marc Rich's loss is one problem Bernard Madoff will not have to sweat.

While the asset report filed by Bernard Madoff with the SEC on New Year's Eve continues to remain under lock and key, it may be possible to discover what that list entails by mid-January. Much to his victims' likely chagrin, however, Madoff appears to be worth only $1 billion, that figure arrived at by estimating the value of his defunct brokerage firm, his Lipstick Building office, his Upper East Side and Wall Street apartments, his three properties in Palm Beach, and his houses in Key Largo, Florida and Antibes, France, his four boats, and three automobiles. According to the trustee charged with liquidating Madoff's brokerage, those possessions have a total value of approximately $830 million. If one then adds the $173 million in checks found in Madoff's desk, one arrives at the total of $1 billion.

In the weeks since Bernard Madoff's arrest, new videos are added daily to the scores of YouTube items related to the scandal, and the mainstream print and broadcast media continue to give the story high priority, with reporters jostling for space outside the Madoffs' apartment building on East 64th Street.

And the media circus goes into overdrive whenever Bernard Madoff heads to a court appearance, with cable news channel anchors breathlessly uttering the words "breaking news," doing so even at the most fragmentary revelation.

Regarding the cliff-hanger question as to whether Madoff's bail would be rescinded, attorney Sorkin claimed in a letter written on January 7 and addressed to U.S. Magistrate Judge Ronald Ellis that his client was not aware that the court order in the civil case against him, freezing his assets, applied to personal items. Sorkin also revealed details of why and how the jewelry had been mailed. It seems that the Madoffs decided on Christmas Eve that they would "reach out" to members of their immediate family, as well as to close friends, by sending them "a few sentimental personal items." Among those items was Madoff's watch collection, as he realized that "due to the sudden change" in his circumstances, he would "never have a chance to wear these watches again."

Is that what really happened?

With the real Santa Claus flying over the rooftops on the Upper East Side, did generous, considerate Bernie Madoff decide to emulate the jolly, stout, bearded man in the red suit?

According to Sorkin, his client, who must surely understand the value of assets—real or imagined—had no idea that gifting diamond-encrusted timepieces from Tiffany and Cartier, as well as diamond brooches, an emerald ring, and other valuables, could possibly violate explicit provisions of an agreement to which he had affixed his signature.

In other words, Sorkin said that the Feds had it all wrong. As he wrote in his letter to Judge Ellis, "Fundamentally, the government's claim that Mr. Madoff could cause harm by dissipating restitution assets is groundless."

And in response to the government's contention that his client is a flight risk, Sorkin, in an apparent rewriting of very recent history, asserted that it was Madoff who advised his sons to contact the authorities following his revelation to them of his Ponzi scheme.

In an earlier version of what transpired on the evening of December 10, 2008, however, Madoff's sons merely "informed" their attorney of their father's confession, and it was the attorney who then made the decision to call the Feds.

As Sorkin described the scene that evening in Apartment 12A, "It was Mr. Madoff himself who encouraged his sons to apprise the authorities of the exact nature of the fraud"—an amazing feat of clairvoyance, as the exact nature of the Ponzi King's scheme is yet to be unraveled—"and told his sons he intended to turn himself in. The risk of Mr. Madoff's fight in this case is virtually zero."

That is, unless Madoff can somehow make his way to a plastic surgeon's office and order up a new face.

One has to feel a tad sorry for Sorkin, an attorney of demonstrable professional skill; one who in his long career has likely never before represented a client quite like good old Bernie Madoff. Oh, to have been a fly on the wall at the very moment of Sorkin's discovery that the Ponzi King had attempted to move pricey jewelry in much the same deceptive way that he has been moving his investors' funds around for years!

As Sorkin's letter to the court was made public, the experts begin to weigh in: Zachary Carter, a former U.S. Attorney for the Eastern District of New York—where the first class action suit against Madoff has been filed—told the *New York Times*, "The argument that I would make as a prosecutor would be that to the extent that Madoff ignored a legal obligation to preserve his assets, it is some indication that he is willing to ignore other obligations, like remaining in the jurisdiction." Madoff's behavior in that instance could, Carter added, "be regarded as a step in the direction of flight."

Or is Carter's theory more than a bit of a stretch? Does attempting to fence one's valuable jewelry presume a direct line to flight risk?

On January 8, acting U.S. Attorney Lev Dassin, in a letter addressed to Judge Ellis in response to Ike Sorkin's fifteen-page, single-spaced opposition brief of the previous day, significantly upped the ante.

It seems that there was yet another shocking revelation: The government claims that Federal investigators searching Madoff's office desk had found a cache of "approximately one hundred signed checks, totaling more than $173 million, ready to be sent out."

To address Sorkin's contention that his client regarded the mailed jewelry as merely "sentimental items," the acting U.S. Attorney wrote, "What may be merely sentimental baubles to the defendant are, in the posture of this case, valuable assets that may comprise a meaningful part of the assets available to be forfeited and applied to the mandatory restitution order that would be entered, upon a conviction, in an effort to recompense the defendant's victims."

The tone of this letter suggests a confident official who knows that he holds all of the important cards. The acting U.S. Attorney concluded by writing:

> Today, the defendant stands in a different position than he did at the times of the prior bail determination in this case. The Government has learned far more now about the nature and extent of the defendant's crimes, and the case against the defendant has grown even stronger. The Government and the Court also know more about the defendant, namely that he was willing to violate an express Court order designed to protect his victims.... In light of all the facts and circumstances now available to the Court, it is clear there is no combination of conditions that reasonably will assure the presence of the defendant and the safety of the community. Accordingly, the defendant should be detained.

The acting U.S. Attorney's response to what could have been a mere indiscretion on Bernard Madoff's part should, however, give the Ponzi King pause. Even if the late Roy Cohn's dictum that "all federal prosecutors are bastards" is somewhat flawed, Bernard Madoff should never doubt the determination of the Southern District's attorneys to nail him. After all, Bernard Madoff's victims, the public, and the American judicial system demand no less.

As if that controversy isn't enough, on Friday, January 9, it was revealed that Madoff had actually confessed to his brother on the evening of Tuesday, December 8, one day before he informed Mark and Andrew of his crimes.

It is possible then that Peter Madoff could himself be in trouble with federal authorities, since he was duty-bound to report the confession to regulatory agency officials as BMIS's senior managing director and chief compliance officer .

And in another development on January 9, the embattled hedge fund manager J. Ezra Merkin resigned as chairman of GMAC, the financial arm of General Motors, which itself had suffered a loss of nearly $8 billion during Merkin's tenure.

That day, as the weekend began, the major players on both sides of the unprecedented scandal dug in their heels—with extreme trepidation on the part of the Madoff camp—in anticipation of Judge Ronald Ellis's announcement, scheduled for noon on Monday, January 12, as to whether the Ponzi King's bail would be revoked, and he would be sent to jail.

The Madoff camp needn't have worried, however.

At twelve minutes past noon on the appointed day, cable news channels interrupted their coverage of the morning's events with breaking news: Judge Ellis had rendered his Opinion and Order (reproduced below with the court's bolding of certain words):

> *Because the Government has failed to meet its legal burden, the motion is **denied**. The Court finds, however, that the following additional conditions shall be imposed to address the identified concerns:*

*[1] The restrictions set forth in the preliminary injunction entered on December 18, 2008, in the civil case brought by the SEC before District Judge Louis L. Stanton, including restrictions on transfer of all property whatsoever, wherever located, in the possession or under the control of Madoff, **shall** be incorporated into the current bail conditions;*

*[2] The restrictions set forth in the voluntary restraint agreement signed by Mrs. Madoff on December 26, 2008, **shall** be incorporated into the current bail conditions; and*

*[3] Madoff **shall** compile an inventory of all valuable portable items in his Manhattan home. In addition to providing this inventory to the Government, Casale Associates, or another security company approved by the Government, **shall** check the inventory once every two weeks. Casale Associates, or another security company approved by the Government, shall search all outgoing physical mail to ensure that no property has been transferred. The Government and Madoff **shall** agree on a threshold value for inventory items within one week of this Order.*

Thus Bernard Madoff—albeit with his ankle bracelet still affixed—will remain amid the luxurious confines of Apartment 12A, where he can order takeout from his favorite restaurants when hungry, recline on freshly laundered and ironed sheets when tired, shave and shower in the privacy of his commodious bathroom at times of his own choosing, and then dress in attire of his own choosing.

Meanwhile, the Ponzi King's victims, many of whom now cannot afford to remain in their own homes—including his own sister—can only pray for the day when Bernard Madoff will be brought to trial and, they hope, found guilty and finally incarcerated.

POSTSCRIPT

Just when Bernard Madoff was settling into his duplex for the long haul following Judge Ellis's decision to continue his bail, the government announced that it would appeal the ruling. The proceeding was scheduled to take place in two days, on the afternoon of Wednesday, January 14.

Early on the appointed day, "Breaking News" alerts began to flash across television screens: The Ponzi King would be heading to court early that afternoon. Within minutes, a crush of television cameras were trained on the entrance to 133 East 64th Street.

Emerging from the building at 1:30 p.m., wearing a bulletproof vest beneath his trench coat, Madoff entered a car and began the approximately six-mile trip down Franklin Delano Roosevelt Drive to the Federal Courthouse. And in a procession reminiscent of the frenzied coverage so many years earlier of O.J. Simpson's attempt to escape arrest, the media was in hot pursuit.

An hour later, as broadcast and print journalists cooled their heels outside the Pearl Street entrance of the courthouse, Federal Judge Lawrence McKenna began to hear arguments. Within the hour, the judge ruled against the government, stating: "The chance of Mr. Madoff fleeing at this point is as close to nil as you can get. The freeze on the assets has made it close to impossible for the defendant to dispose of anything valuable."

Asked by the authors to comment on Judge McKenna's decision, a government spokeswoman uttered two words: "No comment."

Asked by the authors for his comment, Bernard Madoff's lead attorney, Ira Lee Sorkin replied, "The judge ruled and we will abide by the decision."

Now, Bernard Madoff and his attorney must decide whether to seek a plea bargain or to go to trial.

That evening, as Bernard Madoff was likely savoring his courtroom victory amid all the comforts of home on East 64th Street, only blocks away, at 740 Park Avenue, J. Ezra Merkin—lying low in the sumptuous digs he shares with his wife Lauren in the wake of being sued by furious investors claiming losses of more than $2 billion—was about to learn that his legal troubles were escalating.

Working overtime, New York State's attorney general, Andrew M. Cuomo, had just issued after-hours subpoenas to Merkin and the three investment funds under his control—Ascot, Ariel and Gabriel—as well as to the fifteen non-profit institutions that had entrusted the embattled financier with their money.

In doing so, the attorney general sought to determine whether Merkin, already besieged with lawsuits from investors whose funds he had channeled to BMIS but insisting on depicting himself as a victim of the Ponzi king, had defrauded universities and charities by investing their funds with BMIS without their knowledge.

Reacting to his client's having been subpoenaed, Andrew J. Levander, a member of Merkin's legal team, pledged, "We will fully cooperate with any investigation by the New York attorney general's office."

Publishing and real estate mogul Mortimer Zuckerman, one of the boldface personalities who had entrusted considerable funds to Merkin, and whose charitable trust lost $30 million, now says, "Frankly, I was absolutely hoodwinked."

As many of Merkin's other victims grapple with their losses—as well as with their resulting humiliation and anger—among those institutions having filed suits against Merkin and having been subpoenaed by the attorney general is New York University, which has lost more than $24 million. According to the *New York Times*, the university's chief investigative officer had rejected a suggestion made by Merkin in October 2008 that money be invested in a Madoff fund when, in fact, Merkin had been doing so for at least eight years.

Other institutions of higher learning on the attorney general's subpoena list are New York Law School, which lost $3 million; Tufts University, which is out $20 million; and, of course, Yeshiva University, which sustained the spectacular loss of $110 million, and where Merkin not only served as a trustee but headed the investment committee.

As Ezra Merkin's attorneys were responding to the attorney general's action, Bernard Madoff's legal team was dealing with a series of suits filed by irate companies, among them Repex Ventures, a company incorporated in the British Virgin Islands that had entrusted $700,000 to Bank Medici, not realizing, the suit contended, that many other investors never knew of Madoff's role; Bank Austria and its parent company, UniCredit of Italy; HSBC Holdings, the fund's custodian, Ernst & Young, its auditor; and Peter Scheithauer, the former chief executive of Bank Medici.

In an all too familiar pattern that has emerged in the wake of 12/11, both a spokesman for Bank Medici's owner, the missing Sonja Kohn, and Madoff's attorneys have declined to comment.

According to Bank Medici documents that have now surfaced, the *New York Times* reported on Saturday, January 17, that "no mention" is made of BMIS while United States Treasury bills and foreign exchange currency contracts are recorded, and elsewhere, "seemingly blue-chip stocks are listed as having been bought and sold, with millions of shares of companies like General Electric, Microsoft, Exxon, and AT&T changing hands."

Commenting on the arrangement, Drago Indjic, a project manager at the London Business School's Hedge Fund Center, said, "it's a very strange setup.... If you've been in the industry, this doesn't pass the smell test."

Oh, and the missing Ms. Kohn resurfaced late in the week, at least in cyberspace—as one of Bernie Madoff's many victims. In an e-mailed statement, she said, "Having fallen victim to a company supervised by a U.S. regulator, as did many of the world's most illustrious financial institutions, does not ease the pain."

CHAPTER TEN

WHAT PUNISHMENT COULD POSSIBLY FIT THE CRIME?

"Oh God, I hope there will be no wave of sympathy for Bernard Madoff!"—Bette Greenfield, a victim

"I don't care what happens to him. I have to have the energy to get my money back and I really don't want to waste my energy on Bernie Madoff."
—Ronnie Sue Ambrosino, a victim

"Unfortunately, we don't treat white-collar crime with the magnitude we do common crime, yet white-collar crime is often so much worse than holding up a 7-11."
—Lawrence Leamer

"Killing him would be too good."
—Sydelle Meyer, a victim

Bloggers are also weighing in on how they would like to see Bernard Madoff punished:

"Jail for the rest of his poor, poor life. Nothing worse than these white collar thieves."—Regards from Amsterdam

"Without wasting any money and time, 'Hang that SOB.'" —Anonymous

"This person should be in jail. He destroyed so many lives directly and indirectly. What makes him any different than someone who commits mass murder?"
—David

"Pigs get slaughtered."—Kevin

"Why is this man not in jail? If he were a young black man accused of taking $100 from someone, he would be in jail awaiting trial. The fact that he is out on bail is obscene! Of course he can make bail, he stole enough money!"—Jen

"Throw him in jail—and throw away the key—and not a cushy federal prison—let him sit with low-life criminals like himself."—Bob

"...Madoff is under 'house arrest' in his $7m apartment and not in a cold jail cell. A shoplifter stealing food would go directly to jail."—John

"The $10 million Madoff made bail on is a piece of the money that should be going to my family and the other families and charities he stole from. It is disgusting this man is not in jail—he has destroyed and forever changed the lives of countless people. He and his family need to get used to living like paupers because every penny they are currently living on is my family's money and the money of other innocent people that trusted him. He should be thrown in jail for life."
—Rebecca

As investigators pore over thousands of documents related to Bernard Madoff's Ponzi scheme, speculation abounds as to whether he will plea bargain, or if he does stand trial and is convicted, what sort of sentence might be imposed.

"If he goes to trial and is convicted, he would likely receive a thirty-year sentence. If he agrees to plead guilty, while they will bargain back and forth, he will become like an Enron scapegoat. In my opinion," said former federal prosecutor Burns, "he's going to get a high sentence. It will likely be about eighteen months before he actually goes to prison."

Attorney Mark Mulholland said, "In order for him to get what he would consider a soft deal from the government, he is going to have to reveal where all the monies are that he secreted offshore, and truly convince people that he's made as full restitution as he can, with whatever resources that he has."

And, Mulholland believes, "He will have to convince the SEC and the U.S. attorney that he has truly come clean and that he's left penniless and that his children and wife are left penniless."

A source of the authors with FBI contacts, who declined to be identified, has it on good faith that "a deal has already been cut. He is going to walk, that he was told he will have to pay restitution." Of course, the authors' source said, "Everyone in the world knows he is incapable of paying."

"He should receive whatever the law allows," Sydelle Meyer said. "Personally, I believe he must be sick. Someone who could do something like that and turn on his own people, and all the people that needed him so badly is a sick person. What are they going to do with him? I have no idea."

"At the very least, he should be imprisoned for the rest of his life," said Robert Lappin.

Gary Tobin agrees. "He committed a nasty crime. He cheated organizations that are providing heath care, meals on wheels, and education to students. We sometimes soft-pedal these crimes by calling them white-collar crimes. But in its scope and destruction, his is a phenomenally destructive crime. I don't think there is any possibility that he will not spend the rest of his life in jail."

"What about the people who were looking for scholarships, who were getting food?" Harry Taubenfeld asked. "I don't think he calculated just how many people he had hurt.

"Madoff should be sent to a maximum security prison," Taubenfeld insisted. "Let him spend the rest of his life looking behind his back at the rapists and other criminals, because he has destroyed the lives of many people far more than those who lost their money."

"They ought to put him on Rikers Island and let him be somebody's bitch!" said Bette Greenfield. "If there's an afterlife, he's going to get it, only we won't know it. I can't imagine how the poor people feel who get put into jail one-two-three, but see a rich guy in New York sitting in a duplex apartment and having all of the food and all of the lifestyle that he had before. So he can't go out? Everything can come in.

"I have been reading that so many people say, 'He'll get his,' and that's the only way I can think. But it's not what I want to think about. I want to think about what I'm going to do, what my brothers are going to do, what the charities are going to do."

"There's not a place in hell that's probably hot enough for him, given that he did what he himself has alleged that he did," Jon Najarian said. "To steal knowingly for decades, especially from widows, orphans, and charities, there has to be a special spot in hell for you."

"There is no punishment stringent enough for what this man has done. It's beyond punishment," Lawrence Leamer insisted. "It makes you thoroughly wish for a heaven and a hell."

And what of Madoff's sons if they are found to have had knowledge of their father's Ponzi scheme? Victims' attorney Barry

Slotnick predicts that "they could lose their property because it would be considered to be ill-gotten gains."

Lest one fear that Bernie Madoff will one day appear on *Oprah*, crying his eyes out and saying he wants to atone for his terrible sins by giving toys to the grandkids of the people from whom he once stole, Lawrence Leamer assured that he will not.

"Palm Beach is about money. Bernie was revered because he had money," Leamer observed. "Now, he's a pariah, an outcast, finished, gone."

AFTERWORD

At some point during the autumn of 2008, Bernard Madoff knew that the walls supporting his carefully structured Ponzi edifice were about to come tumbling down. Not because he had lost his nerve or had suddenly acquired a conscience. Rather, Bernard Madoff's impending catastrophe was triggered by the deepening economic crisis and the concomitant, precipitous drop in stock prices. He was about to come face-to-face with two immediate and interrelated problems. First, it would become more difficult for him to find investors able to pump fresh money into his firm. Second, some of his clients had already asked for all or part of their funds—and the list would likely grow, perhaps exponentially, in the coming months.

For years Bernie Madoff had succeeded in playing some of the smartest people in the financial world, charming and swindling experienced hedge fund, banking, and private investment leaders, both in the United States and around the world. The roster of his unwitting prey includes Nine West founder Jerome Fisher, American economist and financial consultant Henry Kaufman, chief economist for MarketWatch Irwin Kellner, philanthropist and close friend Carl Shapiro, and real estate and media baron Morton Zuckerman, just to name a few.

Along the way, Madoff had also played government regulatory agencies, most notably the Securities and Exchange

Commission. Whether through intellect, guile, chutzpah, understanding of human nature, or some combination thereof, he would ride the rough waves and contend with the shifting currents of an ever-increasing tide of investment, much as he had mastered the ocean's waves and currents as a lifeguard so many years earlier at Silver Point Beach Club in Atlantic Beach, not far from the town of Far Rockaway, where he attended high school.

It appears now that Bernard Madoff did not distinguish between his wealthy clients and the so-called little people, making him an equal opportunity thief. He played investors of relatively small means, taking their money and promising both significant return and long-term safety. He would deliver on the first promise for the most part while knowing that he might not be able to make good on the latter commitment.

Bernard Madoff reveled in his reputation, whether on the golf links, or in the clubhouses and dining rooms of exclusive country clubs, or in pricey restaurants, or in his inner sanctum in the Lipstick Building, whose special trading floor—cleverly designed to throw due-diligence seekers off guard—evoked for skeptical visitors the deceptive images of a Potemkin village.

The Ponzi schemer knew, however, that most of the individual investors and institutional representatives lusting to gain his attention were not very interested in learning the truth of how he operated. He knew that they ached to buy into his mystique—and at his price. For every Fred Adler or Harry Markopolos or Jon Najarian, there were hordes of apparently sophisticated people only too willing to throw their own or other people's money at him.

Similarly, from his experience with nonprofit entities, Bernard Madoff knew how little governance was exerted by nonprofit boards and lay leaders, some of whom were both clients and go-betweens. It apparently never occurred to him that robbing an organization devoted to education or reforming the justice system or social welfare is a particular *shanda*—"shame" in English—and that is one of the mysteries of his psyche, if not of his soul, providing that he has one.

Now, as Bernard Madoff remains sequestered in his luxurious Upper East Side apartment rather than in the federal lockup just six miles away, he is likely calculating precisely how he can play the criminal justice system.

And, as investigators with the woefully incompetent regulatory system and the tortoise-like federal courts work with the batteries of accountants, attorneys, and advisers to discover what really happened at Bernard L. Madoff Investment Securities, he enjoys the advantage of time—anywhere from eighteen to twenty-four months, it is estimated, before conclusions will be drawn and his fate determined.

Meanwhile Bernard Madoff's ego probably demands that he once again devise a system to thwart his opponents—just as he did years ago, when for a time he bested the major brokerage houses and made his reputation.

He seems to have a deep-seated need to bend this seemingly hopeless situation to his will. Consider what he accomplished in just the first weeks of his downfall and disgrace. While a first offender who sticks up a bodega or robs a taxi driver will be unable to make bail and will surely end up on Rikers Island, the biggest Ponzi schemer ever, the man who pulled off history's greatest white-collar heist, is the recipient of a get-out-of-jail card.

True, it is not a free pass, but for Bernard Madoff the required fee was indeed a bargain, requiring only that family property, rather than cash, be pledged as bond. Whereas a petty criminal awaiting arraignment and disposition of his or her case would not likely have a Manhattan duplex, an oceanfront house on Long Island, or a Palm Beach mansion to put up as surety.

Then, in an almost incomprehensible decision, Madoff was initially granted the privilege of being able to walk the streets of Manhattan during daylight hours. And walk them he did, strolling on Lexington Avenue, window shopping, and acknowledging the greetings and stares from passersby, all the while smiling his enigmatic smile.

It is difficult to assess what enraged Bernard Madoff's victims more: his having been granted bail or his being allowed out of his house at all.

"What is at work here?" they ask. Is it simply that the judge fails to grasp the magnitude of Madoff's crimes? Or do certain federal judges, among them former corporate attorneys, identify with well-connected defendants who wear suits and ties to work, have memberships in all the right clubs, and live in elegant neighborhoods?

The wave of revulsion engendered by the bail fiasco has led the court to modify its initial determination. Thus, Bernard Madoff must now remain in his apartment, meals at his favorite East Side hangouts a pleasure of the past.

Yet the thought of Madoff's now being confined twenty-four hours a day to his duplex while surrounded by costly artworks likely purchased with ill-gotten gains, rather than being forced to endure the stark trappings of the Metropolitan Detention Center, hardly assuages his victims' anguish.

And those of Bernard Madoff's victims who awoke on December 11, 2008, to learn that they can no longer afford to feed their families a decent meal, and would soon learn that the Ponzi King, unlike the denizens of the Detention Center, can either order in or enjoy meals prepared in the kitchen of Apartment 12A by his wife, a cookbook author, must be outraged.

While Bernard Madoff's victims lack the power to revoke his bail or its conditions, they did anticipate being allowed to inspect the list of his assets, which was delivered to the court on December 31, 2008. To say that the victims—as well as the public—have a vested interest in that accounting would be a gross understatement. Yet that crucially vital information remains unavailable to them. The victims' and public's right to know has been trashed—at least for now.

Consider as well that Bernard Madoff, rather than having to rely on the legal skills of an overworked, underpaid, court-appointed attorney, has at his disposal the firepower of the well-connected, white-shoe firm Dickstein Shapiro. Madoff's lead attorney, Ira Lee Sorkin, was the SEC's New York regional enforcement director during the period of the Boesky and Milken investigations in the 1980s. One can safely assume that Sorkin knows how to press the SEC's buttons and will not hesitate to fully utilize his wealth of contacts in both the government and the private sector, established during years of high-level practice on his clients' behalf.

It is interesting to note the ways in which high-profile cases—even some of those considered not winnable—attract high-flying attorneys like moths to the flame. On the face of it, Sorkin would appear to have a sole option: a plea bargain, no luster there to be added to his curriculum vitae.

As appropriately reticent as his client is deceitful, Sorkin, during a telephone conversation with us in December 2008, declined our request for an interview with Madoff, and refused to disclose any information concerning his client's background.

Should attorney and client decide to gamble on a jury trial, however, we wonder: How long will it be until we can click on our TV remotes or our laptops and view good old Bernie Madoff, pulling at our heart strings in interviews with the likes of Barbara Walters or Oprah or *60 Minutes*?

Will we then learn that Bernard Madoff was abused as a child by a parent, a close relative or a trusted family friend? Will Bernard Madoff tell us how, at great personal risk, he pulled a small child from the turbulent Atlantic Ocean years ago during his time as a lifeguard? Will he pause during one of his interviews to pop a pill and then explain to viewers that he is seriously ill? Will he lean into the camera, tears welling in his eyes, and say how truly sorry he is for his "mistakes"?

Or will we awake one morning to learn that Bernard Madoff has been rushed to the hospital in the middle of the night after complaining of chest pains?

The ploys available to this master dissembler are many and varied. Once relatively obscure and known mainly within the financial world—although a legendary figure to his circle of investors—Madoff has emerged on the world stage, his name heard in workplaces, restaurants, and wherever else people congregate.

And he is now more than holding his own in competition for media attention with President Obama, Governor Ron Blagojevich, the Clintons, and Caroline Kennedy. Bernard Madoff must be basking in his newfound notoriety.

Bernard Madoff's predicament has cranked up the New York gossip machine. On New Year's Eve, we were told by the manager of an upscale East Side Manhattan restaurant that Madoff is "very ill." Others speak knowingly of Madoff's fear for his own safety, as well as of his fear of imprisonment.

If and when the Ponzi King is incarcerated, it is not likely that he will be held in a minimum security prison. Rather, he could be sent to the Federal Correctional Center in Butner, North Carolina, where he would be able to go once around the yard daily with one of his peers, Jeffrey Skilling, of Enron notoriety. Or perhaps the Feds will want him to do hard time in Lewisburg or Leavenworth or Marion.

We are jumping ahead of ourselves, however, because Bernard Madoff may just go to trial and be acquitted.

He surely has little to lose by appearing before a jury, providing, of course, that Ira Sorkin or some other top litigator will work for his or her much-less-than-usual fee.

Should Madoff choose to go to trial, the government will likely come up with a long litany of charges that could result, if Madoff is found guilty, in considerable jail time.

Given that he is already seventy years old, however, and according to actuarial tables that he would likely die before having served even a potion of his sentence, Bernard Madoff has little to lose, and much to gain, by gambling on a trial.

Acquittal would put Bernard Madoff back on the street—literally, should all his assets eventually be sold to the benefit of his victims—a far better fate than spending the rest of his life in prison under the conditions of a plea bargain.

Does Bernard Madoff have reason to fear for his life in the coming months?

It is not inconceivable that, lurking in the shadows around the corner from East 64th Street, there is an enraged individual just waiting for the opportunity to take Bernard Madoff out.

Others believe that Madoff will take his own life. We do not believe that he will commit suicide anytime soon or, perhaps, ever.

We predict that a year or two from now, the media—and hence the public—will have moved on to other causes célèbres.

And, God forbid, there may be other Madoffs out there, waiting to be uncovered.

If so, will one of them one day take the Ponzi King's place in the *Guinness Book of Records?*

If the dénouement of other recent scandals is any guide, Madoff may well become a victim himself—that is, of the public's fickleness and poor attention span, as well as its capacity to grant a measure of forgiveness to even the vilest of characters. Led by Dr. Phil, Oprah, and their lesser imitators, Americans are conditioned to forgive—if not necessarily to forget. As time goes on, our interest will likely be captured by the misdeeds of other swindlers. Thus the many sins of Bernard Madoff may fade in the public's perception.

And in the meantime, the greatest Ponzi schemer to date will become older; and if not wiser, still shrewd and determined to off the system.

At the same time, Bernard Madoff's many victims will attempt the difficult and, in some instances, the near impossible task of rebuilding their shattered lives. Most of the victims, lacking high-profile names, will barely be noticed in our celebrity-driven culture, as it is much easier in the society we live in to empathize with one bearing a boldface name, since we are familiar with their careers and personal foibles.

Not so with Madoff's media-faceless victims, unfortunate individuals who are criticized for allowing themselves to be scammed, and as Madoff makes his way through the legal thicket, he can only benefit from the classic tactic of blaming victims for their victimization.

As our conversations with certain victims and media reports about them attest, most of them are in a state of shock, which will likely evolve into anger. Other victims, however, will likely never be able to recover emotionally and get on with their lives.

Whatever the medium or long-term effects of Bernard Madoff's treachery, it is abundantly clear that the government keeps a separate set of books for high-profile offenders. As a friend once said to us, "If you are going to owe money, make sure it's ten thousand dollars rather than one hundred dollars, because your creditor will have a greater incentive to act in an understanding manner."

Madoff's victims realize that unless he has siphoned off and hidden huge amounts of money that can be located and recovered, the most they can hope for is some restitution from the SIPC, a process that will likely take many months. Those who entrusted their money to banks and hedge funds that fed Bernard Madoff's insatiable need for cash can only hope that the SIPC will relax its rules so as to allow them to receive some compensation.

In the unlikely event that Bernard Madoff did it all his way, alone, as he claims, only he knows the full extent of his crimes.

If, as is more likely, Madoff had assistance in executing his nefarious scheme, he will have to decide whether to give up the individual or individuals who abetted him to the Feds.

Should the latter scenario apply, given the fact that Bernard Madoff lured into his web and then betrayed some of his closest friends and longtime associates, he would likely not have the slightest compunction about ratting out his abettors.

The overriding problem for the U.S. Attorney, however, concerns the credibility of anything Madoff might say. Thus, while it is likely that the government will one day unravel the mystery through examination of Madoff's paper trail, final adjudication of the matter requires the Ponzi King's willingness to tell the whole truth.

As we sit here in our apartment, a little more than a mile away from the Madoffs' duplex, we yearn to be flies on the wall in

Apartment 12A. What is the Ponzi King thinking? Is he relieved that the game is all over, that he will not have to begin and end each day waiting for that inevitable knock on the door? Does he read the daily news accounts of his scam? Does he watch coverage of himself on the cable news networks that almost hourly mention his name? Does he relive over and over again in his mind the exact moment—if there was one—when he initiated the Ponzi scheme? Does he look back with satisfaction on all the wonderful days and nights he was able to enjoy as a result of his investors having picked up the tab? Does he consider himself to be an evil man beyond sympathy, understanding, and redemption? Does he regard himself as one who adeptly—albeit criminally—played the cards he was dealt?

Finally, as Bernard Madoff remains secluded in his aerie, does he have any understanding that his misdeeds were so incomprehensible and so destructive that no one seems to grasp the extent of his criminality?

APPENDIX A

THE MISSION STATEMENT OF BERNARD L. MADOFF INVESTMENT SECURITIES LLC

The following is the authors' reproduction of the document exactly as it appeared on Google's cache of http://www.madoff.com on December 15, 2008. Revisiting the site on December 27, the authors discovered that the document had been removed due to the site's seizure by the U.S. government.

Page 1 of 5

MADOFF SECURITIES: QUALITY EXECUTIONS AND SERVICE THROUGH INNOVATIVE TECHNOLOGY

Jump to specific categories:
A Global Leader in Trading US Equities
Providing a complete Dealing Capability for US Securities in Europe
Advanced Technology and Sophisticated Traders
Clearing and Settlement are Rooted in Advanced Technology
Disaster Recovery Facility Reflects the Attention to Every Detail
The Owner's Name is on the Door

A Global Leader in Trading US Equities

Bernard L. **Madoff** Investment **Securities** LLC is a leading international market maker. The firm has been providing quality executions for broker-dealers, banks and financial institutions since its inception in 1960. During this time, **Madoff** has compiled an uninterrupted record of growth, which has enabled us to continually build our financial resources. With more than $700 million in firm capital, **Madoff** currently ranks among the top 1% of US **Securities** firms. Our sophisticated proprietary automation and unparalleled client service delivers an enhanced execution that is virtually unmatched in our industry.

Madoff Securities' clients include scores of leading **securities** firms, banks and financial institutions from across the United States and around the world. The firm is a leading market-maker in all of the S&P 500 stocks as well as over 350 NASDAQ issues. The firm is known for its fine pricing as well as its ability to execute most orders in seconds.

Madoff Securities' superior service is made possible by a sophisticated dealing staff backed by the **securities** industry's most advanced technology. It is underpinned by the personal commitment if founder Bernard L. **Madoff** and his brother Peter B. **Madoff**, who is the senior managing director. Their dedication to providing quality executions has enabled the firm to become a leader in the US "third market," which trades US listed equities away from the exchange floor.

Madoff Securities is a registered US broker/dealer regulated by the **Securities** and Exchange Commission and the Financial Industry Regulatory Authority, Inc.

Page 2 of 5

An Intricate Interweaving of Advanced Technology and Sophisticated Traders

One of the critical ingredients in creating the added value which **Madoff Securities** offers its clients is the firm's intricate interweaving of advanced technology and experienced traders. The firm's position at the forefront of computerized trading is widely acknowledged in the US financial community.

Madoff Securities' leading edge information processing technology means clients can choose to communicate their buy and sell orders to the firm's trading room by electronically inputting them or by making a telephone call. In either case, once an order is received, **Madoff's** systems scan prevailing prices in all markets to establish an execution price. Because this process may take only seconds, clients can receive immediate confirmation of their transactions.

Sophisticated computers are integral to every aspect of the firm's activities, from executing trades to clearing and settling them, from monitoring prices to identifying trading opportunities around the world.

Madoff Securities also utilizes its computers to seek out opportunities for hedging its inventory of **securities**. The firm uses a variety of futures, options, and other instruments to hedge its positions and limit its risks. While these hedging strategies are an important tool in protecting the firm's financial position, ultimately, these highly prudent risk management policies protect the interests of clients as well.

At Madoff Securities, Clearing and Settlement are Rooted in Advanced Technology

The combination of quality and value that is inherent in every **Madoff Securities** transaction continues beyond execution. At **Madoff**, the clearing and settlement process is also rooted in advanced technology, which minimizes errors and maximizes efficient processing and rapid communications.

Madoff Securities is a full clearing firm and a member of all US clearing corporations and depositories. The firm's highly automated clearing and settlement systems interface with the Depository Trust Company, the Options Clearing Corporation, and the National **Securities** Clearing Corporation, of which Bernard **Madoff** is a past chairman. The firm's systems also interface fully with the systems of all major global custodians and clearing & Settlement systems.

Page 3 of 5

Madoff Securities' extensive network of

relationships with other broker/dealers enables the firm to ensure timely delivery and settlement of all client transactions.

Moreover, **Madoff Securities'** computerized transaction processing means that the firm can customize client reports and deliver them electronically in whatever format best meets the needs of clients.

IMPORTANT INFORMATION ABOUT PROCEDURES FOR OPENING A NEW ACCOUNT

To help the government fight the funding of terrorism and money laundering activities, Federal law requires all financial institutions to obtain, verify, and record information that identifies each person who opens an account.

What this means for you: When you open an account, we will ask for your name, address, date of birth and other information that will allow us to identify you. We may also ask to see your driver's license or other identifying documents.

Sophisticated Disaster Recovery Facilities, Reflects he Attention to Every Detail

Madoff Securities has one of the most sophisticated disaster recovery facilities found anywhere in the **securities** industry, In addition to its offices in Manhattan, **Madoff Securities** maintains a fully equipped and staffed facility located near LaGuardia Airport. This office duplicates all the features of the primary **Madoff**

Securities offices. **Madoff Securities'** disaster recovery facility is not just an alternative trading room, but rather a full-fledged office which is equipped to receive and transact orders and to handle the clearing and settlement process as well.

Under the supervision of a facilities manager, this unique on-line facility is tested continuously to ensure that it is prepared to take over the firm's operations if any kind of disaster were to affect the Manhattan office. Members of the firm's staff are rotated through the facility and regularly perform their work from it. Thus, there is always staff on hand in case disaster strikes at the firm's main office.

The disaster recovery facility is on a different electric power grid than the main office, and it is served by a different telephone central office. The facility also has its own electrical generator.

Since this facility was created in 1992, it has been used as an adjunct to **Madoff Securities'** main office, and it has not been confronted with a major emergency. But the

Page 4 of 5

existence of the facility testifies to the high priority the firm places on being available to meet the needs of its clients under all conditions.

The Owner's Name is on the Door

In an era of faceless organizations owned by other equally faceless organizations, Bernard L. **Madoff** Investment **Securities** LLC harks back to an earlier era in the financial world: The owner's name is on the door. Clients know that Bernard **Madoff** has a personal interest in maintaining the unblemished record of value, fair-dealing, and high ethical standards that has always been the firm's hallmark.

Bernard L. **Madoff** founded the investment firm that bears his name in 1960, soon after leaving law school. His brother, Peter B. **Madoff**, graduated from law school and joined the firm in 1970. While building the firm into a significant force in the **securities** industry, they have both been deeply involved in leading the dramatic transformation that has been underway in US **securities** trading.

Bernard L. **Madoff** has been a major figure in the National Association of **Securities** Dealers (NASD), the major self-regulatory organization for US broker/dealer firms. The firm was one of the five broker/dealers most closely involved in developing the NASDAQ Stock Market. He has been chairman of the board of directors of the NASDAQ Stock Market as well as a member of the board of governors of the NASD and a member of numerous NASD committees.

One major US financial publication lauded Bernard **Madoff** for his role in "helping to make NASDAQ a faster, fairer, more efficient and more international system." He has also served as a member of the board of directors of the **Securities** Industry Association.

Reflecting the growing international involvement of the firm, when **Madoff Securities** opened a London office in 1983, it would become one of the first US members of the London Stock Exchange. Bernard **Madoff** was also a founding member of the board of directors of the International **Securities** Clearing Corporation in London.

Peter B. **Madoff** has also been deeply involved in the NASD and other financial services regulatory organizations. He has served as vice chairman of the NASD, a member of its board of governors, and chairman of its New York region. He has also been actively involved in the NASDAQ Stock Market as a member of its board of governors and its executive committee and as chairman of its trading committee. He also has been president of the Security Traders Association of New York. He is a member of the board of

Page 5 of 5

directors of the Depository Trust and Clearing Corp. He is a member of the board of the **Securities** Industry Association.

Bernard and Peter **Madoff** have both played instrumental roles in the development of the fully computerized National Stock Exchange. Peter **Madoff** has been a member of the board of governors and has served on its executive committee. They have helped make the National Exchange the fastest growing regional stock exchange in the United States.

These positions of leadership not only indicate the deep interest **Madoff Securities** has shown in its industry, they also reflect the respect the firm and its management have achieved in the financial community.

APPENDIX B

MARKOPOLOS LETTER
TO THE SEC, NOVEMBER 7, 2005

The World's Largest Hedge Fund is a Fraud

November 7, 2005 Submission to the SEC
Madoff Investment Securities, LLC
www.madoff.com

Opening Remarks:

I am the original source for the information presented herein having first presented my rationale, both verbally and in writing, to the SEC's Boston office in May, 1999 before any public information doubting Madoff Investment Securities, LLC appeared in the press. There was no whistleblower or insider involved in compiling this report. I used the Mosaic Theory to assemble my set of observations. My observations were collected first-hand by listening to fund of fund investors talk about their investments in a hedge fund run by Madoff Investment Securities, LLC, a SEC registered firm. I have also spoken to the heads of various Wall Street equity derivative trading desks and every single one of the senior managers I spoke with told me that Bernie Madoff was a fraud. Of course, no one wants to take undue career risk by sticking their head up and saying the emperor isn't wearing any clothes but....

I am a derivatives expert and have traded or assisted in the trading of several billion $US in options strategies for hedge funds and institutional clients. I have experience managing split-strike conversion products both using index options and using individual stock options, both with and without index puts. Very few people in the world have the mathematical background needed to manage these types of products but I am one of them. I have outlined a detailed set of Red Flags that make me very suspicious that Bernie Madoff's returns aren't real and, if they are real, then they would almost certainly have to be generated by front-running customer order flow from the broker-dealer arm of Madoff Investment Securities. LLC.

Due to the sensitive nature of the case I detail below, its dissemination within the SEC must be limited to those with a need to know. The firm involved is located in the New York Region.

As a result of this case, several careers on Wall Street and in Europe will be ruined. Therefore, I have not signed nor put my name on this report. I request that my name not be released to anyone other than the Branch Chief and Team Leader in the New York Region who are assigned to the case, without my express written permission. The fewer people who know who wrote this report the better. I am worried about the personal safety of myself and my family. Under no circumstances is this report or its contents to be shared with any other regulatory body without my express permission. This report has been written solely for the SEC's internal use.

As far as I know, none of the hedge fund, fund of funds (FOF's) mentioned in my report are engaged in a conspiracy to commit fraud. I believe they are naïve men and women with a notable lack of derivatives expertise and possessing little or no quantitative finance ability.

There are 2 possible scenarios that involve fraud by Madoff Securities:

1. Scenario # 1 **(Unlikely):** I am submitting this case under Section 21A(e) of the 1934 Act in the event that the broker-dealer and ECN depicted is actually providing the stated

returns to investors but is earning those returns by front-running customer order flow. Front-running qualifies as insider-trading since it relies upon material, non-public information that is acted upon for the benefit of one party to the detriment of another party. Section 21A(e) of the 1934 Act allows the SEC to pay up to 10% of the total fines levied for insider-trading. We have obtained approval from the SEC's Office of General Counsel, the Chairman's Office, and the bounty program administrator that the SEC is able and willing to pay Section 21A(e) rewards. This case should qualify if insider-trading is involved.

2. Scenario # 2 **(Highly likely)** Madoff Securities is the world's largest Ponzi Scheme. In this case there is no SEC reward payment due the whistle-blower so basically I'm turning this case in because it's the right thing to do. Far better that the SEC is proactive in shutting down a Ponzi Scheme of this size rather than reactive.

Who: The politically powerful Madoff family owns and operates a New York City based broker-dealer, ECN, and what is effectively the world's largest hedge fund. Bernard "Bernie" Madoff, the family patriarch started the firm.

According to the www.madoff.com website, *"Bernard L. Madoff was one of the five broker-dealers most closely involved in developing the NASDAQ Stock Market. He has been chairman of the board of directors of the NASDAQ Stock Market as well as a member of the board of governors of the NASD and a member of numerous NASD committees. Bernard Madoff was also a founding member of the International Securities Clearing Corporation in London.*

His brother, Peter B. Madoff *has served as vice chairman of the NASD, a member of its board of governors, and chairman of its New York region. He also has been actively involved in the NASDAQ Stock Market as a member of its board of governors and its executive committee and as chairman of its trading committee. He also has been a member of the board of directors of the Security Traders Association of New York. He is a member of the board of directors of the Depository Trust Corporation.*

What:

1. The family runs what is effectively the world's largest hedge fund with estimated assets under management of at least $20 billion to perhaps $50 billion, but no one knows exactly how much money BM is managing. That we have what is effectively the world's largest hedge fund operating underground is plainly put shocking. But then again, we don't even know the size of the hedge fund industry so none of this should be surprising. A super-sized fraud of this magnitude was bound to happen given the lack of regulation of these off-shore entities. My best guess is that approximately $30 billion is involved.
2. However the hedge fund isn't organized as a hedge fund by Bernard Madoff (BM) yet it acts and trades exactly like one. BM allows third party Fund of Funds (FOF's) to private label hedge funds that provide his firm, Madoff Securities, with equity tranch funding. In return for equity tranch funding, BM runs a trading strategy, **as agent**, whose returns flow to the third party FOF hedge funds and their investors who put up equity capital to

fund BM's broker-dealer and ECN operations. *BM tells investors it earns its fees by charging commissions on all of the trades done in their accounts.*

Red Flag # 1: *Why would a US broker-dealer organize and fund itself in such an unusual manner? Doesn't this seem to be an unseemly way of operating under the regulator's radar screens? Why aren't the commissions charged fully disclosed to investors? Can a SEC Registered Investment Advisor charge **both** commissions and charge a principle fee for trades? MOST IMPORTANTLY, why would BM settle for charging only undisclosed commissions when he could earn standard hedge fund fees of 1% management fee + 20% of the profits? Doing some simple math on BM's 12% average annual return stream to investors, the hedge fund, before fees, would have to be earning average annual returns of 16%. Subtract out the 1% management fee and investors are down to 15%. 20% of the profits would amount to 3% (.20 x 15% = 3% profit participation) so investors would be left with the stated 12% annual returns listed in Attachment 1 (Fairfield Sentry Ltd. Performance Data). Total fees to the third party FOF's would amount to 4% annually. Now why would BM leave 4% in average annual fee revenue on the table unless he were a Ponzi Scheme? Or, is he charging a whole lot more than 4% in undisclosed commissions?*

3. The third parties organize the hedge funds and obtain investors but 100% of the money raised is actually managed by Madoff Investment Securities, LLC in a purported hedge fund strategy. The investors that pony up the money don't know that BM is managing their money. That Madoff is managing the money is purposely kept secret from the investors. Some prominent US based hedge fund, fund of funds, that "invest" in BM in this manner include:

   A. Fairfield Sentry Limited (Arden Asset Management) which had $5.2 billion invested in BM as of May 2005; 11th Floor, 919 Third Avenue; New York, NY 10022; Telephone 212.319.606; The Fairfield Greenwich Group is a global family of companies with offices in New York, London and Bermuda, and representative offices in the U.S., Europe and Latin America. Local operating entities are authorized or regulated by a variety of government agencies, including Fairfield Greenwich Advisors LLC, a U.S. SEC registered investment adviser, Fairfield Heathcliff Capital LLC, a U.S. NASD member broker-dealer, and Fairfield Greenwich (UK) Limited, authorized and regulated by the Financial Services Authority in the United Kingdom.

   B. Access International Advisors; www.aiagroup.com; a SEC registered investment advisor, telephone # 212.223.7167; Suite 2206; 509 Madison Avenue, New York, NY 10022 which had over $450 million invested with BM as of mid-2002. The majority of this FOF's investors are European, even though the firm is US registered.

   C. Broyhill All-Weather Fund, L.P. had $350 million invested with BM as of March 2000.

   D. Tremont Capital Management, Inc. Corporate Headquarters is located at 555 Theodore Fremd Avenue; Rye, New York 10580; T: (914) 925-1140 F: (914) 921-3499. Tremont oversees on an advisory and fully discretionary basis over $10.5 billion in assets. Clients include institutional investors, public and private pension plans, ERISA plans, university endowments, foundations, and financial institutions, as well as high net worth individuals. Tremont is owned by Oppenhiemer Funds Inc. which is owned by Mass Mutual Insurance Company so they should have sufficient reserves to make investors whole. Mass Mutual is currently under investigation by the Massachusetts Attorney General, the Department of Justice, and the SEC.

E. During a 2002 marketing trip to Europe every hedge fund FOF I met with in Paris and Geneva had investments with BM. They all said he was their best manager! A partial list of money managers and Private Banks that invest in BM is included at the end of this report in Attachment 3.

4. Here's what smells bad about the idea of providing equity tranch funding to a US registered broker-dealer:

A. The investment returns passed along to the third party hedge funds are equivalent to BM borrowing money. These 12 month returns from 1990 – May 2005 ranged from a low of 6.23% to a high of 19.98%, with an average 12 month return during that time period of 12.00%. Add in the 4% in average annual management & participation fees and BM would have to be delivering average annual returns of 16% in order for the investors to receive 12%. No Broker-Dealer that I've ever heard of finances its operations at that high of an implied borrowing rate (source: Attachment 1; Fairfield Sentry Limited return data from December 1990 – May 2005). Ask around and I'm sure you'll find that BM is the only firm on Wall Street that pays an average of 16% to fund its operations.

B. BD's typically fund in the short-term credit markets and benchmark a significant part of their overnight funding to LIBOR plus or minus some spread. LIBOR + 40 basis points would seem a more realistic borrowing rate for a broker-dealer of BM's size.

C. **Red Flag # 2**: *why would a BD choose to fund at such a high implied interest rate when cheaper money is available in the short-term credit markets? One reason that comes to mind is that BM couldn't stand the due diligence scrutiny of the short-term credit markets. If Charles Ponzi had issued bank notes promising 50% interest on 3 month time deposits instead of issuing unregulated Ponzi Notes to his investors, the State Banking Commission would have quickly shut him down. The key to a successful Ponzi Scheme is to promise lucrative returns but to do so in an unregulated area of the capital markets. Hedge funds are not due to fall under the SEC's umbrella until February 2006.*

5. The third party hedge funds and fund of funds that market this hedge fund strategy that invests in BM don't name and aren't allowed to name Bernie Madoff as the actual manager in their performance summaries or marketing literature. Look closely at Attachment 1, Fairfield Sentry Ltd.'s performance summary and you won't see BM's name anywhere on the document, yet BM is the actual hedge fund manager with discretionary trading authority over all funds, as agent.

Red Flag # 3: *Why the need for such secrecy? If I was the world's largest hedge fund and had great returns, I'd want all the publicity I could garner and would want to appear as the world's largest hedge fund in all of the industry rankings. Name one mutual fund company, Venture Capital firm, or LBO firm which doesn't brag about the size of their largest funds' assets under management. Then ask yourself, why would the world's largest hedge fund manager be so secretive that he didn't even want his investors to know he was managing their money? Or is it that BM doesn't want the SEC and FSA to know that he exists?*

6. The third party FOF's never tell investors who is actually managing their money and describe the investment strategy as: This hedge fund's objective is long term growth on

a consistent basis with low volatility. The investment advisor invests exclusively in the U.S. and utilizes a strategy often referred to as a "split-strike conversion." Generally this style involves purchasing a basket of 30 – 35 large-capitalization stocks with a high degree of correlation to the general market (e.g. American Express, Boeing, Citigroup, Coca-Cola, Dupont, Exxon, General Motors, IBM, Merck, McDonalds). To provide the desired hedge, the manager then sells out-of-the-money OEX index call options and buys out-of-the-money OEX index put options. The amount of calls that are sold and puts that are bought represent a dollar amount equal to the basket of shares purchases.

7. I personally have run split-strike conversion strategies and know that BM's approach is far riskier than stated in 6 above. His strategy is wholly inferior to an all index approach and is wholly incapable of generating returns in the range of 6.23% to 19.98%. BM's strategy should not be able beat the return on US Treasury Bills Due to the glaring weakness of the strategy:

    A. Income Part of the strategy is to buy 30 – 35 large-cap stocks, sell out-of-the-money index call options against the value of the stock basket. There are three possible sources of income in this strategy.

        1) We earn income from the stock's dividends. Let's attribute a 2% average return to this source of funds for the 14 ½ year time period. This explains 2% of the 16% average gross annual returns before fees and leaves 14% of the returns unexplained.

        2) We earn income from the sale of OTC OEX index call options. Let's also assume that we can generate an additional 2% annual return via the sale of OTC out-of-the-money OEX index call options which leaves 12% of the 16% gross returns unexplained. On Friday, October 14, 2005 the OEX (S&P 100) index closed at 550.49 and there were only 163,809 OEX index call option contracts outstanding (termed the "open interest"). 163,809 call option calls outstanding x $100 contact multiplier x 550.49 index closing price = $9,017, 521,641 in stock equivalents hedged.

        3) We can earn income from capital gains by selling the stocks that go up in price. This portion of the return stream would have to earn the lion's share of the hedge fund strategy's returns. We have 12% of the return stream unexplained so far. However, the OTC OEX index puts that we buy will cost AT LEAST <8%> per year (a lot more in most years but I'm giving BM the benefit of every doubt here). Therefore, BM's stock selection would have to be earning an average of 20% per year. That would mean that he's been the world's best stock-picker since 1990 beating out such luminaries as Warren Buffet and Bill Miller. Yet no one's ever heard of BM as being a stock-picker, much less the world's best stock-picker. Why isn't he famous if he was able to earn 20% average annual returns?

        Red Flag # 4: *$9.017 billion in total OEX listed call options outstanding is not nearly enough to generate income on BM's total amount of assets under management which I estimate to range between $20 - $50 billion. Fairfield Sentry Ltd. alone has $5.1 billion with BM. And, while BM may say he only uses Over-the-Counter(OTC) index options, there is no way that this is* *possible. The OTC market should never be several times larger than the exchange listed market for this type of plain vanilla derivative.*

B. Protection Part of the strategy is to buy out-of-the-money OEX index put options. This costs you money each and every month. This hurts your returns and is the main reason why BM's strategy would have trouble earning 0% average annual returns much less the 12% net returns stated in Fairfield Sentry Ltd.'s performance summary. Even if BM earns a 4% return from the combination of 2% stock dividends and 2% from the sale of call options, the cost of the puts would put this strategy in the red year in and year out. No way he can possibly be delivering 12% net to investors. The math just doesn't support this strategy if he's really buying index put options.

Red Flag # 5: *BM would need to be purchasing at-the-money put options because he has only 7 small monthly losses in the past 14 ½ years. His largest monthly loss is only <0.55%>, so his puts would have to be at-the-money. At-the-money put options are very, very expensive. A one-year at-the-money put option would cost you <8%> or more, depending upon the market's volatility. And <8%> would be a cheap price to pay in many of the past 14 ½ years for put protection!! Assuming BM only paid< 8%> per year in put protection, and assuming he can earn +2% from stock dividends plus another +2% from call option sales, he's still under-water <4%> performance wise. <8%> put cost + 2% stock dividends + 2% income from call sales = <4%>. And, I've proven that BM would need to be earning at least 16% annually to deliver 12% after fees to investors. That means the rest of his returns would have to be coming from stock selection where he picked and sold winning stocks to include in his 35-stock basket of large-cap names. Lots of luck doing that during the past stock market crises like 1997's Asian Currency Crises, the 1998 Russian Debt / LTCM crises, and the 2000-2002 killer bear market. And index put option protection was a lot more expensive during these crises periods than 8%. Mathematically none of BM's returns listed in Attachment 1 make much sense. They are just too unbelievably good to be true.*

C. The OEX index (S&P 100) closed at 550.49 on Friday, October 14, 2005 meaning that each put option hedged $55,049 dollars worth of stock ($100 contract multiplier x 550.49 OEX closing index price = $55,049 in stock hedged). As of that same date, the total open interest for OEX index put options was 307,176 contracts meaning that a total of $16,909,731,624 in stock was being hedged by the use of OEX index puts (307,176 total put contracts in existence as of Oct 14th x $55,049 hedge value of 1 OEX index put = $16,909,731,624 in stock hedged). Note: I excluded a few thousand OEX LEAP index put options from my calculations because these are long-term options and not relevant for a split-strike conversion strategy such as BM's.

Red Flag # 6: *At my best guess level of BM's assets under management of $30 billion, or even at my low end estimate of $20 billion in assets under management, BM would have to be over 100% of the total OEX put option contract open interest in order to hedge his stock holdings as depicted in the third party hedge funds marketing literature. In other words, there are not enough index option put contracts in existence to hedge the way BM says he is hedging! And there is no*

way the OTC market is bigger than the exchange listed market for plain vanilla
S&P 100 index put options.

D. Mathematically I have proven that BM cannot be hedging using listed index put and call options. One hedge fund FOF has told me that BM uses only Over-the-Counter options and trades exclusively thru UBS and Merrill Lynch. I have not called those two firms to check on this because it seems implausible that a BD would trade $20 - $50 billion worth of index put options per month over-the-counter thru only 2 firms. That plus the fact that if BM was really buying OTC index put options, then there is no way his average annual returns could be positive!! At a minimum, using the cheapest way to buy puts would cost a fund <8%> per year. To get the put cost down to <8%>, BM would have to buy a one-year at-the-money put option and hold it for one-year. No way his call sales could ever hope to come even fractionally close to covering the cost of the puts.

Red Flag # 7: *The counter-party credit exposures for UBS and Merrill would be too large for these firms credit departments to approve. The SEC should ask BM for trade tickets showing he has traded OTC options thru these two firms. Then the SEC should visit the firms' OTC derivatives desks, talk the to heads of trading and ask to see BM's trade tickets. Then ask the director of operations to verify the tickets and ask to see the inventory of all of the stock and listed options hedging the OTC puts and calls. If these firms can't show you the off-setting hedged positions then they are assisting BM as part of a conspiracy to commit fraud. If any other brokerage firms equity derivatives desk is engaged in a conspiracy to cover for BM, then this scandal will be a doozy when it hits the financial press but at least investors would have firms with deep pockets to sue.*

Red Flag # 8: *OTC options are more expensive to trade than listed options. You have to pay extra for the customization features and secrecy offered by OTC options. Trading in the size of $20 - $50 billion per month would be impossible and the bid-ask spreads would be so wide as to preclude earning any profit whatsoever. These Broker/Dealers would need to offset their short OTC index put option exposure to a falling stock market by hedging out their short put option risk by either buying listed put options or selling short index futures and the derivatives markets are not deep and liquid enough to accomplish this without paying a penalty in prohibitively expensive transaction costs.*

Red Flag # 9: *Extensive and voluminous paperwork would be required to keep track of and clear each OTC trade. Plus, why aren't Goldman, Sachs and Citigroup involved in handling BM's order flow? Both Goldman and Citigroup are a lot larger in the OTC derivatives markets than UBS or Merrill Lynch.*

E. My experience with split-strike conversion trades is that the best a good manager is likely to obtain using the strategy marketed by the third-party FOF's is T-bills less management fees. And, if the stock market is down by more than 2%, the return from this strategy will range from a high of zero return to a low of a few percent depending upon your put's cost and how far out-of-the-money it is.

F. In 2000 I ran a regression of BM's hedge fund returns using the performance data from Fairfield Sentry Limited. BM had a .06 correlation to the equity market's return which confirms the .06 Beta that Fairfield Sentry Limited lists in its return numbers.

7

Red Flag # 10: *It is mathematically impossible for a strategy using index call options and index put options to have such a low correlation to the market where its returns are supposedly being generated from. This makes no sense! The strategy depicted retains 100% of the single-stock downside risk since they own only index put options and not single stock put options. Therefore if one or more stocks in their portfolio were to tank on bad news, BM's index put would offer little protection and their portfolio should feel the pain. However, BM's performance numbers show only 7 extremely small losses during 14 ½ years and these numbers are too good to be true. The largest one month loss was only -55 basis points (-0.55%) or just over one-half of one percent! And BM never had more than a one month losing streak! Either BM is the world's best stock and options manager that the SEC and the investing public has **never** heard of or he's a fraud. You would have to figure that at some point BM owned a WorldCom, Enron, GM or HealthSouth in their portfolio when bad or really bad news came out and caused these stocks to drop like a rock.*

8. **Red Flag # 11** *Two press articles, which came to print well after my initial May 1999 presentation to the SEC, do doubt Bernie Madoff's returns and they are:*
   A. The May 7, 2001 edition of Barron's, in an article entitled, ***"Don't Ask, Don't Tell; Bernie Madoff is so secretetive, he even asks his investors to keep mum,"*** written by Erin Arvedlund, published an expose about Bernie Madoff a few years ago with no resulting investigation by any regulators. Ms. Arvedlund has since left Barron's. I have attached a copy of the Barrons' article which lists numerous red flags.
   B. Michael Ocrant, formerly a reporter for MAR Hedge visited Bernie Madoff's offices and wrote a very negative article that doubted the source of BM's returns. He reported to a colleague that he saw some very unusual things while at Madoff's offices. The SEC should contact him. Michael Ocrant is currently serving as the Director of Alternative Investments; Institutional Investor; New York, NY 10001; Telephone # 212-224-3821 or 212-213-6202; Email: mocrant@iiconferences.com

9. Fund of funds with whom I have spoken to that have BM in their stable of funds continually brag about their returns and how they are generated thanks to BM's access to his broker-dealer's access to order flow. They believe that BM has perfect knowledge of the market's direction due to his access to customer order flow into his broker-dealer.
   Red Flag # 12: *Yes, BM has access to his customer's order flow thru his broker-dealer but he is only one broker out of many, so it is impossible for him to know the market's direction to such a degree as to only post monthly losses once every couple of years. All of Wall Street's big wire houses experience trading losses on a more regular frequency that BM. Ask yourself how BM's trading experience could be so much better than all of the other firms on Wall Street. Either he's the best trading firm on the street and rarely ever has large losing months unlike other firms or he's a fraud.*

10. **Red Flag # 13**: *I believe that BM's returns can be real ONLY if they are generated from front-running his customer's order flow. In other words, yes, if he's buying at a penny above his customer's buy orders, he can only lose one penny if the stock drops but can*

make several pennies if the stock goes up. For example, if a customer has an order to buy 100,000 shares of IBM at $100, BM can put in his own order to buy 100,000 share of IBM at $100.01. This is what's known as a right-tail distribution and is very similar to the payoff distribution of a call option. Doing this could easily generate returns of 30% - 60% or more per anum. He could be doing the same thing by front-running customer sell orders. However, if BM's returns are real but he's generating them from front-running there are two problems with this:

    A. Problem # 1: front-running is one form of insider-trading and is illegal

    B. Problem # 2: generating real returns from front-running but telling hedge fund investors that you are generating the returns via a complex (but unworkable) stock and options strategy is securities fraud.

Some time ago, during different market conditions, I ran a study using the Black-Scholes Option Pricing Model to analyze the value of front-running with the goal of putting a monetary value on front-running where the insider knew the customer's order and traded ahead of it. When I ran the study the model inputs were valued at: OEX component stocks annualized volatility on a cap-weighted basis was 50% (during a bear market period), the T-bill rate was 5.80%, and the average stock price was $46. I then calculated the value of an at-the-money call options over time intervals of 1 minute, 5 minutes, 10 minutes, and 15 minutes. I used a 253 trading day year. The SEC should be able to duplicate these results:

1 minute option = 3 cents worth of trade information value
5 minute option = 7 cents worth of trade information value
10 minute option = 10 cents worth of trade information value
15 minute option = 12 cents worth of trade information value

Conclusion: Bernie Madoff used to advertise in industry trade publications that he would pay 1 cent per share for other broker's order flow. If he was paying 1 cent per share for order flow and front-running these broker's customers, then he could easily be earning returns in the 30% - 60% or higher annually. In all time intervals ranging from 1 minute to 15 minutes, having access to order flow is the monetary equivalent of owning a valuable call option on that order. The value of these implicit call options ranges between 3 – 12 times the one penny per share paid for access to order flow. If this is what he's doing, then the returns are real but the stated investment strategy is illegal and based solely on insider-trading.

NOTE: I am pretty confident that BM is a Ponzi Scheme, but in the off chance he is front-running customer orders and his returns are real, then this case qualifies as insider-trading under the SEC's bounty program as outlined in Section 21A(e) of the 1934 Act. However, if BM was front-running, a highly profitable activity, then he wouldn't need to borrow funds from investors at 16% implied interest. Therefore it is far more likely that BM is a Ponzi Scheme. Front-running is a very simple fraud to commit and requires only access to inside information. The elaborateness of BM's fund-raising, his need for secrecy, his high 16% average cost of funds, and reliance on a derivatives investment scheme that few investors (or regulators) would be capable of comprehending lead to a weight of the evidence conclusion that this is a Ponzi Scheme.

11. **Red Flag # 14**: *Madoff subsidizes down months! Hard to believe (and I don't believe this) but I've heard two FOF's tell me that they don't believe Madoff can make money in big down months either. They tell me that Madoff "subsidizes" their investors in down months, so that they will be able to show a low volatility of returns. These types of stories are commonly found around Ponzi Schemes. These investors tell me that Madoff only books winning tickets in their accounts and "eats the losses" during months when the market sells off hard. The problem with this is that it's securities fraud to misstate either returns or the volatility of those returns. These FOF professionals who heard BM tell them that he subsidizes losses were professionally negligent in not turning BM into the SEC, FSA and other regulators for securities fraud.*
    Red Flag # 15: *Why would a fund of funds investor believe any broker-dealer that commits fraud in a few important areas – such as misstating returns and misstating volatility of returns – yet believe him in other areas? I'd really like to believe in the tooth fairy, but I don't after catching my mother putting a quarter underneath my pillow one night.*
12. **Red Flag # 16**: *Madoff has perfect market-timing ability. One investor told me, with a straight face, that Madoff went to 100% cash in July 1998 and December 1999, ahead of market declines. He said he knows this because Madoff faxes his trade tickets to his firm and the custodial bank. However, since Madoff owns a broker-dealer, he can generate whatever trade tickets he wants. And, I'll bet very few FOF's ask BM to fax them trade tickets. And if these trade tickets are faxed, have the FOF's then matched them to the time and sales of the exchanges? For example, if BM says he bot 1 million shares of GM, sold $1 million worth of OTC OEX calls and bot $1 million worth of OTC OEX puts, we should see prints somewhere. The GM share prints would show on either the NYSE or some other exchange while the broker-dealers he traded OTC options thru would show prints of the hedges they traded to be able to provide BM with the OTC options at the prices listed on BM's trade tickets.*
13. **Red Flag # 17**: *Madoff does not allow outside performance audits. One London based hedge fund, fund of funds, representing Arab money, asked to send in a team of Big 4 accountants to conduct a performance audit during their planned due diligence. They were told "No, only Madoff's brother-in-law who owns his own accounting firm is allowed to audit performance for reasons of secrecy in order to keep Madoff's proprietary trading strategy secret so that nobody can copy it. Amazingly, this fund of funds then agreed to invest $200 million of their client's money anyway, because the low volatility of returns was so attractive!! Let's see, how many hedge funds have faked an audited performance history?? Wood River is the latest that comes to mind as does the Manhattan Fund but the number of bogus hedge funds that have relied upon fake audits has got to number in the dozens.*
14. **Red Flag # 18**: *Madoff's returns are not consistent with the one publicly traded option income fund with a history as long as Madoff's. In 2000, I analyzed the returns of Madoff and measured them against the returns of the Gateway Option Income Fund (Ticker GATEX). During the 87 month span analyzed, Madoff was down only 3 months versus GATEX being down 26 months. GATEX earned an annualized return of 10.27% during the period studied vs. 15.62% for Bernie Madoff and 19.58% for the S&P 500. GATEX has a more flexible investment strategy than BM, so GATEX's returns should be*

superior to BM's but instead they are inferior. This makes no sense. How could BM be better using an inferior strategy?

15. **Red Flag # 19**: *There have been several option income funds that went IPO since August 2004. None of them have the high returns that Bernie Madoff has. How can this be? They use similar strategies only they should be making more than BM in up months because most of these option income funds don't buy expensive index put options to protect their portfolios. Thus the publicly traded option income funds should make more money in up markets and lose more than Madoff in down markets. Hmm....that Madoff's returns are so high yet he buys expensive put options is just another reason to believe he is running the world's largest Ponzi Scheme. A good study for the SEC would be to compare 2005 performance of the new option income funds to Bernie Madoff while accounting for the cost of Bernie's index put option protection. There's no way Bernie can have positive returns in 2005 given what the market's done and where volatility is.*

16. **Red Flag # 20**: *Madoff is suspected of being a fraud by some of the world's largest and most sophisticated financial services firms. Without naming names, here's an abbreviated tally:*

    A. A managing director at Goldman, Sachs prime brokerage operation told me that his firm doubts Bernie Madoff is legitimate so they don't deal with him.

    B. From an Email I received this past June 2005 I now suspect that the end is near for BM. All Ponzi Schemes eventually topple of their own weight once they become too large and it now appears that BM is having trouble meeting redemptions and is attempting to borrow sizeable funds in Europe.

ABCDEFGH and I had dinner with a savvy European investor that studies the HFOF market. He stated that both RBC and Socgen have removed Madoff some time ago from approved lists of individual managers used by investors to build their own tailored HFOFs.

More importantly, Madoff was turned down, according to this source, for a borrowing line from a Euro bank, I believe he said Paribas. Now why would Madoff need to borrow more funds? This Euro Investor said that Madoff was in fact running "way over" our suggested $12-14 billion (Fairfield Sentry is running $5.3 BB by themselves!) . Madoff's 12 month returns is about 7% net of the feeder fund's fees. Looks like he is stepping down the pay out.

    C. An official from a Top 5 money center bank's FOF told me that his firm wouldn't touch Bernie Madoff with a ten foot pole and that there's no way he's for real.

17. **Red Flag # 21:** *ECN's didn't exist prior to 1998. Madoff makes verbal claims to his third party hedge FOF's that he has private access to ECN's internal order flow, which Madoff pays for, and that this is a substantial part of the return generating process. If this is true, then where did the returns come from in the years 1991 – 1997, prior to the ascendance of the ECN's? Presumably, prior to 1998, Madoff only had access to order flow on the NASDAQ for which he paid 1 cent per share for. He would have no such advantage pre-1998 on the large-cap, NYSE listed stocks the marketing literature says he buys (Exxon, McDonalds, American Express, IBM, Merck, etc...).*

18. **Red Flag # 22:** *The Fairfield Sentry Limited Performance Chart (Attachment 1) depicted for Bernie Madoff's investment strategy are misleading. The S&P 500 return line is accurate because it is moving up and down, reflecting positive and negative returns. Fairfield Sentry's performance chart is misleading, it is almost a straight line rising at a 45 degree angle. This chart cannot be cumulative in the common usage of the term for reporting purposes, which means "geometric returns." The chart must be some sort of arithmetic average sum, since a true*

cumulative return line, given the listed monthly returns would be exponentially rising (i.e. curving upward at an increasing rate). My rule of thumb is that if the manager misstates his performance, you can't trust him. Yet somehow Madoff is now running the world's largest, most clandestine hedge fund so clearly investors aren't doing their due diligence. And why does he provide the S&P 500 as his benchmark when he is actually managing using a S&P 100 strategy? Shouldn't the performance line presented be the S&P 100's (OEX) performance?

19. **Red Flag # 23:** *Why is Bernie Madoff borrowing money at an average rate of 16.00% per anum and allowing these third party hedge fund, fund of funds to pocket their 1% and 20% fees bases upon Bernie Madoff's hard work and brains? Does this make any sense at all? Typically FOF's charge only 1% and 10%, yet BM allows them the extra 10%. Why? And why do these third parties fail to mention Bernie Madoff in their marketing literature? After all he's the manager, don't investors have a right to know who's managing their money?*

20. **Red Flag # 24:** *Only Madoff family members are privy to the investment strategy. Name one other prominent multi-billion dollar hedge fund that doesn't have outside, non-family professionals involved in the investment process. You can't because there aren't any. Michael Ocrant, the former MAR Hedge Reporter listed above saw some highly suspicious red flags during his visit to Madoff's offices and should be interviewed by the SEC as soon as possible.*

21. **Red Flag # 25:** *The Madoff family has held important leadership positions with the NASD, NASDAQ, SIA, DTC, and other prominent industry bodies therefore these organizations would not be inclined to doubt or investigate Madoff Investment Securities, LLC. The NASD and NASDAQ do not exactly have a glorious reputation as vigorous regulators untainted by politics or money.*

22. **Red Flag # 26:** *BM goes to 100% cash for every December 31st year-end according to one FOF invested with BM. This allows for "cleaner financial statements" according to this source. Any unusual transfers or activity near a quarter-end or year-end is a red flag for fraud. Recently, the BD REFCO Securities engaged in "fake borrowing" with Liberty, a hedge fund, that made it appear that Liberty owed REFCO over $400 million in receivables. This allowed REFCO to mask its true debt position and made all of their equity ratios look better than they actually were. And of course, Grant Thorton, REFCO's external auditor missed this $400 million entry. As did the two lead underwriters who were also tasked with due-diligence on the IPO - CSFB and Goldman Sachs. BM uses his brother-in-law as his external auditor, so in this case there isn't even the façade of having an independent and vigilant auditor verifying the accounting entries.*

23. **Red Flag # 27:** *Several equity derivatives professionals will all tell you that the split-strike conversion strategy that BM runs is an outright fraud and cannot possibly achieve 12% average annual returns with only 7 down months during a 14 ½ year time period. Some derivatives experts that the SEC should call to hear their opinions of how and why BM is a fraud and for some insights into the mathematical reasons behind their belief, the SEC should call:*

       a. Leon Gross, Managing Director of Citigroup's world-wide equity derivatives research unit; 3rd Floor, 390 Greenwich Street; New York, NY 10013: Tel# 800.492.9833 or 212.723.7873 or leon.j.gross@citigroup.com [Leon can't believe that the SEC hasn't shut down Bernie Madoff yet. He's also amazed that FOF's actually believe this stupid options strategy is capable of earning a positive return much less a 12% net average annual return. He thinks the strategy would have trouble earning 1% net much less 12% net. Leon is a free spirit, so if you ask him he'll tell you but you'd understand it better if you met him at his workplace in a private conference room and tell him he won't need to have Citigroup lawyers present, you're just there for some friendly opinions. He talks derivatives at a high level, so ask simple "yes or no" type questions to start off the interview then drill down.]

    b. Walter "Bud"Haslett, CFA; Write Capital Management, LLC; Suite 455; 900 Briggs Road; Mount Laurel, NJ 08065; Tel#: 856.727.1700 or bud.haslett@writecapital.com www.writecapital.com [Bud's firm runs $ hundreds of millions in options related strategies and he knows all of the math.]

    c. Joanne Hill, Ph.D.; Vice-President and global head of equity derivatives research, Goldman Sachs (NY), 46th Floor; One New York Plaza, New York, NY 10004; Tel# 212.902.2908 [Again, make sure she doesn't lawyer up or this conversation will be useless to you. Tell her you want her opinion and no one will hold her to it or ever tell she gave the SEC an opinion without legal counsel present.]

24. **Red Flag # 28:** *BM's Sharpe Ratio of 2.55 (Attachment 1: Fairfield Sentry Ltd. Performance Data) is UNBELIEVABLY HIGH compared to the Sharpe Ratios experienced by the rest of the hedge fund industry. The SEC should obtain industry hedge fund rankings and see exactly how outstanding Fairfield Sentry Ltd.'s Sharpe Ratio is. Look at the hedge fund rankings for Fairfield Sentry Ltd. and see how their performance numbers compare to the rest of the industry. Then ask yourself how this is possible and why hasn't the world come to acknowledge BM as the world's best hedge fund manager?*

25. **Red Flag # 29:** *BM tells the third party FOF's that he has so much money under management that he's going to close his strategy to new investments. However, I have met several FOF's who brag about their "special access" to BM's capacity. This would be humorous except that too many European FOF's have told me this same seductive story about their being so close to BM that he'll waive the fact that he's closed his funds to other investors but let them in because they're special. It seems like every single one of these third party FOF's has a "special relationship" with BM.*

Conclusions:

1. I have presented 174 months (14 ½ years) of Fairfield Sentry's return numbers dating back to December 1990. Only 7 months or 4% of the months saw negative returns. Classify this as "definitely too good to be true!" No major league baseball hitter bats .960, no NFL team has ever gone 96 wins and only 4 losses over a 100 game span, and you can bet everything you own that no money manager is up 96% of the months either. It is inconceivable that BM's largest monthly loss could only be -0.55% and that his longest losing streaks could consist of 1 slightly down month every couple of years. Nobody on earth is that good of a money manager unless they're front-running.

2. There are too many red flags to ignore. REFCO, Wood River, the Manhattan Fund, Princeton Economics, and other hedge fund blow ups all had a lot fewer red flags than Madoff and look what happened at those places.

3. Bernie Madoff is running the world's largest unregistered hedge fund. He's organized this business as "hedge fund of funds private labeling their own hedge funds which Bernie Madoff **secretly** runs for them using a split-strike conversion strategy getting paid only trading commissions which are not disclosed." If this isn't a regulatory dodge, I don't know what is. This is back-door marketing and financing scheme that is opaque and rife with hidden fees (he charges only commissions on the trades). If this product isn't marketed correctly, what is the chance that it is managed correctly? In my financial industry experience, I've found that wherever there's one cockroach in plain sight, many more are lurking behind the corner out of plain view.

4. Mathematically this type of split-strike conversion fund should never be able to beat US Treasury Bills much less provide 12.00% average annual returns to investors net of fees. I and other derivatives professionals on Wall Street will swear up and down that a split-strike conversion strategy cannot earn an average annual return anywhere near the 16% gross returns necessary to be able to deliver 12% net returns to investors.

5. BM would have to be trading more than 100% of the open interest of OEX index put options every month. And if BM is using only OTC OEX index options, it is guaranteed that the Wall Street firms on the other side of those trades would have to be laying off a significant portion of that risk in the exchange listed index options markets. Every large derivatives dealer on Wall Street will tell you that Bernie Madoff is a fraud. Go ask the heads of equity derivatives trading at Morgan Stanley, Goldman Sachs, JP Morgan and Citigroup their opinions about Bernie Madoff. They'll all tell the SEC that they can't believe that BM hasn't been caught yet.

6. The SEC is slated to start overseeing hedge funds in February 2006, yet since Bernie Madoff is not registered as a hedge fund but acting as one but via third party shields, the chances of Madoff escaping SEC scrutiny are very high. If I hadn't written this report, there's no way the SEC would have known to check the facts behind all of these third party hedge funds.

Potential Fall Out if Bernie Madoff turns out to be a Ponzi Scheme:

1. If the average hedge fund is assumed to be levered 4:1, it doesn't take a rocket scientist to realize that there might be anywhere from a few hundred billion on up in selling pressure in the wake of a $20 - $50 billion hedge fund fraud. With the hedge fund market estimated to be $1 trillion, having one hedge fund with 2% - 5% of the industry's assets under management suddenly blow up, it is hard to predict the severity of the resulting shock wave. You just know it'll be unpleasant for anywhere from a few days to a few weeks but the fall out shouldn't be anywhere near as great as that from the Long Term Capital Management Crises. Using the hurricane scale with which we've all become quite familiar with this year, I'd rate BM turning out to be a Ponzi Scheme as a Category 2 or 3 hurricane where the 1998 LTCM Crises was a Category 5.

2. Hedge fund, fund of funds with greater than a 10% exposure to Bernie Madoff will likely be faced with forced redemptions. This will lead to a cascade of panic selling in all of the various hedge fund sectors whether equity related or not. Long –short and market neutral managers will take losses as their shorts rise and their longs fall. Convertible arbitrage managers will lose as the long positions in underlying bonds are sold and the short equity call options are bought to close. Fixed income arbitrage managers will also face losses as credit spreads widen. Basically, most hedge funds categories with two exceptions will have at least one big down month thanks to the unwinding caused by forced redemptions. Dedicated Short Funds and Long Volatility Funds are the two hedge fund categories that will do well.

3. The French and Swiss Private Banks are the largest investors in Bernie Madoff. This will have a huge negative impact on the European capital markets as several large fund of funds implode. I figure one-half to three-quarters of Bernie Madoff's funds come from overseas. The unwinding trade will hurt all markets across the globe but it is the Private European Banks that will fare the worst.

4. European regulators will be seen as not being up to the task of dealing with hedge fund fraud. Hopefully this scandal will serve as a long overdue wake-up call for them and result in increased funding and staffing levels for European Financial Regulators.

5. In the US Fairfield Sentry, Broyhill, Access International Advisors, Tremont and several other hedge fund, fund of funds will all implode. There will be a call for increased hedge fund regulation by scared and battered high net worth investors.

6. The Wall Street wire house FOF's are not invested in Madoff's strategy. As far as I know the wire house's internal FOF's all think he's a fraud and have avoided him like the plague. But these very same wire houses often own highly profitable hedge fund prime brokerage operations and these operations will suffer contained, but painful nonetheless, losses from loans to some hedge funds that go bust during the panic selling. As a result, I predict that some investment banks will pull out of the prime brokerage business deeming it too volatile from an earnings standpoint. Damage to Wall Street will be unpleasant in that hedge funds and FOF's are a big source of trading revenues. If the

hedge fund industry fades, Wall Street will need to find another revenue source to replace them.

7. US Mutual fund investors and other long-term investors in main stream investment products will only feel a month or two's worth of pain from the selling cascade in the hedge fund arena but their markets should recover afterwards.

8. Congress will be up in arms and there will be Senate and House hearings just like there were for Long Term Capital Management.

9. The SEC's critics who say the SEC shouldn't be regulating private partnerships will be forever silenced. Hopefully this leads to expanded powers and increased funding for the SEC. Parties that opposed SEC entry into hedge fund regulation will fall silent. The SEC will gain political strength in Washington from this episode but only if the SEC is proactive and launches an immediate, full scale investigation into all of the Red Flags surrounding Madoff Investment Securities, LLC. Otherwise, it is almost certain that NYAG Elliot Spitzer will launch his investigation first and once again beat the SEC to the punch causing the SEC further public embarrassment.

10. Hedge funds will face increased due diligence from regulators, investors, prime brokers and counter-parties which is a good thing and long overdue.

Potential Fall Out if Bernie Madoff is found out to be front-running customer order flow:

1. This would be just one more black eye among many for the brokerage industry and the NYSE and NASDAQ. At this point the reputations of both the NYSE and NASDAQ are already at rock bottom, so there's likely little downside left for these two troubled organizations.

2. The industry wouldn't miss a beat other than for the liquidation of Madoff Investment Securities, LLC. Figure it will be similar to REFCO's demise only there won't be a buyer of the firm given that they cheated customers who would all be embarrassed to remain customers once the news they've been ripped off is on the front-pages. These former customers are more likely to sue for damages than remain customers. Unsecured lenders would face losses but other than that the industry would be better off.

3. At least the returns are real, in which case determining restitution could keep the courts busy for years. The Class Action Bar would be thrilled. A lot of the FOF's are registered offshore in places where the long arm of the law might not reach. My guess is that the fight for the money off-shore would keep dozens of lawyers happily employed for many years.

4. The FOF's would suffer little in the way of damage. All could be counted on to say "*We didn't know the manager was generating returns illegally. We relied upon the NYSE and NASDAQ to regulate their markets and prevent front-running therefore we see no reason to return any funds.*"

Attachments:

1. 2 page Summary of Fairfield Sentry Ltd with performance data from December 1990 – May 2005

2. Copy of the May 7, 2001 Barrons' article, ***"Don't Ask, Don't Tell; Bernie Madoff is so secretetive, he even asks his investors to keep mum,"*** written by Erin E. Arvedlund.

3. Partial list of French and Swiss money-managers and private banks with investments in Bernie Madoff's hedge fund. Undoubtedly there are dozens more European FOF's and Private Banks that are invested with BM.

4. 2 page offering memorandum, faxed March 29, 2001, for an investment in what I believe is Fairfield Sentry Ltd., one of several investment programs run by Madoff Investment Securities, LLC for third party hedge fund, fund of funds. I do not know who the source was who faxed this document since the fax heading is blank. The document number listed at the bottom of the page appears to read   I:\Data\WPDOCS|AG_\94021597

ATTACHMENT 1: Fairfield Sentry Performance Data

Fairfield Sentry Ltd

Fund Category(s):
Long/Short Equity

Strategy Description:
The Fund seeks to obtain capital appreciation of its assets principally through the utilization of a nontraditional options trading strategy described as "split strike conversion", to which the Fund allocates the predominant portion of its assets. This strategy has defined risk and profit parameters, which may be ascertained when a particular position is established. Set forth below is a description of the "split strike conversion" strategies ("SSC Investments"). The establishment of a typical position entails (i) the purchase of a group or basket of equity securities that are intended to highly correlate to the S&P 100 Index , (ii) the sale of out-of-the-money S&P 100 Index call options in an equivalent contract value dollar amount to the basket of equity securities, and (iii) the purchase of an equivalent number of out-of-the-money S&P 100 Index put options. An index call option is out-of-the-money when its strike price is greater than the current price of the index; an index put option is out-of-the-money when the strike price is lower than the current price of the index. The basket typically consists of approximately 35 to 45 stocks in the S&P 100. The logic of this strategy is that once a long stock position has been established, selling a call against such long position will increase the standstill rate of return, while allowing upward movement to the short call strike price. The purchase of an out-of-the-money put, funded with part or all of the call premium, protects the equity position from downside risk. A bullish or bearish bias of the positions can be achieved by adjustment of the strike prices in the S&P 100 puts and calls. The further away the strike prices are from the price of the S&P 100, the more bullish the strategy. However, the dollar value underlying the put options always approximates the value of the basket of stocks.

Contact Info		Fees & Structure	
Fund:	Fairfield Sentry Ltd	Fund Assets:	$5100.00million
General Partner:	Arden Asset Management	Strategy Assets:	$5300.00million
Address:	919 Third Avenue	Firm Assets:	$8300million
	11th th Floor	Min. Investment:	$ 0.10million
	New York NY 10022	Management Fee:	1.00%
	USA	Incentive Fee:	20.00%
Tel:	212-319-6060	Hurdle Rate:	
Fax:		High Water Mark:	Yes
Email:	fairfieldfunds@fggus.com	Additions:	Monthly
Contact Person:	Fairfield Funds	Redemptions:	Monthly
Portfolio Manager:		Lockup:	
		Inception Date:	Dec-1990
		Money Invested In:	United States
		Open to New Investments:	Yes

Annual Returns

1990	1991	1992	1993	1994	1995	1996	1997	1998	1999	2000	2001	2002	2003	2004	2005
2.83%	18.58%	14.67%	11.68%	11.49%	12.95%	12.99%	14.00%	13.40%	14.18%	11.55%	10.68%	9.33%	8.21%	7.07%	2.52%

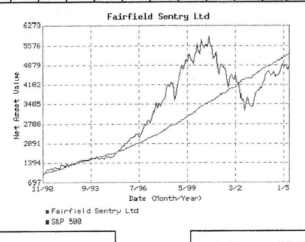

Fairfield Sentry Ltd

- Fairfield Sentry Ltd
- S&P 500

Year To Date:	2.52%
Highest 12 Month Return:	19.98%
Lowest 12 Month Return:	6.23%
Average Annual Return:	12.00%
Average Monthly Return:	0.96%
Highest Monthly Return:	3.36%
Lowest Monthly Return:	-0.55%
Average Gain:	1.01%
Average Loss:	-0.24%
Profitable Percentage:	95.98%
Compounded Monthly Return:	0.96%
Longest Losing Streak:	1 mo.
Maximum Drawdown:	-0.55%

Sharpe Ratio (Rolling 12):	2.56
Sharpe Ratio (Annualized):	2.55
Std. Dev. (Monthly):	0.75%
Std. Dev. (Rolling 12):	2.74%
Beta:	0.06
Alpha:	0.91
R:	0.30
R Squared:	0.09

	Jan	Feb	Mar	Apr	May	Jun	Jul	Aug	Sep	Oct	Nov	Dec
1990	N/A	N/A	N/A	N/A	N/A	N/A	N/A	N/A	N/A	N/A	N/A	2.83% E
1991	3.08% E	1.46% E	0.59% E	1.39% E	1.88% E	0.37% E	2.04% E	1.07% E	0.80% E	2.82% E	0.08% E	1.63% E
1992	0.49% E	2.79% E	1.01% E	2.86% E	-0.19%	1.29% E	0.00% E	0.92% E	0.40% E	1.40% E	1.42% E	1.43% E
1993	0.00% E	1.93% E	1.86% E	0.06% E	1.72% E	0.86% E	0.09% E	1.78% E	0.35% E	1.77% E	0.26% E	0.45% E
1994	2.18% E	-0.36%	1.52% E	1.82% E	0.51% E	0.29% E	1.78% E	0.42% E	0.82% E	1.88% E	-0.55%	0.66% E
1995	0.92% E	0.76% E	0.84% E	1.69% E	1.72% E	0.50% E	1.08% E	-0.16%	1.70% E	1.60% E	0.51% E	1.10% E
1996	1.49% E	0.73% E	1.23% E	0.64% E	1.41% E	0.22% E	1.92% E	0.27% E	1.22% E	1.10% E	1.58% E	0.48% E
1997	2.45% E	0.73% E	0.86% E	1.17% E	0.63% E	1.34% E	0.75% E	0.35% E	2.39% E	0.55% E	1.56% E	0.42% E
1998	0.91% E	1.29% E	1.75% E	0.42% E	1.76% E	1.28% E	0.83% E	0.28% E	1.04% E	1.93% E	0.84% E	0.33% E
1999	2.06% E	0.17% E	2.29% E	0.36% E	1.51% E	1.76% E	0.43% E	0.94% E	0.73% E	1.11% E	1.61% E	0.39% E
2000	2.20% E	0.20% E	1.84% E	0.34% E	1.37% E	0.80% E	0.65% E	1.32% E	0.25% E	0.92% E	0.68% E	0.43% E
2001	2.21% E	0.14% E	1.13% E	1.32% E	0.32% E	0.23% E	0.44% E	1.01% E	0.73% E	1.28% E	1.21% E	0.19% E
2002	0.03% E	0.60% E	0.46% E	1.16% E	2.12% E	0.26% E	3.36% E	-0.06%	0.13% E	0.73% E	0.16% E	0.06% E
2003	-0.27%	0.04% E	1.97% E	0.10% E	0.95% E	1.00% E	1.44% E	0.22% E	0.93% E	1.32% E	-0.08%	0.32% E
2004	0.94% E	0.50% E	0.05% C	0.43% C	0.66% C	1.28% C	0.08% C	1.33% E	0.53% E	0.03% E	0.79% E	0.24% E
2005	0.51% E	0.37% E	0.85% C	0.14% C	0.63% C	N/A	N/A	N/A	N/A	N/A	N/A	N/A

END ATTACHMENT # 1 FAIRFIELD SENTRY LTD. PERFORMANCE DATA

19

APPENDIX C

SEC DOCUMENT FILED DECEMBER 12, 2008

JAMES CLARKSON
ACTING REGIONAL DIRECTOR
Attorney for Plaintiff
SECURITIES AND EXCHANGE COMMISSION
New York Regional Office
3 World Financial Center – RM 400
New York, NY 10281
(212) 336-1020

UNITED STATES DISTRICT COURT
SOUTHERN DISTRICT OF NEW YORK

--x

SECURITIES AND EXCHANGE COMMISSION,   :
                                                                          :
                                      Plaintiff,   :
                                                                          :
                    - against -   :   08 Civ. 10791 (LLS)
                                                                          :   ECF CASE
BERNARD L. MADOFF and   :
BERNARD L. MADOFF INVESTMENT   :
SECURITIES LLC,   :
                                                                          :
                                      Defendants.   :
                                                                          :

--x

ORDER TO SHOW CAUSE,
TEMPORARY RESTRAINING ORDER,
AND ORDER FREEZING ASSETS AND GRANTING OTHER RELIEF

On the Emergency Application of Plaintiff Securities and Exchange Commission (the

"Application") for an Order and upon consent of Defendants Bernard L. Madoff ("Madoff") and

Bernard L. Madoff Investment Securities LLC ("BMIS") (collectively, "Defendants") to an

Order:[1]

---

[1]   Defendants consent to this Order in its entirety, except that they do not object and
otherwise take no position on the portion of Section XII below temporarily enjoining any third
party other than the Securities Investor Protection Corporation from filing a bankruptcy
proceeding against the Defendants without filing a motion on at least three (3) days' notice to the
Plaintiff, and approval of this Court after a hearing.

1.   directing Madoff and BMIS to show cause why an order should not be entered,

pending a final disposition of this action:

        a.   preliminarily enjoining Defendants from violating Sections 206(1) and

            206(2) of the Investment Advisers Act of 1940 ("Advisers Act"), 15

            U.S.C. § 80b-6(1) and (2); Section 17(a) of the Securities Act of 1933

            ("Securities Act"), 15 U.S.C. §§ 77q(a); Section 10(b) of the Securities

            Exchange Act of 1934 ("Exchange Act"), 15 U.S.C. §§ 78j(b), and

            Exchange Act Rule 10b-5, 17 C.F.R. § 240.10b-5.

        b.   directing Defendants to provide a verified accounting immediately,

            including, but not limited to, a verified written accounting of Madoff's

            interests in BMIS and all other entities owned, in whole or in part, or

            controlled by, related to, or associated or affiliated with, Madoff or BMIS;

        c.   freezing the assets of the Defendants;

        d.   appointing Lee Richards as receiver for BMIS' assets;

        c.   prohibiting the destruction, concealment, or alteration of documents by

            Defendants; and

        f.   preliminarily enjoining Defendants and their partners, owners, agents,

            employees, attorneys, or other professionals, anyone acting in concert with

            them, and any third party from filing a bankruptcy proceeding against the

            Defendants without filing a motion on at least three (3) days' notice to the

Plaintiff, and approval of this Court after a hearing; and

2.   pending adjudication of the foregoing, an Order

    a.   temporarily restraining Defendants from violating the aforementioned statutes and rules;

    b.   directing Defendant Madoff to provide a verified accounting immediately, including, but not limited to, a verified written accounting of Madoff's interests in BMIS and all other entities owned, in whole or in part, or controlled by, related to, or associated or affiliated with, Madoff or BMIS;

    c.   freezing the assets of the Defendants, including, without limitation, the accounts listed on the attached Exhibit A;

    d.   appointing Lee Richards, Esq., of Richards Kibbe & Orbe LLP as receiver for the Defendants' assets, including without limitation Madoff Securities International Ltd. ("Madoff International") and Madoff Ltd.;

    e.   prohibiting the destruction, concealment, or alteration of documents by Defendants;

    f.   temporarily restraining Defendants and their partners, owners, agents, employees, attorneys, or other professionals, anyone acting in concert with them, and any third party from filing a bankruptcy proceeding against the Defendants without filing a motion on at least three (3) days' notice to the Plaintiff, and approval of this Court after a hearing; and

    g.   providing that the Commission may take expedited discovery in

3

preparation for a hearing on this Order to Show Cause, and further

providing that the order expediting discovery will remain in place beyond

any hearing on the Commission's application for preliminary injunctions.

The Court has considered (1) the Complaint filed by the Commission on December 11,

2008: (2) the sworn statement of Theodore Cacioppi, executed December 11, 2008; (3) the

Declaration of Alex Vasilescu Pursuant to Local Rule 6.1, executed December 11, 2008; and (4)

the memorandum of law in support of the Application. Based upon the foregoing documents, the

Court finds that a proper showing, as required by Sections 20(b) of the Securities Act, Section

21(d) of the Exchange Act, and Section 209 of the Advisers Act has been made for the relief

granted herein, for the following reasons:

It appears from the evidence presented that Defendants have violated, and, unless

temporarily restrained, will continue to violate, Section 17(a) of the Securities Act, Section 10(b)

of the Exchange Act, Exchange Act Rule 10b-5, and Sections 206(1) and 206(2) of the Advisers

Act, as charged in the Complaint.

It appears from the evidence presented that certain ill-gotten gains derived from the

Defendants' fraudulent conduct have been deposited into the accounts of BMIS and/or Madoff's

personal accounts.

It appears from the evidence presented that BMIS is under the control of Madoff, its

founder.

4

It appears that Defendants may attempt to dissipate or transfer from the jurisdiction of this Court, funds, property and other assets that could be subject to an order of disgorgement or an order imposing civil penalties.

It appears that an order freezing Defendants' assets, as specified herein, is necessary to preserve the status quo, and to protect this Court's ability to award equitable relief in the form of disgorgement of illegal profits from fraud and civil penalties, and to preserve the Court's ability to approve a fair distribution for victims of the fraud.

It appears that an order requiring Defendants to provide a verified accounting of all assets, money and property held directly or indirectly by the Defendants, or by others for Defendants' direct and indirect beneficial interest is necessary to effectuate and ensure compliance with the freeze imposed on the Defendants' assets.

It appears that an order prohibiting Defendants and their partners, agents, employees, attorneys, or other professionals, anyone acting in concert with them or on their behalf, and any third party, from filing a bankruptcy proceeding against the Defendants without filing a motion on at least three (3) days' notice to the Plaintiff, and approval of this Court after a hearing, is necessary to preserve the status quo and to preserve the Court's ability to approve a fair distribution for victims of the fraud.

It appears that the appointment of a receiver for the assets of BMIS is necessary to (i) preserve the status quo, (ii) ascertain the extent of commingling of funds between Madoff and BMIS; (iii) ascertain the true financial condition of BMIS and the disposition of investor funds; (iv) prevent further dissipation of the property and assets of BMIS; (v) prevent the encumbrance

5

or disposal of property or assets of BMIS and the investors; (vi) preserve the books, records and documents of BMIS; (vii) respond to investor inquiries; (viii) protect the assets of BMIS from further dissipation; (ix) determine whether BMIS should undertake bankruptcy filings; and (x) determine the extent to which the freeze should be lifted as to certain assets in the custody of BMIS.

Good and sufficient reasons have been shown why procedure other than by notice of motion is necessary.

This Court has jurisdiction over the subject matter of this action and over Defendants, and venue properly lies in this District.

NOW, THEREFORE,

I.

IT IS HEREBY ORDERED that the Defendants show cause, if there be any, to this Court at 12:00 p.m. on Friday, December 19, 2008, in Courtroom 21C of the United States Courthouse, 500 Pearl Street, New York, New York 10007-1312, why this Court should not enter an Order pursuant to Rule 65 of the Federal Rules of Civil Procedure, Section 20 of the Securities Act, Section 21 of the Exchange Act, and Section 209 of the Advisers Act preliminarily enjoining Defendants from violating Section 17(a) of the Securities Act, Section 10(b) of the Exchange Act, Exchange Act Rule 10b-5, and Sections 206(1) and 206(2) of the Advisers Act.

II.

IT IS FURTHER ORDERED that Defendants show cause at that time why this Court

6

should not also enter an Order directing that, pending a final disposition of this action,

Defendants, and each of their financial and brokerage institutions, agents, servants, employees,

attorneys, and those persons in active concert or participation with either of them who receive

actual notice of such Order by personal service, facsimile service, telephonic notice, notice by e-

mail, or otherwise, and each of them, hold and retain within their control, and otherwise prevent,

any withdrawal, transfer, pledge, encumbrance, assignment, dissipation, concealment or other

disposal of any assets, funds, or other property (including money, real or personal property,

securities, commodities, choses in action or other property of any kind whatsoever) of, held by,

or under the direct or indirect control of, Defendants, whether held in the name of Madoff, BMIS,

Madoff International or Madoff Ltd. or for the direct or indirect beneficial interest of one or both

of them, wherever situated, in whatever form such assets may presently exist and wherever

located, and directing each of the financial or brokerage institutions, debtors and bailees, or any

other person or entity holding such assets, funds or other property of Defendants, to hold or retain

within its control and prohibit the withdrawal, removal, transfer or other disposal of any such

assets, funds or other properties, including, but not limited to: (1) all assets, funds, or other

properties held in the name of, held by, or under the control of one or both of the Defendants; (2)

all accounts in the name of Madoff or BMIS or on which Madoff is a signatory, including the

accounts listed on the attached Exhibit A; (3) all artwork, property, motor vehicles, jewelry and

other items of personalty held in the name of, held by, or under the control of Madoff or BMIS;

and (4) all real property held in the name of, held by, or under the control of Madoff or BMIS.

7

III.

IT IS FURTHER ORDERED that Defendants show cause at that time why this Court should not also enter an Order enjoining them, and any person or entity acting at their direction or on their behalf, from destroying, altering, concealing or otherwise interfering with, the access of the Plaintiff Commission to any and all documents, books and records, that are in the possession, custody or control of Defendants, and each of their partners, agents, employees, servants, accountants, financial or brokerage institutions, attorneys-in-fact, subsidiaries, affiliates, predecessors, successors and related entities that refer, reflect or relate to the allegations in the Complaint, including, without limitation, documents, books, and records referring, reflecting or relating to Defendants' finances or business operations, or the offer or sale of securities by Defendants and the use of proceeds therefrom.

IV.

IT IS FURTHER ORDERED that the Defendant show cause at that time why this Court should not also enter an Order continuing the appointment of Lee Richards, Esq., of Richards Kibbe & Orbe LLP as receiver for BMIS' assets, including, without limitation, the assets of Madoff International and Madoff Ltd.

V.

IT IS FURTHER ORDERED that Defendants show cause at that time why this Court should not also enter an Order preliminarily enjoining Defendants and their partners, agents, employees, attorneys, or other professionals, anyone acting in concert with them or on their behalf, and any third party, from filing a bankruptcy proceeding against the Defendants without

8

filing a motion on at least three (3) days' notice to the Plaintiff, and approval of this Court after a hearing.

VI.

IT IS FURTHER ORDERED that, pending a hearing and determination of the Application, Defendants, and each of their partners, agents, servants, employees, and attorneys, and those persons in active concert or participation with them who receive actual notice of this Order by personal service, facsimile service, telephonic notice, notice by e-mail or otherwise, are temporarily restrained from, directly or indirectly, singly or in concert, in the offer, purchase or sale of any security, by use of any means or instruments of transportation or communication in interstate commerce or by use of the mails:

a.   employing any device, scheme or artifice to defraud;

b.   obtaining money or property by means of an untrue statement of material fact or omitting to state a material fact necessary to make the statements made, in light of the circumstances under which they were made, not misleading; and

c.   engaging in any transaction, practice or course of business which operates or would operate as a fraud or deceit upon the purchaser,

in violation of Section 17(a) of the Securities Act, Section 10(b) of the Exchange Act, and Rule 10b-5 thereunder.

VII.

IT IS FURTHER ORDERED that, pending a hearing and determination of the Application, Defendants, and each of their partners, agents, servants, employees, and attorneys,

9

and those persons in active concert or participation with them who receive actual notice of this

Order by personal service. facsimile service, telephonic notice. notice by e-mail or otherwise, are

temporarily restrained from. directly or indirectly, singly or in concert, by use of any means or

instruments of transportation or communication in interstate commerce or by use of the mails:

    a.   employing any device, scheme or artifice to defraud any client or prospective

        client;

    b.   engaging in any transaction. practice or course of business which operates or

        would operate as a fraud or deceit upon any client or prospective client,

in violation of Sections 206(1) and 206(2) of the Advisers Act.

VIII.

IT IS FURTHER ORDERED that, pending a hearing and determination of the

Application, Defendants. and each of their financial and brokerage institutions, agents, servants,

employees. attorneys, and those persons in active concert or participation with either of them

who receive actual notice of such Order by personal service. facsimile service. telephonic notice,

notice by e-mail, or otherwise, and each of them, hold and retain within their control, and

otherwise prevent, any withdrawal. transfer, pledge, encumbrance, assignment, dissipation,

concealment or other disposal of any assets, funds, or other property (including money, real or

personal property. securities. commodities. choses in action or other property of any kind

whatsoever) of. held by, or under the direct or indirect control of Madoff or BMIS, whether held

in the name of Madoff, BMIS, Madoff International or Madoff Ltd. for the direct or indirect

beneficial interest of either of them, wherever situated, in whatever form such assets may

10

presently exist and wherever located, and direct each of the financial or brokerage institutions, debtors and bailees, or any other person or entity holding such assets, funds or other property of Defendants to hold or retain within its control and prohibit the withdrawal, removal, transfer or other disposal of, any such assets, funds or other properties, including, but not limited to: (1) all assets, funds, or other properties held in the name of, held by, or under the control of one or both of the Defendants; (2) all accounts in the name of Madoff or BMIS or on which Madoff is a signatory, including, without limitation, the accounts listed on Exhibit A; (3) all artwork, property, motor vehicles, jewelry and other items of personalty held in the name of, held by, or under the control of Madoff or BMIS; and (4) all real property held in the name of, held by, or under the control of Madoff or BMIS.

IX.

IT IS FURTHER ORDERED that, pending a hearing and determination of the Commission's Application for a Preliminary Injunction:

1.   Defendants shall each file with this Court and serve upon Plaintiff, two days prior to the hearing on the Commission's Application for a Preliminary Injunction, a verified written accounting, under penalty of perjury, of:

      a.   All assets, liabilities and property currently held, directly or indirectly, by or for the benefit of one or both Defendants, including, without limitation, bank accounts, brokerage accounts, investments, business interests, loans, lines of credit, and real and personal property wherever situated, describing each asset and liability, its current location and amount;

11

b.   All money, property, assets and income received by one or both
Defendants, or for the direct or indirect benefit of one or both Defendants,
at any time through the date of such accounting, describing the source,
amount, disposition and current location of each of the items listed;

c.   The names and last known addresses of all bailees, debtors, and other
persons and entities that currently are holding the assets, funds or property
of Madoff or BMIS; and

d.   All assets, funds, securities, and real or personal property received by
Madoff, BMIS, or any other person or entity controlled by Madoff, from
persons who provided money to him or at his direction in connection with
the offer or sale of any securities by him at any time to the date of the
accounting, and the disposition of such assets, funds, securities, real or
personal property; and

The Defendant shall serve such verified written accountings by hand delivery, facsimile
transmission, email or overnight courier service on the Commission's counsel, Alex Vasilescu,
Esq., Securities and Exchange Commission, 3 World Financial Center, Room 400, New York,
NY 10281, vasilescua@sec.gov.

X.

IT IS FURTHER ORDERED that, pending a hearing and determination of the
Commission's Application for a Preliminary Injunction, Defendants, and any person or entity
acting at their direction or on their behalf, be and hereby are (1) enjoined and restrained from

12

destroying, altering, concealing or otherwise interfering with the access of Plaintiff Commission to any and all documents, books, and records that are in the possession, custody or control of Defendants and each of their partners, agents, employees, servants, accountants, financial or brokerage institutions, or attorneys, subsidiaries, affiliates, predecessors, successors and related entities that refer, reflect or relate to the allegations in the Complaint, including, without limitation, documents, books and records referring, reflecting or relating to Defendants' finances or business operations.

XI.

IT IS FURTHER ORDERED that, pending a hearing and determination of the Commission's Application for a Preliminary Injunction, Lee Richards, Esq., of Richards Kibbe & Orbe LLP is appointed as receiver for the assets of BMIS, including, without limitation, the assets of Madoff Securities International Ltd. ("Madoff International") and Madoff Ltd. to (i) preserve the status quo, (ii) ascertain the extent of commingling of funds between Madoff and BMIS; (iii) ascertain the true financial condition of BMIS and the disposition of investor funds; (iv) prevent further dissipation of the property and assets of BMIS; (v) prevent the encumbrance or disposal of property or assets of BMIS and the investors; (vi) preserve the books, records and documents of BMIS; (vii) respond to investor inquiries; (viii) protect the assets of BMIS from further dissipation; (ix) determine whether BMIS should undertake bankruptcy filings; and (x) determine the extent to which the freeze should be lifted as to certain assets in the custody of BMIS.

To effectuate the foregoing, the receiver is empowered to:

13

(a)   Take and retain immediate possession and control of all of the assets and property,

and all books, records and documents of, BMIS, Madoff International, and

Madoff Ltd.;

(b)   Have exclusive control of, and be made the sole authorized signatory for, all

accounts at any bank, brokerage firm or financial institution that has possession or

control of any assets or funds of BMIS and Madoff International and Madoff Ltd.;

(c)   Conduct business, including making trades, and pay from available funds

necessary business expenses, as required to preserve or maximize the value of the

assets and property of BMIS, Madoff International and Madoff Ltd.,

notwithstanding the asset freeze imposed by paragraph VIII, above;

(d)   Locate assets that may have been conveyed to third parties or otherwise

concealed;

(e)   Engage and employ persons, including accountants, attorneys and experts, to

assist in the carrying out of the receiver's duties and responsibilities hereunder,

including appointing a person or entity to manage any aspect of the business of

BMIS, Madoff International or Madoff Ltd., including its investment adviser

business and its market-making business, and to use available funds as required to

preserve the assets and property of BMIS, notwithstanding the asset freeze

imposed by paragraph VIII, above;

(f)   Report to the Court and the parties within 45 days from the date of the entry of

this Order, subject to such reasonable extensions as the Court may grant, the

14

following information:

1. All assets, money, funds, securities, and real or personal property then held directly or indirectly by or for the benefit of BMIS, Madoff International or Madoff Ltd., including, but not limited to, real property, bank accounts. brokerage accounts, investments, business interests, personal property, wherever situated. identifying and describing each asset, its current location and value;

2. A list of secured creditors and other financial institutions with an interest in the receivership assets;

3. A list of customers and clients of BMIS, Madoff International, and Madoff Ltd., including investment advisory clients, and, to the extent practicable, the amounts received by Madoff from each such customer or client and the amounts withdrawn by each such customer or client;

(g) Develop a preliminary plan for the administration of the assets of the receivership, including a recommendation regarding whether bankruptcy cases should be filed for all or a portion of the assets subject to the receivership and a recommendation whether litigation against third parties should be commenced on a contingent fee basis to recover assets for the benefit of the receivership.

Defendants agree to provide any written authorizations necessary for the receiver to exercise the foregoing powers over Madoff International and Madoff Ltd.

15

XI.

IT IS FURTHER ORDERED that each of the receiver and his advisors be, and they

hereby are, indemnified by each of the Defendants, Madoff International and Madoff Ltd., except

for gross negligence, willful misconduct, fraud, and breach of fiduciary duty determined by final

order no longer subject to appeal or certiorari, for all judgments, losses, costs, and reasonable

expenses including legal fees (which shall be paid under the indemnity after court approval as

they arise), arising from or related to any and all claims of whatsoever type brought against any

of them in their capacities as receiver or advisors to the receiver; provided, however, that nothing

herein shall limit the immunity of the receiver and his advisors allowed by law or deprive the

receiver and his advisors of indemnity for any act or omission for which they have immunity.

XII.

IT IS FURTHER ORDERED that no creditor or claimant against the Defendants, or

any person acting on behalf of such creditor or claimant, shall take any action to interfere with

the control, possession, or management of the assets subject to the receivership.

XIII.

IT IS FURTHER ORDERED that, pending a hearing and determination of the

Commission's Application for a Preliminary Injunction, Defendants and their partners, agents,

employees, attorneys, or other professionals, anyone acting in concert with them or on their

behalf, and any third party, are temporarily enjoined from filing a bankruptcy proceeding against

the Defendants without filing a motion on at least three (3) days' notice to the Plaintiff, and

approval of this Court after a hearing, except that the Securities Investor Protection Corporation

16

may commence a proceeding under the Securities Investor Protection Act.

XIV.

IT IS FURTHER ORDERED that discovery is expedited as follows: pursuant to Rules 26. 30. 31. 33. 34. 36 and 45 of the Federal Rules of Civil Procedure, and without the requirement of a meeting pursuant to Fed. R. Civ. P. 26(f), the parties may:

1. Take depositions, subject to two (2) calendar days' notice by facsimile, email or otherwise;

2. Obtain the production of documents, within three (3) calendar days from service by facsimile. email or otherwise of a request or subpoena from any persons or entities. including non-party witnesses;

3. Obtain other discovery. including further interrogatories. requests for admissions. and requests to inspect the premises and files of Defendant within three (3) calendar days from the date of service by facsimile, email or otherwise of such other discovery requests, interrogatories. requests for admissions or requests for inspection; and

4. Service of any discovery requests, notices. or subpoenas may be made by personal service, facsimile, overnight courier, e-mail, or first-class mail on an individual, entity or the individual's or entity's attorney.

This order expediting discovery will remain in place beyond any hearing on the Commission's application for preliminary injunction.

17

XV.

IT IS FURTHER ORDERED that a copy of this Order and the papers supporting the Commission's Application be served upon the Defendants, or their respective counsel, on or before December 12, 2008 by personal delivery, facsimile, overnight courier, electronic mail, or first-class mail to their last known addresses.

XVI.

IT IS FURTHER ORDERED that the Defendant shall deliver any opposing papers in response to the Order to Show Cause above no later than December 16, 2008, at 11:59 p.m. Service shall be made by delivering the papers, using the most expeditious means available, by that date and time, to the New York Regional Office of the Commission at 3 World Financial Center, Room 400, New York, New York 10281, Attn: Alex Vasilescu, Esq., or such other place as counsel for the Commission may direct in writing. The Commission shall have until December 18, 2008, at 5:00 p.m., to serve, by the most expeditious means available, any reply papers upon the Defendant, or upon their respective counsel.

XVII.

IT IS FURTHER ORDERED that this Order shall be, and is, binding upon Defendants and their partners, agents, servants, employees, attorneys, subsidiaries, affiliates and those persons in active concert or participation with them who receive actual notice of this Order by personal service, facsimile service, telephone, e-mail or otherwise.

Consented to by Defendants Bernard L. Madoff and Bernard L. Madoff Investment Securities LLC and by Madoff Securities International Ltd. and Madoff Ltd.:

Dated: 12 - 12 , 2008
New York, New York

By _____

Ira Lee Sorkin, Esq.
Dickstein Shapiro LLP
1177 Avenue of the Americas
New York, NY 10036
(212) 277-6576

Attorney for Defendants Bernard L. Madoff
and Bernard L. Madoff Investment
Securities LLC and for Madoff Securities
International Ltd. and Madoff Ltd.

_____
Louis L. Stanton
UNITED STATES DISTRICT JUDGE

Issued at :   4 : 51 p.m.
December 12 2008
New York, NY

19

Exhibit A

JP Morgan Chase Account No. 000000140081703
Account in the Name of: Bernard L. Madoff Investment Securities

JP Morgan Chase Account No. 000000066709466
Account in the Name of: Bernard L. Madoff Investment Securities

The Bank of New York Mellon Account No. 890-0402-393
Account in the Name of: Benard J. Madoff Investment Securities

The Bank of New York Mellon Account No. 030-0951050
Account in the Name of: Bernard L Madoff

The Bank of New York Mellon Account No. 866-1126-621
Account in the Name of: Bernard L Madoff Investment Securities LLC

APPENDIX D

SEC DOCUMENT FILED DECEMBER 15, 2008

STANTON, F.

SECURITIES INVESTOR PROTECTION
   CORPORATION
JOSEPHINE WANG (JW0674)
General Counsel
KEVIN H. BELL (KB2260)
Senior Associate General Counsel
805 Fifteenth Street, N.W., Suite 800
Washington, DC 20005-2207
Telephone: (202) 371-8300

UNITED STATES DISTRICT COURT
SOUTHERN DISTRICT OF NEW YORK

SECURITIES AND EXCHANGE COMMISSION,   )
)
                 Plaintiff,   )
      v.   )   Civ. 08-10791
)
BERNARD L. MADOFF, and   )
BERNARD L. MADOFF INVESTMENT   )
SECURITIES LLC,   )
                 Defendants.   )
)
)
_____)
)
SECURITIES INVESTOR PROTECTION   )
   CORPORATION,   )
)
                 Applicant,   )
)
      v.   )
)
BERNARD L. MADOFF INVESTMENT   )
SECURITIES LLC,   )
                 Defendant.   )
_____)

ORDER

On the Complaint and Application of the Securities Investor Protection Corporation ("SIPC"), it is hereby:

     I.   ORDERED, ADJUDGED and DECREED that the customers of the Defendant,

Bernard L. Madoff Investment Securities LLC, are in need of the protection afforded by the Securities Investor Protection Act of 1970, as amended ("SIPA", 15 U.S.C. §78aaa *et seq.*).

II.   ORDERED that pursuant to 15 U.S.C. §78eee(b)(3), Irving H. Picard, Esquire is appointed trustee for the liquidation of the business of the Defendant with all the duties and powers of a trustee as prescribed in SIPA, and the law firm of Baker & Hostetler LLP is appointed counsel for the trustee. The trustee shall file a fidelity bond satisfactory to the Court in the amount of $250,000. ⁰⁰   LLS

III.   ORDERED that all persons and entities are notified that, subject to the other provisions of 11 U.S.C. §362, the automatic stay provisions of 11 U.S.C. §362(a) operate as a stay of:

A.   the commencement or continuation, including the issuance or employment of process, of a judicial, administrative or other proceeding against the Defendant that was or could have been commenced before the commencement of this proceeding, or to recover a claim against the Defendant that arose before the commencement of this proceeding;

B.   the enforcement against the Defendant or against property of the estate of a judgment obtained before the commencement of this proceeding;

C.   any act to obtain possession of property of the estate or property from the estate;

D.   any act to create, perfect or enforce any lien against property of the estate;

E.   any act to create, perfect or enforce against property of the Defendant any lien to the extent that such lien secures a claim that arose before the commencement of this proceeding;

F.   any act to collect, assess or recover a claim against the Defendant that arose before the commencement of this proceeding;

G.   the setoff of any debt owing to the Defendant that arose before the commencement

-2-

of this proceeding against any claim against the Defendant; and

H.   the commencement or continuation of a proceeding before the United States Tax Court concerning the Defendant's tax liability for a taxable period the Bankruptcy Court may determine.

IV.   ORDERED that all persons and entities are stayed, enjoined and restrained from directly or indirectly removing, transferring, setting off, receiving, retaining, changing, selling, pledging, assigning or otherwise disposing of, withdrawing or interfering with any assets or property owned, controlled or in the possession of the Defendant, including but not limited to the books and records of the Defendant, and customers' securities and credit balances, except for the purpose of effecting possession and control of said property by the trustee.

V.   ORDERED that pursuant to 15 U.S.C. §78eee(b)(2)(B)(i), any pending bankruptcy, mortgage foreclosure, equity receivership or other proceeding to reorganize, conserve or liquidate the Defendant or its property and any other suit against any receiver, conservator or trustee of the Defendant or its property, is stayed.

VI.   ORDERED that pursuant to 15 U.S.C. §§78eee(b)(2)(B)(ii) and (iii), and notwithstanding the provisions of 11 U.S.C. §§362(b) and 553, except as otherwise provided in this Order, all persons and entities are stayed, enjoined and restrained for a period of twenty-one (21) days, or such other time as may subsequently be ordered by this Court or any other court having competent jurisdiction of this proceeding, from enforcing liens or pledges against the property of the Defendant and from exercising any right of setoff, without first receiving the written consent of SIPC and the trustee.

VII.   ORDERED that, pursuant to 15 U.S.C. §78eee(b)(2)(C)(ii), and notwithstanding 15 U.S.C. §78eee(b)(2)(C)(i), all persons and entities are stayed for a period of twenty-one (21) days, or such other time as may subsequently be ordered by this Court or any other court having competent jurisdiction of this proceeding, from foreclosing on, or disposing of, securities collateral pledged by the Defendant, whether or not with respect to one or more of such contracts or agreements, securities sold by the Defendant under a repurchase agreement, or securities lent under a securities lending agreement, without first receiving the written consent of SIPC and the trustee.

VIII. ORDERED that the stays set forth above shall not apply to:

A.   any suit, action or proceeding brought or to be brought by the United States Securities and Exchange Commission ("Commission") or any self-regulatory organization of which the Defendant is now a member or was a member within the past six months; or

B.   the exercise of a contractual right of a creditor to liquidate, terminate, or accelerate a securities contract, commodity contract, forward contract, repurchase agreement, swap agreement, or master netting agreement, as those terms are defined in 11 U.S.C. §§101, 741, and 761, to offset or net termination values, payment amounts, or other transfer obligations arising under or in connection with one or more of such contracts or agreements, or to foreclose on any cash collateral pledged by the Defendant, whether or not with respect to one or more of such contracts or agreements; or

C.   the exercise of a contractual right of any securities clearing agency to cause the liquidation of a securities contract as defined in 11 U.S.C. §741(7); or

D.   the exercise of a contractual right of any stockbroker or financial institution, as defined in 11 U.S.C. §101, to use cash or letters of credit held by it as collateral, to cause the liquidation of its contract for the loan of a security to the Defendant or

-4-

for the pre-release of American Depository Receipts or the securities underlying such receipts; or

E. the exercise of a contractual right of any "repo" participant, as defined in 11 U.S.C. §101, to use cash to cause the liquidation of a repurchase agreement, pursuant to which the Defendant is a purchaser of securities, whether or not such repurchase agreement meets the definition set forth in 11 U.S.C. §101(47); or

F. the exercise of a contractual right, as such term is used in 11 U.S.C. §555, in respect of (i) any extension of credit for the clearance or settlement of securities transactions or (ii) any margin loan, as each such term is used in 11 U.S.C. §741(7), by a securities clearing bank. As used herein, "securities clearing bank" refers to any financial participant, as defined in 11 U.S.C. §101(22A), that extends credit for the clearance or settlement of securities transactions to one or more Primary Government Securities Dealers designated as such by the Federal Reserve Bank of New York from time to time; or

G. any setoff or liquidating transaction undertaken pursuant to the rules or bylaws of any securities clearing agency registered under section 17A(b) of the Securities Exchange Act of 1934, 15 U.S.C.§78q-1(b), or by any person acting under instructions from and on behalf of such a securities clearing agency; or

H. any settlement transaction undertaken by such securities clearing agency using securities either (i) in its custody or control, or (ii) in the custody or control of another securities agency with which it has a Commission approved interface procedure for securities transactions settlements, provided that the entire proceeds thereof, without benefit of any offset, are promptly turned over to the trustee; or

I. any transfer or delivery to a securities clearing agency by a bank or other depository, pursuant to instructions given by such clearing agency, of cash, securities, or other property of the Defendant held by such bank or depository subject to the instructions of such clearing agency and constituting a margin payment as defined in 11 U.S.C. §741(5).

IX. ORDERED that pursuant to 15 U.S.C. §78eee(b)(4), this liquidation proceeding is removed to the United States Bankruptcy Court for the Southern District of New York.

X. ORDERED that the trustee is authorized to take immediate possession of the property of the Defendant, wherever located, including but not limited to the books and records of the Defendant, and to open accounts and obtain a safe deposit box at a bank or banks to be chosen by the trustee, and the trustee may designate such of his representatives who shall be authorized to have access to such property.

Date: December *15*, 2008

    4:08 PM

           Louis L. Stanton

           UNITED STATES DISTRICT JUDGE

-6-

APPENDIX E

SEC DOCUMENT FILED DECEMBER 18, 2008

UNITED STATES DISTRICT COURT
SOUTHERN DISTRICT OF NEW YORK

---x

SECURITIES AND EXCHANGE COMMISSION,   :
                                       :
                        Plaintiff,   :
                                       :
            - against -   :
                                       :
BERNARD L. MADOFF and   :
BERNARD L. MADOFF INVESTMENT   :
SECURITIES LLC,   :
                                       :
                        Defendants.   :
                                       :
---x

08 Civ. 10791 (LLS)
ECF CASE

ORDER ON CONSENT IMPOSING PRELIMINARY INJUNCTION, FREEZING ASSETS AND GRANTING OTHER RELIEF AGAINST DEFENDANTS

The Securities and Exchange Commission ("SEC") having filed a Complaint in this

matter on December 11, 2008; the SEC that same day having filed an Application for Emergency

Preliminary Relief Against Defendants Bernard L. Madoff ("Madoff") and Bernard L. Madoff

Investment Securities LLC ("BMIS") (collectively, "Defendants"); Defendants that same day

having entered a general appearance and consented to the Court's jurisdiction over the

Defendants and the subject matter of this action; Defendants on December 12, 2008 having

consented to the entry of a temporary restraining order, asset freeze, appointment of a receiver

and other relief against Defendants; the Court that same day having entered such an Order; the

Court on December 15, 2008 having issued an Order appointing Irving H. Picard, Esq. ("SIPC

Trustee"), as trustee for the liquidation of the business of Defendants with all the duties and

powers of a trustee described in the Securities Investor Protection Corporation ("SIPC"), and

appointing the law firm of Baker & Hostetler LLP as appointed counsel for the trustee; and

Defendants having consented to the entry of this Order On Consent Imposing Preliminary

Injunction, Freezing Assets And Granting Other Relief Against Defendants, waived findings of fact and conclusions of law, and waived any right to appeal from this P.I. Order:

I.

IT IS HEREBY ORDERED, pending a final disposition of this action, that Defendants, and each of their partners, agents, servants, employees, and attorneys, and those persons in active concert or participation with them who receive actual notice of this Order by personal service, facsimile service, telephonic notice, notice by e-mail or otherwise, are preliminarily enjoined from, directly or indirectly, singly or in concert, in the offer, purchase or sale of any security, by use of any means or instruments of transportation or communication in interstate commerce or by use of the mails:

    a.   employing any device, scheme or artifice to defraud;

    b.   obtaining money or property by means of an untrue statement of material fact or omitting to state a material fact necessary to make the statements made, in light of the circumstances under which they were made, not misleading; and

    c.   engaging in any transaction, practice or course of business which operates or would operate as a fraud or deceit upon the purchaser,

in violation of Section 17(a) of the Securities Act, Section 10(b) of the Exchange Act, and Rule 10b-5 thereunder.

II.

IT IS FURTHER ORDERED, pending a final disposition of this action, that Defendants, and each of their partners, agents, servants, employees, and attorneys, and those persons in active concert or participation with them who receive actual notice of this Order by

2

personal service, facsimile service, telephonic notice, notice by e-mail or otherwise, are

preliminarily enjoined from, directly or indirectly, singly or in concert, by use of any means or

instruments of transportation or communication in interstate commerce or by use of the mails:

    a.   employing any device, scheme or artifice to defraud any client or prospective

              client;

    b.   engaging in any transaction, practice or course of business which operates or

              would operate as a fraud or deceit upon any client or prospective client,

in violation of Sections 206(1) and 206(2) of the Advisers Act.

III.

IT IS FURTHER ORDERED, pending a final disposition of this action, that

Defendants, and each of their financial and brokerage institutions, agents, servants, employees,

attorneys, and those persons in active concert or participation with either of them who receive

actual notice of this Order by personal service, facsimile service, telephonic notice, notice by e-

mail, or otherwise, and each of them, hold and retain within their control, and otherwise prevent,

any withdrawal, transfer, pledge, encumbrance, assignment, dissipation, concealment or other

disposal of any assets, funds, or other property (including money, real or personal property,

securities, commodities, choses in action or other property of any kind whatsoever) of, held by,

or under the direct or indirect control of, Defendants, whether held in the name of Madoff,

BMIS, Madoff International or Madoff Ltd. or for the direct or indirect beneficial interest of one

or both of them, wherever situated, in whatever form such assets may presently exist and

wherever located, and directing each of the financial or brokerage institutions, debtors and

bailees, or any other person or entity holding such assets, funds or other property of Defendants,

3

to hold or retain within its control and prohibit the withdrawal, removal, transfer or other

disposal of any such assets, funds or other properties, including, but not limited to: (1) all assets,

funds, or other properties held in the name of, held by, or under the control of one or both of the

Defendants; (2) all accounts in the name of Madoff or BMIS or on which Madoff is a signatory,

including the accounts listed on the attached Exhibit A; (3) all artwork, property, motor vehicles,

jewelry and other items of personalty held in the name of, held by, or under the control of

Madoff or BMIS; and (4) all real property held in the name of, held by, or under the control of

Madoff or BMIS.

IV.

IT IS FURTHER ORDERED, pending a final disposition of this action, that

Defendants, and any person or entity acting at their direction or on their behalf, are preliminarily

enjoined from destroying, altering, concealing or otherwise interfering with, the access of the

Plaintiff Commission and/or SPIC Trustee to any and all documents, books and records, that are

in the possession, custody or control of Defendants, and each of their partners, agents,

employees, servants, accountants, financial or brokerage institutions, attorneys-in-fact,

subsidiaries, affiliates, predecessors, successors and related entities that refer, reflect or relate to

the allegations in the Complaint, including, without limitation, documents, books, and records

referring, reflecting or relating to Defendants' finances or business operations, or the offer or

sale of securities by Defendants and the use of proceeds therefrom.

V.

IT IS FURTHER ORDERED that Defendants and their partners, agents, employees,

attorneys, or other professionals, anyone acting in concert with them or on their behalf, and any

4

third party, are preliminarily enjoined from filing a bankruptcy proceeding against Defendants without filing a motion on at least three (3) days' notice to the Plaintiff, and approval of this Court after a hearing.

VI.

IT IS FURTHER ORDERED that:

1.   Defendant Madoff shall serve upon Plaintiff, on or before December 31, 2008, a verified written accounting, under penalty of perjury, of:

       a.   All assets, liabilities and property currently held, directly or indirectly, by or for the benefit of Defendant Madoff, including, without limitation, bank accounts, brokerage accounts, investments, business interests, loans, lines of credit, and real and personal property wherever situated, describing each asset and liability, its current location and amount;

       b.   All money, property, assets and income received by Defendant Madoff, or for the direct or indirect benefit of Defendant Madoff, at any time through the date of such accounting, describing the source, amount, disposition and current location of each of the items listed;

       c.   The names and last known addresses of all bailees, debtors, and other persons and entities that currently are holding the assets, funds or property of Defendant Madoff; and

       d.   The names and locations of all entities where Defendant BMIS, or entities controlled by, or related to, BMIS, held, without limitation, bank accounts, brokerage accounts, investments, or assets.

5

Defendant Madoff shall serve such verified written accountings by hand delivery, facsimile

transmission, email or overnight courier service on the Commission's counsel, Alex Vasilescu,

Esq., Securities and Exchange Commission, 3 World Financial Center, Room 400, New York,

NY 10281, vasilescua@sec.gov.

VII.

IT IS FURTHER ORDERED that Lee Richards, Esq., of Richards Kibbe & Orbe LLP,

continues as the appointed receiver for the assets of Madoff Securities International Ltd.

("Madoff International"), Madoff Ltd., and any other broker-dealer, market making, or

investment advisory businesses (the "Foreign Entities") not located in the United States of

America that are owned or controlled, in whole or in part, by Madoff, BMIS and their partners,

agents, employees, attorneys, or other professionals, anyone acting in concert with them or on

their behalf, and any third party, to (i) preserve the status quo, (ii) ascertain the extent of

commingling of funds between Madoff, BMIS and the Foreign Entities; (iii) ascertain the true

financial condition of the Foreign Entities and the disposition of investor funds; (iv) prevent

further dissipation of the property and assets of the Foreign Entities; (v) prevent the

encumbrance or disposal of property or assets of the Foreign Entities and the investors; (vi)

preserve the books, records and documents of the Foreign Entities; (vii) respond to investor

inquiries regarding the foreign entities; (viii) protect the assets of the Foreign Entities from

further dissipation; (ix) determine whether the Foreign Entities should undertake bankruptcy

filings; and (x) determine the extent to which the freeze should be lifted as to certain assets in the

custody of the Foreign Entities.

To effectuate the foregoing, the receiver is empowered to:

6

(a)   Take and retain immediate possession and control of all of the assets and
property, and all books, records and documents of, the Foreign Entities;

(b)   Have exclusive control of, and be made the sole authorized signatory for, all
accounts at any bank, brokerage firm or financial institution that has possession or
control of any assets or funds of the Foreign Entities;

(c)   Conduct business, including making trades, and pay from available funds
necessary business expenses, as required to preserve or maximize the value of the
assets and property of the Foreign Entities, notwithstanding the asset freeze
imposed by paragraph III, above;

(d)   Locate assets that may have been conveyed to third parties or otherwise concealed
by the Foreign Entities;

(e)   Engage and employ persons, including accountants, attorneys and experts, to
assist in the carrying out of the receiver's duties and responsibilities hereunder,
including appointing a person or entity to manage any aspect of the business of
the Foreign Entities, including any investment adviser business and market-
making businesses of the Foreign Entities, and to use available funds as required
to preserve the assets and property of the Foreign Entities, notwithstanding the
asset freeze imposed by paragraph III, above;

(f)   Report to the Court and the parties by January 26, 2009, subject to such
reasonable extensions as the Court may grant, the following information:

1.   All assets, money, funds, securities, and real or personal property then
held directly or indirectly by or for the benefit of the Foreign Entities,

7

including, but not limited to, real property, bank accounts, brokerage

accounts, investments, business interests, personal property, wherever

situated, identifying and describing each asset, its current location and

value;

2.   A list of secured creditors and other financial institutions with an interest

in the receivership assets of the Foreign Entities;

3.   A list of customers and clients of the Foreign Entities, including

investment advisory clients, and, to the extent practicable, the amounts

received by Madoff from each such customer or client and the amounts

withdrawn by each such customer or client;

(g)   Develop a preliminary plan for the administration of the assets of the receivership

of the Foreign Entities, including a recommendation regarding whether

bankruptcy cases should be filed for all or a portion of the assets subject to the

receivership and a recommendation whether litigation against third parties should

be commenced on a contingent fee basis to recover assets of the Foreign Entities

for the benefit of the receivership.

Defendants agree to provide any written authorizations necessary for the receiver to

exercise the foregoing powers over the Foreign Entities.

As this Court has entered an Order (referenced above) appointing the SIPC Trustee, and

as the SIPC Trustee has roles and responsibilities with respect to BMIS, the receiver will have no

authority over BMIS, except to the extent that such authority is necessary to carry out his

responsibilities with respect to the Foreign Entities and that such authority is exercised with the

8

prior consent and approval of the SIPC Trustee.

VIII.

IT IS FURTHER ORDERED that each of the Receiver and his advisors be, and they hereby are, indemnified by each of the Defendants, Madoff International and Madoff Ltd., except for gross negligence, willful misconduct, fraud, and breach of fiduciary duty determined by final order no longer subject to appeal or certiorari, for all judgments, losses, costs, and reasonable expenses including legal fees (which shall be paid under the indemnity after court approval as they arise), arising from or related to any and all claims of whatsoever type brought against any of them in their capacities as receiver or advisors to the receiver; provided, however, that nothing herein shall limit the immunity of the receiver and his advisors allowed by law or deprive the receiver and his advisors of indemnity for any act or omission for which they have immunity.

IX.

IT IS FURTHER ORDERED that no creditor or claimant against the Defendants, or any person acting on behalf of such creditor or claimant, shall take any action to interfere with the control, possession, or management of the assets subject to the receivership.

X.

IT IS FURTHER ORDERED that, pending final disposition of this action or such

further order of the Court, Plaintiff may conduct expedited discovery, pursuant to Rules 26, 30,

31, 33, 34, 36 and 45 of the Federal Rules of Civil Procedure and without the requirement of a

meeting pursuant to Fed. R. Civ. P. 26(f).

XI.

IT IS FURTHER ORDERED that this Order shall be, and is, binding upon Defendants

and their partners, agents, servants, employees, attorneys, subsidiaries, affiliates and those

persons in active concert or participation with them who receive actual notice of this Order by

personal service, facsimile service, telephone, e-mail or otherwise.

XII.

IT IS FURTHER ORDERED that the Consent of Defendants to Preliminary Injunction

Order filed herewith is incorporated herein with the same force and effect as if fully set forth

herein, and that Defendants shall comply with all of the undertakings and agreements set forth

therein.

Louis L. Stanton

UNITED STATES DISTRICT JUDGE

Issued at :   **6** : **35** **p**.m.
December **18**, 2008
New York, NY

10

Exhibit A

JP Morgan Chase Account No. 000000140081703
Account in the Name of: Bernard L. Madoff Investment Securities

JP Morgan Chase Account No. 000000066709466
Account in the Name of: Bernard L. Madoff Investment Securities

The Bank of New York Mellon Account No. 890-0402-393
Account in the Name of: Benard L Madoff Investment Securities

The Bank of New York Mellon Account No. 030-0951050
Account in the Name of: Bernard L Madoff

The Bank of New York Mellon Account No. 866-1126-621
Account in the Name of: Bernard L Madoff Investment Securities LLC

APPENDIX F

LAWSUIT FILED BY IRWIN KELLNER, DECEMBER 12, 2008

UNITED STATES DISTRICT COURT
EASTERN DISTRICT OF NEW YORK

– x

IRWIN KELLNER, on behalf of himself and on behalf
of all others similarly situated,

                Plaintiff,

    -against-

BERNARD L. MADOFF, BERNARD L. MADOFF
INVESTMENT SECURITIES LLC, and JOHN DOES
1-100 Consisting of Individuals, Corporations,
Partnerships and Entities To Be Determined,

                Defendants.

– X

**CLASS ACTION
COMPLAINT**

Civil Action No. 08-5026 (ADS)(ART)

JURY TRIAL DEMANDED

Plaintiff Irwin Kellner on behalf of himself and on behalf of all others similarly

situated, as and for his complaint against defendants Bernard L. Madoff ("Madoff"),

Bernard L. Madoff Investment Securities LLC ("BMIS") and John Does 1-100 consisting

of individuals, corporation, partnerships and entities to be determined (collectively, along

with Madoff and BMIS, "Defendants"), alleges upon personal knowledge as to himself

and his own acts, and upon information and belief as to all other matters, as follows:

PRELIMINARY STATEMENT

1.   This case arises from one of the most damaging Ponzi schemes in the

history of Wall Street and the United States, a massive fraud through which individual

defendant Madoff and his accomplices swindled investors out of monies estimated to

exceed $50 billion. Plaintiff's claims include fraud based on misrepresentations in

connection with the sale of securities in violation of the Securities and Exchange Act of

1934, violation of the Racketeer Influenced and Corrupt Organizations Act, and related state and common law charges.

2.   According to news reports, shortly before his stunning arrest, defendant Madoff admitted that BMIS is insolvent and has been for years, and has publicly admitted that losses from this fraud are at least $50 billion.

3.   Upon information and belief, at all relevant times defendant Madoff's fraudulent conduct was concealed from plaintiffs – who believed that they were actually purchasing legitimate securities from an enterprise engaged in lawful business activities. On the basis of the giant Ponzi scheme that lies at the heart of this case, plaintiffs allege violations of the securities laws and related federal laws, as well as claims of fraud, fraudulent misrepresentation, negligent misrepresentation, breach of contract, conversion, unjust enrichment, fraudulent conveyance and breach of fiduciary duty.

JURISDICTION AND VENUE

4.   Jurisdiction of this Court is pursuant to § 27 of the Securities Exchange Act of 1934 (the "Exchange Act"), 15 U.S.C. § 788 *et seq.*; the Racketeer Influenced and Corrupt Organizations Act ("RICO"), 18 U.S.C. § 1961 *et. seq.*; and § 1331 of Title 28 of the U.S. Code. The Court has jurisdiction over the common law claims alleged herein pursuant to principles of supplemental jurisdiction, 28 U.S.C. § 1367(a).

5.   Venue is proper pursuant to 28 U.S.C. § 1391(b) because upon information and belief, individual defendant Bernard L. Madoff resides in the Town of East Hampton, New York. Further, a substantial part of the events giving rise to this claim, including

2

solicitation of many individuals who became victims of Defendants' Ponzi scheme, occurred in the Eastern District of New York.

PARTIES

6.   Plaintiff Irwin Kellner is an individual residing at 40 Angler Lane, Port Washington, New York.

7.   Defendant Bernard L. Madoff ("Madoff") is a resident of Suffolk County, New York, with a residence located in the Town of East Hampton, New York.

8.   Madoff is the owner of defendant Bernard L. Madoff Investment Securities LLC ("BMIS"), a New York Limited Liability Company that maintains its principal place of business within the district at 885 Third Avenue, New York, New York.

9.   John Does "1" through "100" consist of individuals, corporations, partnerships and entities to be determined, each of whom is believed to have violated Plaintiffs' rights; and to have aided, abetted and conspired to violate Plaintiffs' rights; or is the successor in interest to one or more of Defendants, the identities of which will be determined through discovery in this matter.

FACTS

10.   Upon information and belief, Madoff is an attorney who founded BMIS in the early 1960s.

11.   Upon information and belief, Madoff is a former Chairman of the board of directors of the NASDAQ stock market.

12.   Upon information and belief, BMIS is both a broker-dealer and investment advisor registered with the Securities and Exchange Commission ("SEC").   BMIS engaged in three different operations, namely investment advisor services, market making services and proprietary trading.

13.   Upon information and belief, Madoff oversees and controls the investment advisor services at BMIS as well as the overall finances of BMIS.

14.   Upon information and belief, the most recent filings by BMIS with the SEC in January 2008 listed BMIS as having over $17 billion in assets under management.

15.   BMIS' website states that it has been "providing quality executions for broker-dealers, banks and financial institutions since its inception in 1960"; and that BMIS, "[w]ith more than $700 million in firm capital[,] currently ranks among the top 1% of US Securities firms."

16.   Upon information and belief, Madoff conducts certain investment advisory business for clients that is separate from the BMIS' proprietary trading and market making activities.

17.   In truth and in fact, unbeknownst to plaintiffs, upon information and belief at all relevant times, Madoff and BMIS have been conducting a Ponzi-scheme through the investment advisor services of BMIS, and through their scheme have defrauded investors out of monies estimated to exceed $50 billion.

18.   Upon information and belief, Madoff ran his investment advisor business from a separate floor in the offices of BMIS, Madoff kept the financial statement for the

firm under lock and key, and was "cryptic" about the firm's investment advisory business when discussing the business with other employees of BMIS.

19.   Upon information and belief, in or about the first week of December, Madoff told a senior employee that there had been requests from clients for approximately $7 billion in redemptions, and that Madoff was struggling to obtain the liquidity necessary to meet those obligations.

20.   Upon information and belief, on or about December 9, 2008, Madoff informed another senior employee that he wanted to pay bonuses to employees of the firm in December, which was earlier than employee bonuses are usually paid.

21.   Upon information and belief, also during December 2008 in a meeting with one of his senior employees, Madoff stated that his investment advisory business was a fraud, that "it's all just one big lie," and that it was "basically, a giant Ponzi scheme."

22.   Upon information and belief, Madoff further communicated to his senior employees that he had for years been paying returns to certain investors out of the principal received from other, different, investors. Upon information and belief, Madoff further stated that the business was insolvent, and that it had been for years, and he estimated the losses from this fraud to be at least approximately $50 billion.

23.   Upon information and belief, on or about December 9, 2008, Madoff also informed his senior employees that he planned to surrender to the authorities, but before he did that, he had approximately $200-300 million left, and he planned to use that money to make payments to certain selected employees, family and friends.

24.   The plaintiff class, as defined and alleged further hereinbelow, is believed to have lost $50 billion dollars, all as a result of Defendants' knowing deception, through which members of the plaintiff class were deceived into investing in a fraudulent Ponzi scheme.

CLASS REPRESENTATIVE CLAIMS

25.   Plaintiff Kellner individually entrusted monies to BMIS for investment on his behalf based upon materially false and misleading information disseminated by Defendants, to the effect that BMIS was a legitimate enterprise engaged in the lawful brokerage and sale of investment securities, when in truth BMIS was a fraudulent Ponzi scheme predicated upon the satisfaction of interest and dividend commitments through the distribution of investor principal.

26.   Plaintiff Kellner first entrusted monies to BMIS in or about December 1998, in the amount of $1,248,838, ostensibly for establishment of an Individual Retirement Account ("IRA"), to be supervised and controlled by BMIS.

27.   At the time plaintiff Kellner first invested funds with BMIS, defendant Madoff acting through BMIS falsely misrepresented that BMIS was a legitimate enterprise operating as a lawful broker and dealer, when in truth and in fact BMIS was a fraudulent Ponzi scheme, which could remain solvent only by paying out interest and dividend commitments through the distribution of investor principal.

28.   Upon information and belief, when defendant Madoff acting through BMIS misrepresented the nature of BMIS, defendant Madoff did so deliberately and with the

6

intention of inducing plaintiff Kellner to invest monies with BMIS, and so as to conceal Defendants' Ponzi scheme.

29.   Plaintiff Kellner naturally, reasonably, and justifiably relied upon Defendants' misrepresentations concerning the nature of BMIS, in determining to invest plaintiff Kellner's monies with BMIS.

30.   Plaintiff Kellner later entrusted additional monies to BMIS in the additional amount of $1,000,000 in or about April 2000, for establishment of an ordinary investment account, to be supervised and controlled by BMIS.

31.   In determining to invest additional monies in BMIS in April 2000, plaintiff Kellner again acted based upon false and materially misleading statements, by defendants Madoffs and BMIS, to the effect that BMIS was a legitimate enterprise engaged in lawful broker dealer operations.

32.   And just as in December 1998, in determining to invest further monies in April 2000, plaintiff Kellner naturally, reasonably, and justifiably relied upon Defendants' misrepresentations concerning the nature of BMIS, in determining to make such investment.

33.   At all relevant times, in or about each month between January 1989 and December 2008, plaintiff Kellner received account statements from BMIS, delivered to plaintiff Kellner's home in Port Washington, New York (the "Monthly Account Statements").

34.   The Monthly Account Statements were delivered to plaintiff Kellner via the United States Mail.

35.   The Monthly Account Statements contained materially false statements, and were an integral part of Defendants' overall scheme to defraud, insofar as the Monthly Account Statements implicitly and explicitly created the false and misleading impression that BMIS was a legitimate enterprise engaged in lawful broker dealer operations, and thus acted to conceal the fact that BMIS in truth and in fact was actually a fraudlent Ponzi scheme, which could remain solvent only by paying out interest and dividend commitments through the distribution of investor principal.

36.   As a consequence of Defendants' fraud as alleged here, plaintiff Kellner has been damaged in an amount to be proven at trial and estimated to exceed $3 million.

CLASS ACTION ALLEGATIONS

37.   Plaintiffs bring this action pursuant to Rules 23(a) and 23(b)(3) of the Federal Rules of Civil Procedure on behalf of the following:

a.   All persons and entities who purchased securities sold by or through defendants Madoff or BMIS, or other selling agents affiliated with Madoff or BMIS, from as early as the formation of BMIS in the 1960's until December 12, 2008 inclusive (the "Class Period"), excluding Defendants, all officers and directors of Defendants during the Class Period, the immediate family of the Individual Defendants and any BMIS subsidiary (the "Class").

8

APPENDIX G

DECISION TO DENY GOVERNMENT'S MOTION TO REVOKE MADOFF'S BAIL, JANUARY 12, 2009

UNITED STATES DISTRICT COURT
SOUTHERN DISTRICT OF NEW YORK

UNITED STATES OF AMERICA,	:
	:
	: **OPINION AND ORDER**
- against -	:
	: **08 Mag. 2735**
BERNARD L. MADOFF,	:
	:
Defendant.	:

RONALD L. ELLIS, United States Magistrate Judge:

I. INTRODUCTION

Before the Court is a motion by the Government to detain Defendant Bernard L. Madoff

pending trial on the grounds that: 1) the facts in this case present a clear risk of flight and

obstruction of justice and 2) neither the current conditions of release, nor any other conditions

that could be imposed, are sufficient to protect the safety of the community. The Government

argues that Madoff's recent transfers of valuable items to third parties constitutes a change in

circumstances that render his current bail conditions, and any other bail conditions that might

subsequently be imposed, insufficient to insure against risk of flight and danger to the

community. Because the Government has failed to meet its legal burden, the motion is **DENIED**.

The Court finds, however, that the following additional conditions shall be imposed to address

the identified concerns:

> (1) The restrictions set forth in the preliminary injunction entered on December 18, 2008, in the civil case brought by the SEC before District Judge Louis L. Stanton, including restrictions on transfer of all property whatsoever, wherever located, in the possession or under the control of Madoff, **SHALL** be incorporated into the current bail conditions;
>
> (2) The restrictions set forth in the voluntary restraint agreement signed by Mrs. Madoff on December 26, 2008, **SHALL** be incorporated into the current bail conditions; and

(3) Madoff **SHALL** compile an inventory of all valuable portable items in his Manhattan home. In addition to providing this inventory to the Government, Casale Associates, or another security company approved by the Government, **SHALL** check the inventory once every two weeks. Casale Associates, or another security company approved by the Government, **SHALL** search all outgoing physical mail to ensure that no property has been transferred. The Government and Madoff shall agree on a threshold value for inventory items within one week of this Order.

II. BACKGROUND

On December 11, 2008, the Government initiated the instant criminal case via a

Complaint charging Madoff with one count of securities fraud in violation of 15 U.S.C. §§

78j(b), 78ff; 17 C.F.R. § 240.10b-5. Upon his arrest, Madoff was interviewed by Pretrial

Services, which did not recommend pretrial detention. (Defendant's Memorandum in Opposition

("Def. Opp."), Jan. 8, 2009, at 1-2.) At presentment, the Government did not seek detention, and

the Parties jointly proposed a set of bail conditions, so ordered by the Honorable Douglas F.

Eaton on December 11, 2008.[1] (*Id.*) After a series of amendments,[2] which added conditions to

bail or adjusted dates by which certain conditions were to be met, the bail conditions currently in

effect were entered on December 19, 2008.[3] They are:

(1) a $10 million personal recognizance bond secured by Madoff's Manhattan apartment,

---

[1]The original conditions presented by the Parties were: (1) a $10 million personal recognizance bond to be secured by Madoff's Manhattan apartment (valued at approximately $7 million), and to be co-signed by four financially responsible persons, including Madoff's wife; (2) surrender of Madoff's passport; (3) travel restricted to the Southern and Eastern Districts of New York and the District of Connecticut; and (4) release upon Madoff's signature and that of his wife, with the remaining conditions to be fulfilled by December 16 at 2:00 p.m. (Government's Memorandum ("Gov. Mem."), Jan. 6, 2009, at 1-2.).

[2]On December 17, 2008, the Government presented the Parties' joint proposal of certain additions and modifications. This joint proposal was so ordered by the Honorable Gabriel W. Gorenstein. (*See* Marc O. Litt's Letter to the Court, Dec. 17, 2008 (Docket No. 7).)

[3]By letter dated December 19, 2008, the Government submitted the jointly proposed bail conditions modifications. (Marc O. Litt's Letter to the Court, Dec. 19, 2008 (Docket No. 10).) The Government provided a comprehensive list of the bail terms, including proposed additional conditions, and The Honorable Theodore H. Katz so ordered this joint proposal. (*Id.*)

and Madoff's wife's properties in Montauk, New York, and Palm Beach, Florida, and co-signed by two financially responsible persons, Madoff's wife and brother;

(2) the filing of confessions of judgment with respect to Madoff's Manhattan apartment and his wife's properties in Montauk, New York, and Palm Beach, Florida;

(3) other than for scheduled court appearances, Madoff is subject to home detention at his Manhattan apartment, 24 hours per day, with electronic monitoring;

(4) Madoff employs, at his wife's expense, a security firm acceptable to the Government, to provide the following services to prevent harm or flight:

> (a) the security firm provides round-the-clock monitoring at Madoff's building, 24 hours per day, including video monitoring of Madoff's apartment doors, and communications devices and services permitting it to send a direct signal from an observation post to the Federal Bureau of Investigation in the event of the appearance of harm or flight;
> (b) the security firm will provide additional guards available on request if necessary to prevent harm or flight;

(5) Madoff and his wife have surrendered their passports.

(*See* Docket No. 10.)

In a related civil proceeding before The Honorable Louis L. Stanton brought by the Securities and Exchange Commission ("SEC") against Madoff and Bernard L. Madoff Investment Securities LLC, the Parties entered into a preliminary injunction on December 18, 2008, pursuant to which Madoff was explicitly enjoined from transferring any assets belonging to him or his company. (Order on Consent Imposing Preliminary Injunction, Freezing Assets and Granting Other Relief Against Defendants, Dec. 18, 2008, *SEC v. Madoff, et al.*, No. 08 Civ. 10791 (LLS) (Docket No. 8).) This injunction requires Madoff to "prevent any withdrawal, transfer, pledge, encumbrance, assignment, dissipation, concealment or other disposal of any assets, funds, or other property (including money, real or personal property, securities, commodities, choses in action or other property of any kind whatsoever) of, held by or under the

3

direct or indirect control of, Defendant . . . ." (*Id.* at 3.) This preliminary injunction was not a condition of bail, nor was it incorporated into Madoff's conditions of release on bail.

Subsequently, on or around December 24, 2008, Madoff and his wife mailed packages to family and to friends. The contents of these packages have been characterized by Madoff as "gifts" and items of "sentimental value."[4] (Def. Opp. at 3-4.) Upon learning of these transfers, the Government sought a hearing to request that Madoff be detained pending trial. According to the Government, the transfers at issue contained personal property that was clearly under Madoff's control, and the value of the items may exceed $1 million.[5] The Government argues that a handwritten note contained in one package and authored by Madoff presents further proof that these items were in Madoff's possession and control. (Transcript of January 5, 2009, Hearing ("Tr.") at 4-5.) The Government concludes that these actions, which it describes as the dissipation of personal assets, violated the preliminary injunction in place in the civil case against Madoff, and constitute an obstruction of justice cognizable under 18 U.S.C. § 3142. (*Id.* at 30 ("Here the obstruction that we see is the inability to get restitution and forfeiture proceedings to victims . . . .").) Building on this argument, the Government asserts that this type of economic harm represents a danger to the community as contemplated by § 3142 of the Bail Reform Act.

The Government further maintains that Madoff's violation of the preliminary injunction has heightened significance because it occurred within one week of the issuance of the injunction

---

[4]The Government is rightly skeptical of this claim. It is highly suspect that a man as sophisticated as Madoff appears to be did not pause to consider the possible ramifications of this proposed course of action on his release conditions. Given Madoff's failing in this regard, it is appropriate that his ability to transfer property be restricted as completely as possible.

[5]Madoff does not take issue with this valuation. Indeed, the force of the Government's argument would not be materially diminished if the value were less than suggested unless the value clearly was negligible.

4

and clearly indicates his lack of respect for the limits put in place by the Court. (Tr. at 4-5.) The

Government concludes that the continued pretrial release of Madoff poses a clear risk of flight

and obstruction of justice, as well as a danger to the safety of the community, which includes

victims of Madoff's alleged fraud.

Madoff argues that he has not violated the conditions of his bail. He admits that personal

items, several of which belonged to his wife, who is not a party to either the criminal or civil case

against him, were mailed to some family members and one couple – friends of Madoff and his

wife. Madoff asserts that these items were holiday gifts and heirloom pieces of sentimental value,

and were sent without an intent to violate any court order. Madoff's counsel acknowledges that it

was a mistake, and that as soon as the impropriety of the action became known to Madoff, he

began working to get the items back. (*Id.* at 12-14.) Moreover, Mrs. Madoff has now voluntarily

agreed to a freeze on her assets, including her jewelry. (*Id.* at 11.)

Following a hearing on the Government's application, the Parties submitted briefs

elaborating on their respective positions. While apparently conceding that there has been no

violation of the specific conditions of bail in the instant case,[6] the Government reiterates that no

bail conditions can be set that adequately address the flight risk or potential harm to the

community. The Government articulates this harm as the dissipation of assets that will arguably

become part of Madoff's restitution debt for victim recovery. (Gov. Mem. at 5-6.) The

Government argues it is not practical to monitor all of Madoff's assets to prevent further

---

[6]The Government does not identify any violation of the conditions of release, and no violation is apparent. If Madoff had violated a condition of his release, the Government would have been entitled to move for detention pursuant to 18 U.S.C. § 3148(b). While this would have provided a clear basis for the motion, it likely would not have changed the result herein as the Court would still be required to address the questions of flight and danger.

dissemination contravening the civil case's preliminary injunction. (*Id.*) Thus, it concludes that

detention is necessary because there are no conditions of release that can assure the safety of the

community. Madoff counters that most of the items have been recovered, and that he is in the

process of recovering the outstanding items at this time. (Def. Opp. at 4.) He argues that the

Government failed to make the threshold showing to allow for a consideration of detention, and

that it failed to make any showing under the law that Madoff is a flight risk of the caliber

mandating detention, or that he can disseminate assets in any fashion that could be considered a

harm cognizable under § 3142 of the Bail Reform Act.

III. DISCUSSION

A. Legal Standard

Generally, a court must release a defendant on bail on the least restrictive condition or

combination of conditions that will reasonably assure the defendant's appearance when required

and the safety of the community. *See* 18 U.S.C. § 3142(c)(1)(B). The issue at this stage of the

criminal proceedings is not whether Madoff has been charged in perhaps the largest Ponzi

scheme ever, nor whether Madoff's alleged actions should result in his widespread

disapprobation by the public, nor even what is appropriate punishment after conviction. The legal

issue before the Court is whether the Government has carried its burden of demonstrating that no

condition or combination of conditions can be set that will reasonably assure Madoff's

appearance and protect the community from danger.[7] 18 U.S.C. § 3142(e).

Under 18 U.S.C. § 3142(b),

> The judicial officer shall order the pretrial release of the person [charged with

---

[7]Were the Court to issue a detention order against Madoff in the context of a bail hearing, the object would not be to punish him, but to achieve these twin goals under the Bail Reform Act.

> an offense] on personal recognizance, or upon the execution of an unsecured appearance bond in an amount specified by the court . . . unless the judicial officer determines that such release will not reasonably assure the appearance of the person as required or will endanger the safety of any other person or the community.

Id. The Government may move for detention under either § 3142(f)(1) or § 3142(f)(2). Under subsection (f)(1) of the Act, the Government may seek a detention hearing in cases where the defendant has been charged in a case involving certain crimes, including: 1) a crime of violence, which carries a maximum term of ten years or more; 2) an offense which carries a maximum sentence of life imprisonment or death; 3) serious drug offenses; 4) felonies committed by certain repeat offenders; and 5) felonies that are not otherwise crimes of violence that involve a minor victim or the possession or use of a firearm, destructive device, or any other dangerous weapon. 18 U.S.C. § 3142(f)(1). As the Government appears to concede, there is no evidence that any of the enumerated bases in this subsection are applicable to Madoff's situation.

The Government may also seek detention under § 3142(f)(2) in a case that involves: either "A) a serious risk that the defendant will flee; or B) a serious risk that [the defendant] will obstruct or attempt to obstruct justice . . . ." 18 U.S.C. § 3142(f)(2). The Government relies on both of these bases, and alleges that it has demonstrated both a serious risk of flight and a serious risk of obstruction of justice.

Presented with a motion for detention, the Court undertakes a two-step inquiry. "First, the court must determine whether the Government has established 'by a preponderance of the evidence that [Madoff] . . . presents a risk of flight or obstruction of justice.'" *United States v. Khashoggi*, 717 F. Supp. 1048, 1049 (S.D.N.Y. 1989) (quoting *United States v. Friedman*, 837 F.2d 48, 49 (2d Cir. 1988)). If the Government carries this initial burden, the Court must

7

determine whether there are reasonable conditions of release that can be set or whether detention

is appropriate. *Friedman*, 837 F.2d at 49; *United States v. Berrios-Berrios*, 791 F.2d 246, 250 (2d

Cir. 1986), *cert. dismissed*, 479 U.S. 978; 18 U.S.C. § 3142(e). To support detention based on

danger, the Government's proof must be clear and convincing, 18 U.S.C. § 3142(f)(2), while

detention based on risk of flight must be proven by a preponderance of the evidence. *United*

States v. Shakur, 817 F.2d 189, 195 (2d Cir. 1987) (citing *United States v. Chimurenga*, 760 F.2d

400, 405 (2d Cir. 1985); *United States v. Gotti*, 794 F.2d 773, 777 (2d Cir. 1986)). Furthermore,

in making this determination, the Court must consider a set of four factors established by

Congress. *See* 18 U.S.C. § 3142(g). These include "'the nature of the offense, the weight of the

evidence against the suspect, the history and character of the person charged, and the nature and

seriousness of the risk to the community.'" *Khashoggi*, 717 F. Supp. at 1049 (quoting

Chimurenga, 760 F.2d at 403). The Government's task is not insubstantial at this second stage.

In most cases, release is the presumptive state. *See* 18 U.S.C. §§ 3142 (b) and (c). "The court

should also 'bear in mind that it is only a 'limited group of offenders' who should be denied bail

pending trial.'"[8] *Khashoggi*, 717 F. Supp. at 1049 (quoting *Shakur*, 817 F.2d at 195).

Thus, under the Bail Reform Act, the Government must first establish by a preponderance

of the evidence that the new circumstances presented in this application demonstrate that there is

a serious risk that Madoff will flee or that there is a serious risk that he will obstruct or attempt to

obstruct justice.

---

[8]Even for the most serious offenses, more than half of all defendants are released on bail conditions, including 51% for violent offenses, 57% for property offenses, and 73% for fraud. *See, e.g.*, U.S. DEPT. OF JUSTICE, BUREAU OF JUSTICE STATISTICS, FELONY DEFENDANTS IN LARGE URBAN COUNTIES, 2004 - STATISTICAL TABLES, TABLE 9. FELONY DEFENDANTS RELEASED BEFORE OR DETAINED UNTIL CASE DISPOSITION, BY MOST SERIOUS ARREST CHARGE (2004), http://www.ojp.gov/bjs/pub/html/fdluc/2004/tables/fdluc04st09.htm (last visited Jan. 10, 2009).

B. The New Information Provided by the Government Does Not Demonstrate Either a Serious Risk of Flight or Serious Risk of Obstruction of Justice

1. Risk of Flight

The Government's burden regarding risk of flight is made more difficult because the record reflects that conditions have already been put in place to address this concern and, until this motion was filed, the Parties had agreed that the measures in place were adequate. The Government did not initially seek detention of Madoff at presentment; rather, bail conditions were set and Madoff was released. (Gov. Mem. at 1-2.) Subsequently, at the request of the Government and with Madoff's consent, these bail conditions were modified on December 17 and again on December 19. (*Id.* at 2. Each time, the Government and the Court agreed with Madoff that adequate and reasonable measures were in place.) The Government contends, nevertheless, that "circumstances have changed markedly since the defendant's bail was set on December 19, 2008," and that detention is now warranted. (*Id.* at 4.)

To support its contention that Madoff presents a serious risk of flight, the Government cites: 1) the scope and nature of the alleged crime; 2) the attendant probability that the applicable Sentencing Guidelines in the circumstance of a conviction will likely result in an advisory range at the top of the Guidelines; 3) the fact that Madoff has assets that cannot be effectively restrained; 4) the severance of Madoff's ties to New York to such an extent that only his wife and brother are willing to sign his bond; and 5) finally, Madoff's recent act of distributing valuable personal property to third parties. (Gov. Mem. at 5-6; Government's Reply ("Gov. Reply"), Jan. 8, 2009, at 4.) The Court agrees with the Government that it should consider "changed" circumstances, but three of these factors – 1, 2 and 4 – are not new, and presumably have been

9

taken into account in the current bail conditions.[9] In addition, factors 3 and 5 are aspects of the

same argument, as the Government argues that factor 5 illustrates how factor 3 comes into play.

More importantly, the Government fails to explain how the transfers in question change the

calculus with respect to the question of risk of flight.

Finally, the Government's concession during the January 5, 2009, hearing severely

undermines any claim that there is a *serious* risk of flight as required by § 3142(f)(2) of the Bail

Reform Act. On this point, the Government admitted that "the prior bail orders substantially

diminished [the risk of flight] by home detention, electronic monitoring and then subsequently by

order of the Court the imposition of a 24 hour guard. But that doesn't make the flight risk zero.

There is still some flight risk . . . ." (Tr. at 22.) In this regard, however, the Government

articulates an erroneous legal standard. The Act does not require that the risk be zero, but that

conditions imposed "reasonably assure" appearance. The Government points to the

unprecedented nature of the charges in this case. However, the conditions imposed for release are

unique in their own right, and appear reasonably calculated to assure Madoff's appearance when

required.

Aside from the bare assertion that there remains some risk of flight, the Government has

failed to articulate any flaw in the current conditions of release. This omission is important

because it does not permit the Government to demonstrate, or the Court to assess, the second part

of the Government's burden, that there are "no condition or combination of conditions" which

---

[9]This case contains many unusual tidbits, most of which present no new or changed information. Thus, while the Government notes in its Reply Brief that Madoff was arrested with $173 million in signed checks in his desk apparently waiting to be sent out (Gov. Reply at 2), this was obviously known at the initial bail setting. It may be interesting and provocative, but has limited probative value regarding the issues before the Court.

could address this identified risk. *Shakur*, 817 F.2d at 195. Given that the Government 1) has

conceded that the flight risk has been "substantially diminished" with the current conditions of

release and 2) is constrained to the mere contention that the flight risk is not "zero," this Court

finds that the Government has failed to carry its burden of showing by a preponderance of the

evidence that Madoff presents a serious risk of flight. (Tr. at 22.)

2. Obstruction of Justice

Absent a showing of a serious risk of flight, the Government must show a serious risk of

obstruction of justice to merit a detention hearing. 18 U.S.C. § 3142(f)(2). The Government sets

forth two potential theories on its claim of obstruction of justice. First, it maintains that

Madoff's "release on bail presents a clear risk of further obstruction of justice" because the

dissipation of his assets through transfers to third parties obstruct justice within the meaning of

the bail statute, insofar as it makes it more difficult to recover all available forfeitable assets to

recompense victims. (Gov. Mem. at 6.) Alternatively, the Government maintains that the transfer

of assets violated the injunction in the civil case before Judge Stanton, and this constitutes

obstruction of justice. (*Id.*)

Madoff argues that neither theory is supportable. First, he urges that the alleged

dissipation of assets here at issue does not constitute obstruction of justice within the plain

meaning of 18 U.S.C. § 3142(f)(2)(B). To support this contention, Madoff notes that the

Government has made no showing that any of the distributed items could constitute a part of

potential victim restitution funds. (Def. Opp. at 10.) With respect to the second theory on

obstruction, Madoff asserts that the alleged violation of Judge Stanton's order in the civil action

related to this case does not constitute obstruction of justice, as the violation of a civil court order

11

carries its own set of remedies– such as contempt proceedings. (Def. Opp. at 7.) Madoff

elaborates on this point, noting that the Bail Reform Act does not define obstruction of justice,

and that the statutory provision detailing the power of the federal courts to punish contempt, 18

U.S.C. § 401, differentiates between obstruction of the administration of justice and disobedience

or resistance to lawful court order in its description of contempt offenses. (Def. Opp. at 7.)

The Parties cite no caselaw to support their respective assertions about the meaning of

"obstruction of justice" within the context of the Bail Reform Act. The question of whether

Madoff's distribution of assets, whether characterized as "sentimental effects" (Def. Opp. at 10)

or "$1 million worth of valuable property" (Gov. Mem. at 8), constitutes a serious risk of

obstruction of justice is a threshold question in the inquiry in this matter. The Bail Reform Act

"does not permit detention on the basis of dangerousness in the absence of risk of flight . . . [or]

obstruction of justice . . . ." *United States v. Friedman*, 837 F.2d 48, 49 (2d Cir. 1988). While the

Parties' positions each seem to have some merit with respect to the definition of "obstruction,"

what constitutes obstruction only propels the Government halfway to its objective. The question

is not simply whether Madoff's actions can be considered obstruction, but whether there is a

serious risk of obstruction in the future. The statute, by its nature, is always looking forward. To

be sure, the Court should consider past behavior in assessing the likelihood of prohibited

behavior in the future, but the Government needs to show that there is a serious risk that these

potential harms exist going forward. While substantial questions remain as to whether the

Government has met its burden of showing that Madoff poses a serious risk of obstruction of

justice, the Court does not find it necessary to resolve this issue in order to decide the

Government's application. As set forth below, even if there were obstruction, and even if there remains potential for obstruction in the future, the Government has failed to demonstrate that no conditions can be set to reasonably protect the community from this form of obstruction.

C. The Government's Proffer that No Conditions Will Reasonably Assure the Safety of the Community

Were the Court to conclude that the Government had carried its initial burden of demonstrating a serious risk of flight or obstruction of justice, it would have to assess "whether any condition or combination of conditions of release will protect the safety of the community and reasonably assure the defendant's appearance at trial." *United States v. Friedman*, 837 F.2d 48, 49 (2d Cir. 1988) (citing *United States v. Berrios-Berrios*, 791 F.2d 246, 250 (2d Cir. 1986), *cert. dismissed*, 479 U.S. 978); 18 U.S.C. § 3142(e). For the Government's detention application to succeed, the Court would have to find that the Government has met its burden of showing 1) by clear and convincing evidence, that no condition or combination of conditions will reasonably assure the safety of any other person and the community; or 2) by a preponderance of the evidence, that there is no condition or combination of conditions that would reasonably assure the "presence of the defendant at trial if released." *United States v. Shakur*, 817 F.2d 189, 195 (2d Cir. 1987) (citing *United States v. Chimurenga*, 760 F.2d 400, 405 (2d Cir. 1985); *United States v. Gotti*, 794 F.2d 773, 777 (2d Cir. 1986)). In its determination, the Court must consider available information concerning the following factors: 1) nature and circumstances of the offense charged; 2) weight of the evidence against the accused; 3) history and characteristics of the defendant, including physical and mental condition, family ties, employment, financial resources, length of residence in the community, community ties, and past conduct and record of past appearances; and 4) nature and seriousness of danger to any person or the community that

13

would be posed by the person's release. 18 U.S.C. 3142(g). Despite having concluded that the Government has failed to carry its burden with respect to risk of flight, the Court considers the issue of danger.

1. Safety of the Community

The Bail Reform Act provides that "the facts the judicial officer uses to support a finding . . . that no condition or combination of conditions will reasonably assure the safety of any other person and the community shall be supported by clear and convincing evidence." 18 U.S.C. § 3142(f)(2). However, even if the Government can meet this burden, "the Bail Reform Act does not permit detention on the basis of dangerousness in the absence of risk of flight, obstruction of justice or an indictment for the offenses enumerated [in 18 U.S.C. § 3142(f)(1)]." *Friedman*, 837 F.2d 48, 49 (remanding so the district court could set conditions for defendant's release on bail). Were the Government to succeed under the serious risk of flight or obstruction of justice test discussed above, to prove its burden here it must affirmatively answer each prong of a three part inquiry. First, the Government must show economic harm is a danger to the community cognizable under the Bail Reform Act, as codified in 18 U.S.C. § 3142; succeeding in that, the Government must next establish the potential for Madoff to execute actions that would merit economic harm for these purposes; proving that, the Government must then prove by the relevant standard of clear and convincing evidence that no "condition or combination of conditions" can adequately mitigate the danger, save detention of Madoff.

a. Is Economic Harm a Danger Cognizable Under the Bail Reform Act; Do the Potential Actions of Madoff Rise to the Level of Economic Harm

The Government argues that Congress intended the "safety of the community" language

14

in the Bail Reform Act to be given broad construction. (Gov. Mem. at 3.) The Government uses

this foundation to argue that courts have "construed the statute to find that protection of the

community from economic harm is a valid objective of bail conditions." (*Id.*) Citing a series of

cases to support its assertion, the Government concludes the danger to the community based on

the possibility that Madoff may attempt to distribute restitution assets rises to the level of a safety

concern as contemplated by § 3142 of the Bail Reform Act.

Madoff notes that the Government's argument is conspicuously lacking in references to

Second Circuit authority on the extension of the concept of danger to the community to

encompass economic or pecuniary harm sufficient to justify a revocation of release. Madoff

specifically attacks the Government's reliance on cases concerning post-conviction detention,

where the standard is governed by 18 U.S.C. § 3143, which provides a more lenient burden of

proof to the Government, and its use of cases where the crimes at issue fell under the felonies

enumerated under 18 U.S.C. § 3142(f)(1), pursuant to which a rebuttable presumption in favor of

detention may arise under certain circumstances, *see* 18 U.S.C. § 3142(e). (Def. Opp. at 7, 12-

13.) Madoff argues that the Government has failed to establish that the dissipation of restitution

funds rises to the level of endangering the community for purposes of a pretrial detention

application.

In urging the Court to adopt its interpretation, the Government asserts that the legislative

history of the Bail Reform Act makes clear that Congress intended that the "safety of the

community" concern in § 3142 was expected to be construed as broader than merely danger of

harm involving physical violence. (Gov. Mem. at 3 (quoting S. Rep. No. 225, 98th Cong., 1st

Sess. 12 (1983), *reprinted in* 1984 U.S.C.C.A.N. 3182, 3195) ("The reference to safety of any other person is intended to cover the situation in which the safety of a particular identifiable

individual, perhaps a victim or witness, is of concern, while the language referring to the safety

of the community refers to the danger that the defendant might engage in criminal activity to the

detriment of the community. The committee intends that the concern about safety be given a

broader construction than merely danger of harm involving physical violence.").)

Courts should approach such "invitations" to broadly construe statutes with caution. The

line between construing a statute and judicial lawmaking can become blurred. Because the

Committee indicates that "harm" to the community should not be limited to "physical violence,"

it does not mean a court should be able to identify other types of harm and read them into the

statute. Indeed, if one were attempting to construe the Committee's intention, the sentence

immediately preceding the one the Government has focused on would suggest that, as an initial

matter, the Committee's proposition would apply only to activities which are in fact crimes. *See

id.*; *see also* GORDON MEHLER, JOHN GLEESON, AND DAVID C. JAMES, FEDERAL CRIMINAL

PRACTICE: SECOND CIRCUIT HANDBOOK 107-08 (8th ed. 2007-2008) (hereinafter "MEHLER,

GLEESON & JAMES, SECOND CIRCUIT HANDBOOK") ("The Bail Reform Act's concept of

dangerousness covers the effect of a defendant's release on the safety of identifiable individuals,

such as a victim or witness, as well as 'the danger that the defendant might engage in criminal

activity to the detriment of the community.'" (quoting *United States v. Millan*, 4 F.3d 1038, 1048

(2d Cir. 1993) (quoting legislative history))).

In reviewing all the cases referenced by the Parties, the Court concludes there is support

for considering economic harm in evaluating danger to the community under § 3142 of the Bail

Reform Act. The Government identifies *United States v. Reynolds*, 956 F.2d 192 (9th Cir. 1992),

16

which asserts that "danger may, at least in some cases, encompass pecuniary or economic harm." *Id.* at 192 (referencing *United States v. Provenzano*, 605 F.2d 85, 95 (3rd Cir. 1979) (danger not limited to physical harm; the concept includes the opportunity to exercise a substantial and corrupting influence within a labor union)); *see also United States v. Parr*, 399 F. Supp. 883, 888 (W.D. Tex. 1975) ("The 'danger to . . . the community' [language in the Bail Reform Act] permits consideration of the defendant's propensity to commit crime generally, even where only pecuniary and not physical harm might result to the community at large."). The only case from the Southern District of New York referenced by the Government is *United States v. Stein*, 2005 WL 3071272 (S.D.N.Y. Nov. 15, 2005). In *Stein*, the Honorable Lewis A. Kaplan arguably infers an economic harm as danger to the community pursuant to § 3142 of the Bail Reform Act by addressing the potential danger to others and to the community if one of the defendants were released on bail. *Id.* at *2. However, Judge Kaplan concludes that "[w]hile the government's proffer certainly supports the assertion that the defendant has engaged in fraudulent activities in the past, it has made no real effort to suggest that there is a substantial risk that he will continue to do so if released pending trial, particularly given the change in his personal circumstances. So the danger argument comes down to an assertion that [the defendant] is likely to tamper with witnesses or attempt to obstruct justice if released on bail." *Id.* at *2 (granting the defendant conditioned release pending trial).

While the Court does not accept the post-conviction/pre-conviction distinction[10] urged by

---

[10] While the burden of proof and standard may differ when the presumption of innocence remains with the defendant in the context of pretrial detention, bail decisions are made pursuant to the Bail Reform Act, and the terms used should be given the same meaning.

17

Madoff to dispense with cases cited by the Government,[11] the Court does consider that a

presumption of innocence may be a factor in determining the weight of an alleged economic

harm and whether it would rise to the level of danger to the community. For example, in

Reynolds, the court concluded that the defendant had failed to show by clear and convincing

evidence that he did not constitute an economic danger to the community after a jury had

convicted him of mail fraud and witness tampering. *Reynolds*, 956 F.2d at 192 (denying bail

pending appeal of convictions).[12] The question appears to become one of propensity to commit

further crimes, even if the resulting harm is solely economic. *See Provenzano*, 605 F.2d at 95.

This seems to be true even in the cases where pretrial detention is the relevant question. *See, e.g.,*

United States v. Persaud, 2007 WL 1074906, at *1 (N.D.N.Y. Apr. 5, 2007) (agreeing that

"economic harm qualifies as a danger within the contemplation of the Bail Reform Act" but

ultimately granting the defendant pretrial release); *see also Gentry*, 455 F. Supp. 2d at 1032

("[d]anger . . . may be recognized in terms other than the use of force or violence[]" but

ultimately concluding that possibility of defendant perpetrating further economic crimes weighed

neither in favor of release or detention).[13] In general, concern about future nonphysical harm to

---

[11]Ultimately, the Court accepts that in certain circumstances an economic or pecuniary harm may give rise to a consideration of danger for purposes of detention, either prior to trial or where the convicted awaits appeal. *See, e.g., Stein*, 2005 WL 3071272, at *2 (pretrial); *United States v. Schenberger*, 498 F. Supp. 2d 738, 742 (D.N.J. 2007) (pretrial); *Parr*, 399 F. Supp. at 888 (pretrial); *United States v. Gentry*, 455 F. Supp. 2d (D. Ariz. 2006) (pretrial).

[12]*United States v. Zaragoza*, 2008 WL 686825, at *3 (N.D. Cal. Mar. 11, 2008), is in a similar procedural posture and also notes that danger to community can include narcotics activity or even encompass pecuniary or economic harm. *Id.* (citing *Reynolds*, 956 F.2d at 192).

[13]The Government additionally presents *United States v. LeClercq*, 2007 WL 4365601, at *4 (S.D. Fla. Dec. 13, 2007). "The reference to safety of the community in the Bail Reform Act of 1984 'refers to the danger that the defendant might engage in criminal activity to the detriment of the community. The [Senate Judiciary] Committee intends that the concern about safety be given a broader construction than merely danger of harm involving physical violence.'" *See id.* at *4, n.5 (quoting *United States v. King*, 849 F.2d, 485, 487, n.2 (11th Cir. 1988)).

18

the community has been primarily considered where the charges or convictions fall under the enumerated felonies articulated in 18 U.S.C. §3142(f)(1), in particular in the context of child pornography or drug trafficking charges. *See, e.g., Zaragoza*, 2008 WL 686825; *Provenzano*, 605 F.2d at 95-96 (acknowledging the possibility of nonphysical harm but reviewing the two defendants' criminal records, histories of violence and the great possibility of extensive and continual undue influence, and other considerations, before denying them bail); *Schenberger*, 498 F. Supp. 2d 738 (finding danger is not just physical harm or violent act, but includes non physical harm within the concept of safety, here in the context of child pornography allegations).

The Court recognizes, therefore, that there is jurisprudence to support the consideration of economic harm in the context of detention to protect the safety of the community. Although the scope of this factor remains uncertain,[14] the Court proceeds to the second step of this analysis. Here, the Government fails to provide sufficient evidence that any potential future dissemination of Madoff's assets would rise to the level of an economic harm cognizable under § 3142 of the Bail Reform Act. Further, it is far too great an extension to reach from the cases presented by the Government that narrowly recognize the possibility of economic harm (and rarely conclude the economic harm presented rises to the level of a danger to the community for which someone should be detained) to such a conclusion based on the minimal evidence presented here by the Government.

---

[14]For example, in instances where courts have acknowledged economic harm and the convictions have not included the "enumerated felonies" or other crimes where the Court presumes a danger to the community, as aforementioned, they have ultimately made their determination based on consideration of the flight risk and not as a result of finding the accused or convicted individual will perpetrate a pecuniary or economic harm that requires detention. *See, e.g., Parr*, 399 F. Supp. at 888 (assessing the likelihood of flight risk as primary reason for detention and noting accused's violation of a material condition of his bail bond to support conclusion of need for detention); *Gentry*, 455 F. Supp. 2d 1018 (analyzing the factors relevant to determination of flight risk and ultimately denying bail); *see also Stein*, 2005 WL 3071272.

designed as further protections:

(1) The restrictions set forth in the preliminary injunction entered on December 18, 2008, in the civil case brought by the SEC before District Judge Louis L. Stanton, including restrictions on transfer of all property whatsoever, wherever located, in the possession or under the control of Madoff, **SHALL** be incorporated into the current bail conditions;

(2) The restrictions set forth in the voluntary restraint agreement signed by Mrs. Madoff on December 26, 2008, **SHALL** be incorporated into the current bail conditions; and

(3) Madoff **SHALL** compile an inventory of all valuable portable items in his Manhattan home. In addition to providing this inventory to the Government, Casale Associates, or another security company approved by the Government, **SHALL** check the inventory once every two weeks. Casale Associates, or another security company approved by the Government, **SHALL** search all outgoing physical mail to ensure that no property has been transferred. The Government and Madoff shall agree on a threshold value for inventory items within one week of this Order.

III. CONCLUSION

The Government seeks an order detaining Defendant Madoff prior to trial based on risk of flight and danger to the community. On this matter, the Government has the burden of proof — by a preponderance of the evidence with respect to the question of flight, and by clear and convincing evidence with respect to question of danger — that there are no conditions which can be set to address these concerns. The Court finds that the Government has failed to meet its burden as to either ground. Accordingly, its motion is **DENIED**.

SO ORDERED this 12th day of January 2009
New York, New York

The Honorable Ronald L. Ellis
United States Magistrate Judge

22

b. Whether Detention is the Appropriate Ameliorative Measure

While the Court finds that the Government takes too great a leap in concluding that the potential dissemination of restitution assets rises to the level of danger to the community as contemplated by § 3142 of the Bail Reform Act, the Court also finds that the Government has failed to carry its burden of showing that no condition or combination of conditions of pretrial release will reasonably assure the safety of the community.

The Government argues that, given Madoff's failure to abide by the preliminary injunction so ordered by Judge Stanton in the civil case, and the fact that there is no practical way to prevent future dissipation of certain of his assets, no condition short of remand will suffice to protect the safety of the community. (Gov. Mem. at 5.) It argues that Madoff's actions constitute a change in circumstances, and that the current bail conditions are insufficient. (Gov. Mem. at 6.)

Madoff responds by describing his current state of affairs, including 24 hour-a-day confinement; no access to any bank account held by him, his wife, or joint accounts; his real property in the United States pledged as collateral for the personal recognizance bond he executed as part of his bail;[15] and his name, face and circumstance known to every financial institution in the world. (Def.'s Mem. at 7.) Further, Madoff notes that since the entry of his current bail conditions, his wife has voluntarily consented to a restraint agreement with the United States Attorney's Office that prohibits her dissemination of any of her personal property. Finally, Madoff provides suggestions for further methods to secure any valuable portable

---

[15]The Second Circuit recognizes that a court may "hold a hearing to ensure that whatever assets are offered to support a bail package are derived from legitimate sources." MEHLER, GLEESON & JAMES, SECOND CIRCUIT HANDBOOK 102 (referencing *United States v. Nebbia*, 357 F.2d 303, 304 (2d Cir. 1966)). As the Government has failed to raise this issue or request any such hearing, the Court presumes that the Government has no basis to question the assets provided for the recognizance bond or any of the conditions of release.

property without the need for his detention. (Def.'s Mem. at 10, 17.)

The Government has failed to meet the additional burden of proving by clear and convincing evidence that there is no condition or combination of conditions that will reasonably prevent dissipation of such property. *See* 18 U.S.C. § 3142(e). In fact, its failure to respond to the various additional bail conditions presented by Madoff further supports the weakness of its argument and its inability to show why Madoff's detention would markedly ameliorate any alleged danger to the community that may result from dissipation of his assets.

D. Determination of Bail Conditions

The Court rejects the Government's proposition that the setting of bail conditions is "based, fundamentally, on the trustworthiness of the defendant." (Def.'s Reply at 4.) Indeed, implicit in the bail condition analysis is the assumption that the defendant cannot be trusted on his own. The Bail Reform Act provides that the Court "shall order the pretrial release of the [defendant] on personal recognizance, or execution of an unsecured bond." 18 U.S.C. § 3142(b). Only if the Court determines that trust of the defendant is insufficient to assure appearance and maintain safety should the Court impose additional conditions. One need only review the conditions enumerated in § 3142(c)(1)(B) to conclude that these measures are designed for situations in which the Court has determined that additional safeguards are necessary to control the defendant. The Court finds it difficult to conclude, for example, that the current conditions of release are based on Madoff's trustworthiness.

The specific harm identified by the Government is the pretrial dissipation of assets. While the Court believes that the prior restrictions on Madoff appear well-considered and have greatly diminished Madoff's ability to effectuate any kind of transfer, the following added conditions are

21

APPENDIX H

WALL STREET JOURNAL LIST OF MAJOR VICTIMS, UPDATED AS OF JANUARY 5, 2009

Today's Paper   Columns   Blogs   Graphics   Newsletters & Alerts   New! Journal Community

HOME   U.S.   WORLD   BUSINESS   MARKETS   TECH   PERSONAL FINANCE   LIFE & STYLE   OPINION   CAREERS   REAL ESTATE   SMALL BUSINESS

QUICK LINKS :   OBAMA'S TRANSITION   MADOFF   BLAGOJEVICH   2008 REVIEW   FUNDS REPORT   DETROIT CRISIS   HEARD ON THE STREET   MARKET DATA

JANUARY 5, 2009

Madoff's Victims

The fallout from Bernard Madoff's alleged Ponzi scheme reverberated around the world as the list of investors facing losses widened. Among the biggest losers were charities, hedge funds, and banks in Europe and Asia. Below, see some of the most exposed investors and sort by the amount of potential losses. --Updated 01/05/09

Investor	Description	Amount of Exposure	Comment
Fairfield Greenwich Advisors	An investment management firm	$7,500,000,000	More than half of Fairfield Greenwich's $14.1 billion in assets under management, or about $7.5 billion was connected to Madoff.
Tremont Group Holdings	Asset management firm	$3,300,000,000	The investment firm is owned by OppenheimerFunds and Massachusetts Mutual Life Insurance Co. Tremont's Rye Investment Management business had $3.1 billion invested, and its fund of funds group invested another $200 million. The loss is more than half of all assets overseen by Tremont.
Banco Santander	Spanish bank	$2,870,000,000	In euros, the figure is 2.33 billion. Of that, 2.01 billion euros belongs to institutional investors, Optimal Strategic hedge fund investors (international private banking customers); 320 million euros belongs to other private banking customers.
Bank Medici	Austrian bank	$2,100,000,000	The bank had two funds with $2.1 billion (1.5 billion euros) invested with Madoff. Bank Medici is 25% owned by Unicredit SpA and 75% owned by chairwoman Sonja Kohn. Hedge funds run by the bank had almost all their money invested with Madoff.
Ascot Partners	A hedge fund founded by billionaire investor, philanthropist and GMAC chief J. Ezra Merkin	$1,800,000,000	The hedge fund had $1.8 billion under management as of Sept. 30, had substantially all of its assets invested with Mr. Madoff. Austria's government named Gerhard Altenberger to manage the bank, but won't supply it with funds.
Access International Advisors	A New York-based investment firm	$1,500,000,000	The investment-advisory firm's co-founder Thierry Magon de La Villehuchet, 65, was found dead in his Manhattan office on Dec. 24, 2008, in an apparent suicide. Mr. De La Villehuchet lost about $50 million, the bulk of his personal wealth.
Fortis	Dutch bank	$1,350,000,000	Fortis Bank and its subsidiaries have no direct exposure to Bernard Madoff Investment Securities LLC, but parts of the group do have a risk exposure to certain funds it provides collateralized lending to. If, as a result of the alleged fraud, the value of the assets of these funds is nil and the respective clients cannot meet their obligations, Fortis Bank Nederland (Holding) N.V.'s loss could amount to around EUR 850 million to EUR 1 billion. The continuity of Fortis Bank Nederland (Holding) N.V. and its subsidiaries is not at stake in any way.
Union Bancaire Privee	Swiss bank	$700,000,000	Half of UBP's 22 funds of funds put at least some of their money into Madoff-related investment vehicles, including one run by J. Ezra Merkin. The principal fund, Dinvest Total Return, had about 3% of its more than $1 billion of assets in Madoff-related funds. One fund of funds had as much as 6.9% of assets in Madoff-related funds. The bank had most recently met with Madoff Nov. 25 as part of an ongoing vetting process.
HSBC	British bank	$1,000,000,000	HSBC provided financing to a small number of institutional clients who invested in funds with Madoff; some clients in its global custody business have invested with Madoff, but the company doesn't believe these arrangements should be a source of exposure to the group.
Natixis SA	A French investment bank	$554,400,000	The company says it didn't make direct investment in Madoff-managed funds; some investments made on behalf of customers could have ended up being managed by Madoff. Exposure is about 450 million euros.
Carl Shapiro	The founder and former chairman of apparel company Kay Windsor Inc., and his wife	$545,000,000	Mr. Shapiro, a 95-year-old apparel entrepreneur and investor, had $545 million with Mr. Madoff, creating what could become the largest personal loss yet in the scandal. A spokeswoman for the family confirmed that Mr. Shapiro's charitable foundation, the Carl and Ruth Shapiro Family Foundation, invested $145 million with Mr. Madoff. Mr. Shapiro and his family had an additional $400 million or more invested with Mr. Madoff. Mr. Shapiro, a widely respected philanthropist, was one of Mr. Madoff's earliest and largest investors.
Royal Bank of Scotland Group PLC	British bank	$492,760,000	The bank had exposure of about 400 million pounds to Madoff through trading, collateralized lending.
BNP Paribas	French bank	$431,170,000	The company said it has no investment of its own in Madoff-managed hedge fund but it does have risk exposure (up to 350 million euros) through its trading business and collateralized lending to funds of hedge funds.
BBVA	Spanish bank	$369,570,000	The company reiterated it doesn't have direct exposure to Madoff but would face losses of 300 million euros if Madoff funds were found not to exist.
Man Group PLC	A U.K. hedge fund	$360,000,000	Invested in funds directly/indirectly sub-advised by Madoff Securities
Reichmuth & Co.	A Swiss private bank	$327,000,000	The Lucerne-based private bank warned investors that around 385 million Swiss francs, or 3.5% of its assets under management, were affected.
Nomura Holdings	Japanese brokerage firm	$304,000,000	The 27.5 billion yen exposure is through Fairfield Sentry; That amount represents 0.2% of assets under management.
Maxam Capital Management	A fund of funds based in Darien, Connecticut	$280,000,000	The fund reported a combined loss of $280 million on funds they had invested.
EIM SA	A European investment manager with about $11 billion in assets	$230,000,000	The European investment manager with about $11 billion in assets. Overall, EIM assets at risk are less than 2% of what it manages.
AXA SA	French insurance giant	N/A	Exposure is well below 100 million euros.
			The company's total exposure is about 75 million euros. Dublin-based Pioneer Alternative

UniCredit SpA	Italian Bank	$92,390,000	Investments is indirectly exposed to Madoff via feeders; Italian clients have zero exposure.
Nordea Bank AB	Swedish Bank	$59,130,000	The amount of exposure is about 48 million euros.
Hyposwiss	A Swiss private bank owned by St. Galler Kantonalbank	$50,000,000	Hyposwiss said roughly 0.1% of its overall assets was invested in Madoff products through managed accounts. Another $100 million is exposed through clients who chose to invest in Madoff funds. St. Galler Kantonalbank said its financial situation and liquidity aren't hurt by Hyposwiss' exposure.
Banque Benedict Hentsch & Cie. SA	A Swiss-based private bank	$48,800,000	Banque Benedict Hentsch said its clients have 56 million Swiss francs at risk. Benedict Hentsch had also recently agreed to merge with Fairfield Greenwich Group, a major Madoff distributor. When the news of Mr. Madoff's arrest broke, it scrambled to undo that deal.
Fairfield, Conn.	town pension fund	$42,000,000	The town's employees board and police and fire board, which cover 971 workers, had $41.9 million invested with Madoff, said Paul Hiller, Fairfield's chief fiscal officer.
Bramdean Alternatives	An asset manager	$31,200,000	The exposure is about 9.5% of assets.
Jewish Community Foundation of Los Angeles	The largest manager of charitable gift assets for Los Angeles Jewish philanthropists	$18,000,000	The amount invested with Madoff represented less than 5% of the Foundation's assets.
Harel Insurance Investments & Financial Services Ltd.	Israel-based insurance firm	$14,200,000	N/A
Baloise Holding AG	Swiss insurer	$13,000,000	N/A
Societe Generale	French Bank	$12,320,000	The company says its exposure, which is less than 10 million euros, is "negligible."
Groupama SA	French insurer	$12,320,000	Exposure is around 10 million euros.
Credit Agricole SA	French bank	$12,320,000	Exposure is less than 10 million euros.
Richard Spring	individual investor	$11,000,000	A Boca Raton resident and former securities analyst, says he had about 95% of his net worth invested with Mr. Madoff. Mr. Spring said he was also one of the unofficial agents who connected Mr. Madoff with dozens of investors, from a teacher who put in $50,000 to entrepreneurs and executives who would put in millions.
RAB Capital	hedge fund	$10,000,000	N/A
Banco Popolare	Italian bank	$9,860,000	The company says it had indirect exposure of up to 8 million euros; maximum lost on funds distributed to institutional, private clients is about 60 million euros.
Korea Teachers Pension	A 10 trillion won Korean pension fund	$9,100,000	N/A
Swiss Life Holding	Swiss insurer	$78,900,000	Swiss Life said it has indirectly invested assets worth around 90 million Swiss francs through funds of funds managed by Madoff Investment Securities.
North Shore-Long Island Jewish Health System	health system	$5,700,000	Exposure represents less than 1% of the health system's investment portfolio. A donor agreed to reimburse the system for any losses.
Neue Privat Bank	Swiss bank	$5,000,000	The bank invested in a certificate based on a hedge fund with exposure to Madoff
Clal Insurance Enterprise Holdings	An Israel-based financial services company	$3,100,000	N/A
Ira Roth	individual investor	$1,000,000	Mr. Roth, a New Jersey resident, says his family has about $1 million invested through Mr. Madoff's firm.
Mediobanca SpA	via its subsidiary Compagnie Monegasque de Banque.	$671,000	Limited to $671,000 via its Compagnie Monegasque de Banque. via its subsidiary Compagnie Monegasque de Banque.
Fred Wilpon	owner of New York Mets	N/A	N/A
Steven Spielberg	The Spielberg charity -- the Wunderkinder Foundation	N/A	N/A
JEHT Foundation	A New York foundation focused on electoral and criminal justice reform	N/A	The foundation, which stands for Justice, Equality, Human dignity and Tolerance, will close its doors at the end of January 2009. Major donors Jeanne Levy-Church and Kenneth Levy-Church had all their funds managed through Madoff.
Mortimer B. Zuckerman Charitable Remainder Trust	The charitable trust of real-estate magnate, who owns the Daily News and U.S. News & World Report	N/A	Funds exposed represented 11% of the value of that charitable trust.
Robert I. Lappin Charitable Foundation	A Massachusetts-based Jewish charity	N/A	The group, which financed trips for Jewish youth to Israel, was forced to close because the money that supported its programs was invested with Madoff.
Chais Family Foundation	A charity that gave to Jewish causes	N/A	Money manager Stanley Chais managed investments he called "the arbitrage partnerships," according to investors and firm correspondence. His California-based charity group invested entirely with Madoff, and was forced to shut down operations after years of donating some $12.5 million annually to Jewish causes in Israel and Eastern Europe.
KBC Group NV	Belgian banking and insurance group	N/A	No direct exposure; some indirect exposure through collateralized loans, but the exposure is very limited and immaterial to KBC's earnings. KBC has also made some loan advances to institutional customers who have invested in funds managed by Madoff Investment Securities, but this shouldn't have any material impact either, the company said.
Barclays PLC	British bank	N/A	The bank says it has "minimal" exposure and is "fully collateralized"
Dexia	French bank	N/A	No direct investments in funds managed by Madoff,; private banking clients have total exposure of 78 million euros to funds primarily invested in Madoff funds. Indirectly, Dexia is exposed through partially collateralized lending operations to funds exposed to Madoff funds for a gross amount of 164 million euros. If the assets managed by Madoff Investment Securities were nil, the above mentioned lending operations could trigger an after tax loss of about 85 million euros for Dexia.
Allianz Global Investors	The asset management unit of German insurer Allianz SE	N/A	The unit says exposure "is not significant."
Banco Espanol de Credito SA (Banesto)	A Spanish bank controlled by Banco Santander	N/A	Its clients have a total 2 million euro exposure. The amount is included in the 2.33 billion euros already disclosed by parent company Banco Santander.
CNP Assurances	French insurer	N/A	No direct exposure. Indirect exposure of 3 million euros via a fund of funds
UBS AG	Swiss bank	N/A	The bank says has "no material exposure." It declined to comment on press reports that its funds-of-funds for clients had $1.4 billion in exposure
			The university's chief financial officer said that the school's actual principal investment in a hedge fund

Yeshiva University	A New York-based private university	$14,500,000	linked to Madoff had been only $14.5 million. On paper, that stake had exploded in value over the past 15 years to $110 million. Although the university had "no direct investments" in Madoff's firm, a portion of its endowment had been invested for 15 years with Ascot Partners, which had "substantially all its assets invested with Madoff." J. Ezra Merkin had been a University trustee but has resigned. Madoff was also on the school's board but has resigned.
The Elie Wiesel Foundation for Humanity	The charitable foundation of Nobel laureate	$15,200,000	The foundation, established to combat anti-Semitism, said it invested "substantially all" of its assets.
Leonard Feinstein	The co-founder of retailer Bed Bath & Beyond	N/A	N/A
Sen. Frank Lautenberg	The charitable foundation of the New Jersey Senator's family	N/A	N/A
Norman Braman	former owner of Philadelphia Eagles	N/A	N/A
Jeffrey Katzenberg	The chief executive of DreamWorks Animation SKG Inc.	N/A	Mr. Katzenberg's financial affairs along with those of Mr. Spielberg were managed by Mr. Breslauer. Mr. Katzenberg has suffered millions in Madoff-connected losses, say people familiar with the matter.
Gerald Breslauer	The Hollywood financial advisor to Steven Spielberg and Jeffrey Katzenberg	N/A	Along Messrs Katzenberg and Spielberg, Mr. Breslauer himself has likely sustained heavy losses in the Madoff affair. He customarily invests alongside his clients, say these people, and has sometimes been a larger investor than the people he represented
Kingate Management	hedge fund	N/A	Kingate's $2.8 billion hedge fund Kingate Global Fund reportedly invested heavily with Madoff
Julian J. Levitt Foundation	Texas-based charity	N/A	N/A
Loeb family	N/A	N/A	N/A
Lawrence Velvel	individual investor	N/A	Mr. Velvel is dean of the Massachusetts School of Law
Fix Asset Management.	hedge fund	N/A	reportedly invested heavily in Madoff's portfolios
Genevalor, Benbassat & Cie.	money manager in Geneva	N/A	Members of the Benbassat family, which run the firm, have long known Mr. Madoff. In a statement on its Web site, Genevalor said it "has been reviewing the potential damages caused to its clients" by the alleged Madoff fraud. A statement from the Thema fund said it had assets with Madoff that were now frozen, but did not elaborate.
Banco Espirito Santo	Portugese bank	$21,400,000	The amount represents about 0.1% of assets under management.
Great Eastern Holding	Singapore insurer	$44,266,000	Great Eastern said S$7.7 million of its S$64 million exposure is invested from its Life Fund. Great Eastern is 87% owned ny Oversea-Chinese Banking Corp.
M&B Capital Advisers	Spanish brokerage	$52,800,000	The firm is run by the son and son-in-law of the chairman of Banco Santander. Through M&B, private and institutional investors bought more than $214 million in Madoff's funds.
Royal Dutch Shell pension fund	Global energy and petrochemical company	N/A	The pension fund fund has an indirect investment that may be affected. The fund originally invested $45 million. The alleged fraud won't affect the financial position and funding status of the fund.
Phoenix Holdings	Israeli financial services company	$12,600,000	Phoenix's insurance unit invested $15 million over the last three years in funds managed by Thema, which made investments through Madoff. In November, the company requested to redeem $10 million. The payment was due Dec. 12 but Phoenix hasn't received it.
Credicorp	Peruvian financial services company	$4,500,000	Credicorp's Atlantic Security Bank unit has $1 million in direct exposure and up to $3.5 million in potential contingencies "related to transactions secured by these investments."
Fukoku Mutual Life Co.	Japanese insurer	N/A	The company said it holds similar investments trusts to those held by Sumitomo Life Insurance Co. but declined to specify the balance. Sumitomo disclosed that it has about 2 billion yen, or about $22 million, exposed via trusts.
New York Law School	law school in New York City	$300,000	The school invested the money through its endowment entity. The school filed an investor lawsuit against J. Ezra Merkin, Ascot Partners and BDO Seidman.
Nipponkoa Insurance	Japanese insurer	N/A	The company said it holds similar investments trusts to those held by Sumitomo Life Insurance Co. but declined to specify the balance. Sumitomo disclosed that it has about Y2 billion exposed via trusts.
Sumitomo Life Insurance Co.	Japanese insurer	$22,000,000	Sumitomo Life didn't invest directly in the Madoff fund but part of its investment trust holdings were linked to it.
Swiss Reinsurance Co.	Swiss insurer	$3,000,000	Indirect exposure, less than $3 million, is through hedge fund investments; no direct exposure.
Aozora Bank Ltd	Japanese lender	$137,000,000	Aozora entrusted 12.4 billion yen to investment funds, which invested with Madoff. Cerberus Capital Management LP owns a majority stake in Aozora.
UBI Banca	Italian bank	$86,000,000	The bank said the exposure is linked to proprietary investments. UBI Pramerica and Capitalgest Alternative Investments, the assets-under-management units, have no exposure.
Taiyo Life Insurance Co.	Japanese insurer	$221,000	Taiyo Life didn't invest directly in the Madoff fund.
Caisse d'Epargne	French bank	$11,100,000	Caisse d'Epargne said 1 million euros was for Caisse Nationale des Caisses d'Epargne, the central hub, and "under 7 million euros" was from its regional level.
J Gurwin Foundation	Charity	N/A	$28 million charity invested heavily in Madoff funds. Gurwin said, "We got a body blow. We did not get killed."
EFG International	Swiss private bank	N/A	EFG clients have $130 million invested in Madoff through third-party funds sold by EFG. In addition, 0.3% of the bank's total invested assets, held in custody, are invested in Madoff.
Fire and Police Pension Association of Colorado	Pension fund	N/A	Fund, with $2.5 billion under management, had $60 million invested with Fairfield Greenwich until six months ago
International Olympic Committee	Olympic organizer	$4,800,000	The IOC's exposure represents about 1% of its total investment portfolio. Organizing committee confirmed they will be able to meet their obligations.
Support Organization for the Madison Cultural Arts District	Wisconsin cultural organization	N/A	$18 million invested with Fairfield Greenwich until September. A spokesman for the Overture Center in Madison, Wis., built with SOMCAD funds, said, "Speculation that SOMCAD could be on the hook is not outlandish."
Credit Industrial et Commercial	French financial-services group	$125,400,000	The bank has no direct exposure to Madoff but could be affected through an intermediary.
Hadassah	U.S. women's zionist organization	$90,000,000	N/A
United Association Plumbers & Steamfitters Local 267 in Syracuse	Local union pension and health care funds	N/A	The union is still trying to determine the extent of its losses. Its investments with Mr. Madoff go back 15 years.

Ramaz School	A Jewish school in New York	$6,000,000	N/A
Congregation Kehilath Jeshurun	A synagogue in New York	$3,500,000	N/A
The Maimonides School	A Jewish day school in Brookline, Mass.	$3,000,000	The school did not directly invest with Madoff, but the school was the sole beneficiary of a trust that lost about $3 million.
Yad Sarah	An Israeli nonprofit	$1,500,000	With a $21 million budget in 2008, Yad Sarah likely won't expand operations or develop any new services or projects in 2009.
Kevin Bacon and wife Kyra Sedgwick	Hollywood actors	N/A	Mr. Bacon's publicist, Allen Eichhorn, confirmed that the couple had investments with Madoff, but wouldn't say how much money they might have lost.
Eric Roth	Hollywood screenwriter	N/A	His credits include "Forrest Gump" and "The Curious Case of Benjamin Button."
Henry Kaufman	Individual investor, former Salomon Brothers chief economist	N/A	The former Salomon Brothers chief economist's bearish views decades ago earned him the nickname "Dr. Doom." Mr. Kaufman, 81 years old, lost several million dollars. He had the money in a brokerage account with Bernard L. Madoff Investment Securities for more than five years. Mr. Kaufman said the amount was "no more than a couple percent of my entire net worth," estimated to be several hundred million dollars.
New York University	University	$24,000,000	NYU filed a lawsuit claiming J. Ezra Merkin turned over his investment responsibilities to Madoff's funds and lost $24 million of the school's money. The suit names as defendants Merkin's Ariel Fund Ltd., the fund's investment manager, Gabriel Capital Corp.; and Fortis Bank. NYU had invested $94 million in Ariel, a partnership between Merkin and Fortis. Ariel plans to liquidate due to Madoff-related losses.
Aioi Insurance Co.	Japanese insurer	$1,100,000	Aioi said it didn't make a direct investment in the Madoff fund.
Meiji Yasuda Life Insurance Co.	Japanese insurer	$1,100,000	Meiji Yasuda didn't invest directly in the Madoff fund.
Mitsui Sumitomo Insurance Co.	Japanese insurer	$8,800,000	Mitsui Sumitomo didn't invest directly in the Madoff fund.
Burt Ross	former mayor of a town in New Jersey	$5,000,000	Mr. Ross believes he has lost about $5 million, the bulk of his net worth, investing with Madoff.
Genium Advisors	Swiss money manager	$281,400	Exposure is nearly 6.7% of a E$4.2 million fund invested in Fairfield Sentry Roland Priborsky, Genium's chief, said he was comfortable with the Fairfield Sentry investment in part because it was included in a list of funds on which Union Bancaire Privee said it had done due diligence.
Sterling Stamos Capital Management LP	Investment firm with offices in New York City and Menlo Park, Calif.	N/A	Six funds each have 1.5%-3% of assets exposed to Madoff. In a Dec. 30 letter sent to clients, the investment firm said it has "some limited indirect exposure" to Madoff. This came after the firm issued a press release on Dec. 12 denying any Madoff investments. The exposure was through Gabriel Capital LP or Gabriel's offshore affiliate Ariel Fund Ltd.
Gabriel Partners	Money-management firm run by GMAC Chairman Ezra Merkin.	N/A	Gabriel Capital Corp. is the investment manager for Merkin's Ariel fund. The Ariel hedge fund plans to liquidate because of losses to Madoff's alleged fraud.
The Diocese of St. Thomas	Catholic church in the U.S. Virgin Islands	$2,000,000	Most of the money represented endowment funds for youngsters at two Catholic elementary schools in St. Croix, the poorest of the U.S. Virgin Islands.
Phyllis Molchatsky	individual investor	$17,000,000	Ms. Molchatsky, a 61-year-old retiree Valley Cottage, N.Y., from filed a claim against the Securities and Exchange Commission alleging the agency was negligent in failing to detect an alleged decades-long fraud.
Members of the Hillcrest Golf Club of St. Paul, Minn. and Oak Ridge Country Club in Hopkins, Minn.	country clubs	N/A	Investors from the two clubs may have invested more than $100 million combined
Bard College	University in New York	$3,000,000	Bard College, a liberal arts school in Annandale-on-Hudson, N.Y., said it lost about $3 million that J. Ezra Merkin's Ariel Fund had invested with Mr. Madoff without the school's knowledge. The losses on the investment includes profits. A lawyer for Mr. Merkin did not immediately respond to a request for comment.
Martin Rosenman	New York City-based heating oil distributor	$10,000,000	Mr. Rosenman, managing member of Rosenman Family LLC, wired $10 million to Madoff via a JPMorgan Chase Bank account on Dec. 5, just six days before Madoff's arrest. The funds weren't supposed to be touched until Jan. 1, according to a suit filed in bankruptcy court, but Mr. Rosenman received a statement Dec. 5 explaining the money was used to sell short $10 million in U.S. Treasuries. There is no record that the Treasury short ever occurred.

Sources: WSJ reporting; Associated Press; the companies and charities

Write to the Online Journal's editors at newseditors@wsj.com
Return To Top

Search News, Quotes, Companies

APPENDIX I

AUTHORS' LIST OF INTERVIEWEES

The following individuals were interviewed by telephone:

Fred Adler, attorney, venture capitalist, on 12/31/08

Ronnie Sue Ambrosino, Madoff victim, on 12/31/08

Marshall Blume, professor, Wharton School, University of Pennsylvania, on 12/31/08

Douglas Burns, former federal prosecutor, on 12/26/08

Ron Gefner, attorney, expert on hedge funds, on 12/30/08

Bette Greenfield, resident of Deerfield Beach, Florida, a victim, on 12/29/08

David Harris, executive director, American Jewish Committee, on 12/23/08

Morton Klein, economist and president, Zionist Organization of America, on 12/23/08

Lawrence Leamer, writer, on 12/24/08

Robert L. Lappin, founder, The Robert L. Lappin Charitable Foundation, on 12/24/08

Carol Solomon Marston, classmate of Bernard Madoff at Far Rockaway High School, on 12/27/08

Sydelle Meyer, resident of Palm Beach, Florida, a victim, on 12/28/08

Mark Mulholland, victims' attorney, on 12/30/08

Robert Nessoff, classmate of Bernard Madoff at Far Rockaway High School, on 12/ 28/08

Jon Najarian, professional investor, founder, optionMONSTER, on 12/30/08

Rev. John Pawlikowski, O.S.M., professor of ethics, Catholic Theological Union, Chicago, on 1/5/09

Tara Pearl, prominent Palm Beach, Florida, realtor and businesswoman, on 12/24/08

Stephen Pine, classmate of Bernard Madoff at Far Rockaway High School, on 12/28/08

Rabbi A. James Rudin, senior interreligious adviser, AJC, on 12/31/08

Ira Lee Sorkin, partner, Dickstein Shapiro, lead attorney to Bernard Madoff, on 12/27/08

Dr. Donald Shriver, president emeritus, Union Theological Seminary, on 12/31/08

Harry Taubenfeld, New York attorney, former member of the Board of Governors, Jewish Agency for Israel, on 12/27/08

Gary Tobin, president, Institute for Jewish and Community Research, on 12/28/08

Arthur Traiger, English teacher, Far Rockaway High School, 1949–56, on 12/28/08

Dr. Andrew Twardon, director, Center for Intensive Treatment of Personality Disorders, St. Luke's-Roosevelt Hospital, New York City, on 1/5/09